Budgeting Entitlements

The Politics of Food Stamps

Budgeting Entitlements

The Politics of Food Stamps

RONALD F. KING

GEORGETOWN UNIVERSITY PRESS
WASHINGTON, DC

Georgetown University Press, Washington, D.C.

Printed in the United States of America

10 9 8 7 6 5 4 3 2 1 2000

This volume is printed on acid-free offset book paper.

Library of Congress Cataloging-in-Publication Data

King, Ronald Frederick, 1949–
Budgeting entitlements : the politics of food stamps / Ronald F. King.
p. cm. — (American governance and public policy)
Includes index.
ISBN 0-87840-797-9 (cloth : acid-free paper)
1. Food stamps—Political aspects—United States. 2. Food relief—United States—Finance. 3. Budget—United States. I. Title. II. Series.

HV696.F6 K56 2000
363.8'83'0973—dc21 00-026374

Contents

Preface and Acknowledgments

Tawney once wrote that inequality is in the air that we breathe, surrounding us continuously but so common that we pass through it almost without noticing. I grew up in New York City, and from my bedroom window I could see both the magnificent skyline across the river and the public housing project across the street. To me, the two images are indelibly linked. It is a constant reminder not to overlook the extremes of dominance and destitution within our society.

This book examines the food stamp program in the United States, using it as a lens through which the broader issues of substantive and procedural justice can be considered. It is absurd in this nation of affluence that certain individuals, especially young children, suffer from hunger or malnutrition. By implication, needy recipients of food assistance should be deemed entitled to their benefits, protected against the ever-shifting tides of political opinion and fiscal fortune. However, entitlement also entails some constraint upon democratic discretion, mandating the allocation of government funds sufficient to provide full benefits to all enrolled program recipients regardless of competing policy priorities or popular preferences. Recent attacks upon the American welfare state, prompted largely by concerns over federal government finance, have made the subject particularly salient. A central finding from this study is that budget mechanisms that seek to cap the growth of entitlement spending have perverse yet predictable effects. It is a sobering lesson to a nation often promised that it can limit the cost yet maintain its conscience.

I would like to thank the Twentieth Century Fund/The Century Foundation, the Murphy Institute of Political Economy, and the Tulane University Committee on Research for their generous support. A version of the basic model was published previously in the *Journal of Public Policy,* vol. 18 (1998); an earlier version of chapter 9 was published in *Political Science Quarterly,* vol. 114 (1999). They are reprinted here with permission.

In the process of writing this book, I spoke with many people who offered helpful comments, recommendations, and suggestions. While apologizing in advance for any oversights and omissions, I express my appreciation to Richard Beth, John Bode, Michael Brown, Demetrios Caraley, Sandy Davis, Susan Ellis, Adriana Filip, Michael Fishman, Laura Jensen, Bruce Katz, Ira Katznelson, John Kramer, Carie Lewis, William Ludwig, Roy Meyers, Andrew Moellmer, Bonny O'Neil, Paul Pierson, Jill Quadagno, James Quinn, Mark Rom, Richard Rose, Irene Rubin, Allen Schick, Paul Sum, David Super, Kent Weaver, Joseph White, Christopher Wlezien, and the anonymous referees. A special acknowledgment is made in the memory of Aaron Wildavsky.

Little research could ever proceed without the aid of librarians. I am indebted to the professional staffs at the National Archives and at the Ford and Carter Presidential Libraries. Eric Weding and his colleagues in the Government Documents department of Tulane's Howard-Tilton Memorial Library have contributed enormously to this project, demonstrating remarkable patience while I pestered them about sources and camped out among the stacks. Their wealth of information and continual good cheer merit high praise.

I would like to thank John Samples, director, and Gail Grella, Deborah Weiner, and Ivan Osorio, of Georgetown University Press, and Barry Rabe, editor of the Press's American Governance and Public Policy series. Trina King did a fabulous job with the index.

My daughters, Allison and Meredith, have long become accustomed to my absent-mindedness and distraction when working on a particularly difficult paragraph. I appreciate their tolerance, irreverence, and wit, for they remind me what is truly important in my life. Rona Lehman King for years has provided inspiration and intelligence. Her unswerving dedication to the idea that nurture and justice advance together gives her the moral strength that I find so admirable. I would like to dedicate this book to my father-in-law, Samuel Lehman, for the hours we spent sitting over coffee and beignets, arguing about politics as a means of expressing love.

ONE

Introduction: Budget Politics and Welfare Politics

Increasingly, U.S. welfare politics has become entwined with U.S. budgetary politics. It is now impossible to address the issues of annual government spending and total government indebtedness without considering the amounts required under current law to be outlayed as transfer payments to individuals. It is unreasonable to discuss public sector assistance to the poor without first asking the price. The fiscalization of welfare has had an impact upon the tenor of the policy debate. Attention has largely shifted from the obligations of society toward the less fortunate to the ability of society to satisfy those obligations, from the adequacy of public expenditures to the availability of public resources, from the level of individual need to the level of societal commitment. Fiscalization has affected the array of political forces, reducing the number of potential allies for welfare liberalization. It has also affected the design and implementation of welfare programs, including those with little individual impact upon budget aggregates. Thus we have seen the rise of such procedural mechanisms as expenditure caps and block grants, which have the potential to constrain payments to households otherwise entitled to benefits.

This book addresses a dimension of the American welfare state that has not received sufficient attention in many contemporary accounts. It discusses how the growing integration of welfare and budgeting has affected both strategic play and anticipated outcomes, using the food stamp program as a relevant illustration. The book is intended as a companion to existing explanations based on competing interests and ideologies, for it observes that the logic through which interests are calculated and the language through which beliefs are expressed will change given different contexts. The formulation of welfare as fundamentally a budgetary problem has therefore transformed the terrain within which policy struggles occur. The book is generally consistent with those recent theories concerned with state capacity, although it shows that the extent of such capacity varies over time and that limited capacity still admits a variety of possible policy options. It is focused largely upon the design of institutional rules, on the assumption that such rules can influence the character of political deliberations and the protection of basic rights.

Attention to the problem of welfare budgeting reminds us that the funds used for transfer payments comprise a share of the total amount extracted from the private economy and then allocated among the various functions of the federal government. Intensified conflict over extraction and allocation has arisen in part because of the expanded size of the federal welfare function. Reciprocally, intensified budget conflict has helped alter the politics, process, and policy of welfare provision.

In particular, this book examines the adoption and effect of three different forms of budget rule applied to welfare transfers—discretion, entitlement, and expenditure caps. Discretion is the procedure of normal agency budgeting, in which annual appropriations determine the maximum outlay for a given fiscal year. Entitlement guarantees that funds are made available sufficient to satisfy the claims of all eligible and enrolled persons to the extent established by prevailing statute. Caps permit government welfare outlays up to some specified limit, at which point benefits must be reduced or enrollments curtailed unless the limit is overridden by explicit legislation. Methodologically, the operation of these three forms of budget-making and the contrasts across them will be depicted by a set of formal models. Grounded upon the institutional and ideological dynamics of U.S. politics, the models will be used to interpret the events in food stamp history. In turn, the events in that history will be used to test specific hypotheses derived from the models, helping to establish the plausibility of the general analytic framework. The established rules of the political game structure the patterns of strategic play and the expected outcomes from that play.

Beyond empirical content and methodological rigor, the intended contribution of this book is normative. As a matter of public policy, budgeting welfare presents an inherent tension. Budgeting is fundamental to discretionary democratic choice. Its subject is the total amount allocated to public sector projects and the relative priorities established among them. Its politics are intended to produce acceptable collective decisions across competing goals and claimants. Welfare, by contrast, concerns only a segment, both of the total budget and of the total population. It is, however, a segment of the budget essential to our self-image as an ethical society, affecting a portion of the population identified as especially needy and deserving of aid.

The problem of welfare budgeting, at the most basic level, concerns the relationship between substantive and procedural justice. On the one hand, contemporary federal policy accepts some degree of protection for impoverished individuals against the fragmentation and fluctuations of ordinary political conflict. On the other hand, it celebrates inclusive democratic deliberation over the multiple tasks of government. The two principles are not necessarily reconciled. Americans generally like the idea of secure assistance to the needy but dislike the idea of undisciplined federal spending. They wish for a budget that can be adapted consciously to changing demands and changing conditions, but they fear that such openness also brings opportunities for political bias and manipulation. They welcome greater fiscal responsibility but do not want to expose critical programs to risk.

The tension between welfare and budgeting is visible in the legal concept of entitlement. Social welfare in modern America occupies an ambiguous conceptual space somewhere between a right and a kindness. There is no constitutional guarantee to a minimum subsistence income, although some have sought to assert such a right based on the government's obligation to ensure individual life and liberty. Nevertheless, welfare as entitlement entails more than a gift from society to the needy, given merely at the option of the donor. Access to benefits, under most existing U.S. welfare programs, is guaranteed by the authorizing legislation and thus cannot be impeded, qualified, or denied on the basis of inadequate funding. The government is obligated to make full payment to all qualified recipients, even if the sum far exceeds budget expectations. Welfare programs established under entitlement rules are therefore classified as "mandatory spending" and are exempted from the annual process of appropriation and review.

From the perspective of individual living standards, entitlement status ensures program benefits for designated households. The authorizing statute can always be changed, for example through the use of omnibus reconciliation bills, but this requires a motion approved by majorities in both chambers of Congress and accepted by the president. Inaction cannot threaten recipient allotments, nor can the vagaries of annual appropriations. From the perspective of aggregate budgeting, however, entitlement status carves off a portion of total outlays and establishes them as relatively uncontrollable, responsive automatically to shifting social and economic conditions, not directly contingent on congressional specification, oversight, and adjustment. Primacy to the part reduces integration for the whole. It establishes a critical asymmetry among the different projects of government and constrains the range of normal political choice. Ironically, entitled individuals are declared privileged by virtue of their presumed vulnerability. The question is, who should enjoy this entitlement privilege, for what level and types of benefit, and do the financial circumstances of government provide sufficient grounds for restricting it?

The implication, essential to the argument in this book, is that the form of budget rule affects the conduct and content of welfare policy. The adoption of a rule—or of a particular combination of rules for different programs and different circumstances—is among the fundamental choices constituting a nation's social welfare system. Discretion as a budget arrangement entails procedural priority, in which decisions regarding the amount of transfer payments are responsive to changes in public opinion and to the disposition of the median voter in Congress. Entitlement as a budget arrangement entails substantive priority. Eligible recipients are clients of the government, dependent on public assistance to supplement their incomes. Yet, unlike ordinary beneficiaries of government programs, entitled segments of the population are granted budgetary special standing because their claims must be paid regardless of other community functions or desires.

Predictably, entitlement status for welfare programs has been granted most easily in times when budget resources seem plentiful and society is confident it can afford its commitment to the needy. By contrast, in times when spending conflicts intensify and deficit fears grow, entitlements become susceptible to attack. In recent years, as America became immersed in budget pessimism, there was much less talk about the adequacy of benefits, and far more about the availability of funding and the necessity for spending restraint. Entitlement has come to be portrayed more as a collective fetter than as an individual bulwark. There has been increasing concern regarding its inherent limits to discretionary democratic choice, and comparably less defense of its value as a barrier against economic deprivation. Virtually across the ideological spectrum, budget control has become a relevant issue. Sometimes this has led to proposals to remove entitlement status from particular programs. More often it has led to the consideration of new budgetary mechanisms. Congress has begun experimenting with institutional reforms intended to improve legislative supervision over welfare items that otherwise may automatically expand.

One instrument often considered as a means of budget control is some form of fixed ceiling that caps the amount of available appropriations. Ostensibly, budget caps allow for incremental program growth but, unless expressly overridden, prohibit expenditures greater than anticipated. Ideally, they are an incentive for administrators to promote savings and avoid waste in order to ensure full benefits to qualified recipients. In less than ideal situations when sufficient administrative savings cannot be found, the cap procedures would push legislators to confront the tradeoff between individual claimants and aggregate costs, to make a choice, and to justify it. Welfare entitlements were deliberately left out of the Gramm-Rudman-Hollings deficit reduction process of the late 1980s. They are included under the Budget Enforcement Act of 1990 but only to limit the growth in mandatory spending caused by explicit policy changes; expenditure growth resulting from the utilization of existing entitlement provisions is wholly accommodated. This is the alleged gap in the system of budget decision-making that some fiscal reformers have sought to close.

In different versions, expenditure caps upon welfare assistance have been proposed for individual programs and for broad segments of the U.S. budget. General entitlement caps were recommended by Democrats in the House Budget Committee in 1991. Caps for most means-tested welfare programs were endorsed by the House Republican Conference as part of the 1994 "Contract with America." President Bush proposed spending caps for all welfare entitlements except Social Security in his budget submission of January 1992. President Clinton contemplated a cap on medical costs as part of his health care package in 1993. The Bipartisan Commission on Entitlement and Tax Reform developed a cap option, recommended in its 1994 chairmen's report, that limited spending increases to the change in consumer prices and total population. Federal entitlement caps were contemplated seriously during the welfare and budget reform debates of the 104th Congress. Although none ultimately were enacted into law, such proposals remain on the policy agenda and will most likely return to active consideration if ever the prospects for deficit reduction appear in jeopardy.

For the purposes of empirical study, it is important to note that a quite stringent form of expenditure cap once existed for the food stamp program, which between FY 1978 and FY 1990 had a fixed ceiling imposed by Congress that limited the maximum appropriation for each given fiscal year. Moreover, the program operated under discretionary funding during its formative period, and under entitlement funding from FY 1972 to FY 1977 and from FY 1991 to the present (see Appendix for a detailed chronology). The sequential application of these different forms of budget rule within a single policy arena establishes a natural experiment, altering the structure within which choices occur while holding the context relatively constant. Food stamp history thus provides a perfect case for use in this study. The data will be organized according to the form of budget rule functioning at each stage in food stamp program development. The effect of the different rules can thus be analyzed and their practical consequences for food stamp politics and policy examined.

This chapter has been intended as a general introduction to the main themes of the book. The next chapter briefly discusses the complications of budgeting welfare in contemporary America, emphasizing the nature and kinds of entitlement programs. It then presents a formal analysis of the three alternative versions of budget rule—ordinary discretion, entitlement protection, and spending caps—and highlights certain entailed propositions regarding actor strategies and expected outcomes, establishing hypotheses for later testing. Chapter 3 begins the chronological account. It discusses the origins and early development of the food stamp program, investigating the impact of budget discretion on program expansion and the conditions leading to the establishment of entitlement status in FY 1972. Chapter 4 addresses the consequences of entitlement for the food stamp program during the mid-1970s, as it affected both the growth of total spending and the intense controversies that emerged regarding such growth, leading to the imposition of fixed caps upon permissible appropriations beginning in FY 1978. Chapter 5 examines the operation of those caps during the Carter administration, a period of unified party control and general consensus regarding the value of protecting recipient benefits when welfare obligations and spending targets diverged. Chapter 6 examines the operation of the caps during the early Reagan years, a period of divided party control and relatively high disagreement over the proper balance between welfare and total spending. Together, these chapters provide a comparative analysis regarding the effectiveness of the food stamp budget caps under different partisan political configurations.

Food stamp budget caps became less of a constraint during the mid-1980s, and they were allowed to expire without controversy starting with FY 1991. It is difficult in American politics to sustain the threat of automatic program sacrifices by an identifiable and sympathetic constituency, especially when the compensating gain is diffuse and uncertain. Ironically, food stamp caps disappeared as a salient policy issue during an era when federal deficit concerns were rising and overall spending restraints were installed. Chapter 7 studies these two contradictory movements during the second Reagan administration and their consequences for deficit control. Chapter 8 examines the return of food stamps to entitlement status during the early 1990s, which entailed a return to previous patterns of intransigent political conflict and the revival of proposals for fixed expenditure caps. Ideas in politics never quite seem to die. As a substitute for block grants, specified dollar caps upon annual food stamp appropriations were incorporated into the initial versions of the 1995–96 welfare reform bill, vetoed by President Clinton, although they were absent from the final compromise version later enacted into law. This is the subject of chapter 9. The tension between welfare protection and spending control remains an unresolved item on the American policy agenda. Without a clear, national determination to protect individuals against economic deprivation, including the dedication to ensure adequate food and nutrition, it is likely that periodic budget fluctuations and deficit fears will again bring forth complaints regarding the need for more stringent entitlement restraint and will again revive proposals for fixed caps on program spending.

To preview the main policy conclusion, the focus of chapter 10, the net effect of budget caps on food stamp politics and policy was not positive. Fiscal reformers concerned about the rise of budgeting by accretion and drift have asserted that procedural rules that impose, unless expressly overridden, ceilings on maximum spending would facilitate greater political competition at the margin, coercing legislators to confront competing priorities and to make the hard decisions necessary for cost control. This study of the food stamp program shows that budgetary rules do seem to matter, but not always in the manner desired by reform proponents.

The caps did sometimes force greater attention to issues of welfare cost. The tension between benefit protection and budget responsibility, however, is fundamental and thus cannot be resolved simply as a result of greater attention. In practice, caps function effectively only to the extent that they can restrict entitlement spending during times of cost explosion; welfare protections function effectively only to the extent that they can guarantee essential benefits regardless of budget cost. When decision-makers could not agree regarding appropriate balance, conflict was displaced from substance to procedures, creating prolonged logjams and calling into question the basic capacities of government. Even when decision-makers could agree, the cap arrangement added to legislative complexities, providing the opportunity for brinkmanship and other tricks of political maneuver. Moreover, politicians did not always appreciate a tight cap framework that compelled them to confront difficult policy choices, resulting in efforts to relax or evade it. These consequences of welfare spending caps, evident in the food stamp case study, are logical and predictable, easily derived from the models of budgetary rule. Mechanistic expenditure ceilings do not dissolve inherent policy tensions we do not wish to confront, nor can they mandate that we confront them in a careful and reasonable manner.

Although the detailed story told in this book focuses upon one specific welfare program, the use of methodological models and normative theory establishes broader relevance. From the perspective of social science, this is a study of the causal impact of rules upon results, a topic familiar to the literature on government institutions. Politics might be essentially contested, but it is a contest shaped and molded by the organized structure within which it proceeds. The assumption is that actors respond rationally to the opportunities and incentives constructed into the institutional arena of political play, that the construction of various arenas offer different opportunities and incentives to interested actors, and that in turn the actors sometimes seek to reconstruct those arenas in order to alter their inherent patterns of benefit and bias. One goal of this project is to demonstrate the value of such an approach to the systematic study of social welfare.

From the perspective of policy analysis, this study explores the dynamics of welfare budgeting, as the federal government attempts to deal with the inherent tension between aggregate cost control and individual income protection. The strain between fiscal flexibility and guaranteed entitlement increased in recent years and has spawned reform proposals promising rationalized expenditure restraint. The lessons learned from this case study of a single U.S. food assistance program can be extended, by analogy, to a wider range of budget experiments that have been contemplated.

Finally, this book can be seen as an exercise in engaged citizenship. Its arguments can be located within the classic debate, dating back to the Greeks, of the obligations of distributive justice and the extent to which such obligations are enhanced or encumbered by those state institutions promoting democratic accountability. Democracy is always on trial for the choices it makes. Ordinary voters and their elected representatives become responsible for producing sound collective decisions and for resisting the temptation toward irresponsible ones. Through an investigation of nutrition entitlement and the caps sometimes placed upon it, this study can help Americans to better define and satisfy the commitments incurred—especially the financial commitments incurred—under the modern welfare state.

At the core of this study is an issue of governance—the ability of the American political system to manage effectively its welfare state, providing at an acceptable cost and reasonable efficiency adequate levels of income support to deserving individuals over time. Each of these goals is itself undefined, and together they are not easily reconciled. Americans have a deep ambivalence about welfare, supporting targeted aid to the needy while suspecting waste and fraud, dependency, and immorality. Meanwhile, the U.S. poverty rate remains high. Expenditure caps are, in essence, the expression of a hesitant fiscal conservatism, unwilling to adequately finance its welfare obligations yet equally unwilling to renege on them. The promises are as contradictory as the society that establishes them.

TWO

Model Behavior: The Problem of Costs and the Forms of Budget Control

Effective policy discussion proceeds on the basis of common concepts, a common understanding of the problem, and a common framework for analysis. The object of this chapter is to provide such necessary background. It first presents a brief introduction to the American welfare state and its budgetary cost. It then examines the concept of entitlement, and it contrasts entitlement rules with ordinary discretionary budgeting and with expenditure caps that limit program growth. Last, it develops a set of analytic models that highlight behavioral differences across these three forms of budget rule. At the core of the models is the notion of a "reversion point," the outcome that will prevail by default if no cooperative agreement is reached. A shift in the reversion point should alter the bargaining strategies of the players in the legislative game over welfare appropriations and thus the probable results from play. The models provide pictorial representations of policy options and political outcomes, useful in hypothesis formation and data interpretation.

The American Welfare State

The foundations of American welfare policy were established during the New Deal. Despite shifts in party power, mounting popular discontent, and certain widely heralded legislative reforms, much of that New Deal foundation remains in place today. The past decade has seen extensive study regarding the characteristics of the American poverty population, the causes and duration of poverty spells, and the impact of current programs. The result has been a high degree of academic consensus regarding the organization and effects of the U.S. welfare state.

In 1997, more than 35.5 million Americans lived under the poverty threshold, as defined by the U.S. Census Bureau.[1] This was 13.3% of the resident population. Approximately one-fifth of all children lived in poverty, more than one-quarter of all African Americans and Hispanics. The Census Bureau definition is based on a minimum nutrition diet and a minimum consumption standard for goods and services, adjusted for the size of the household unit and the annual rate of price inflation. In 1997, for example, the poverty threshold for a family of four was $16,400. Income is computed from total household cash receipts, including government transfer payments. Even under more favorable poverty definitions, using different inflation calculations and considering the value of noncash government support, the overall U.S. poverty rate was still approximately 9%. The poverty rate for market incomes alone, absent the effect of public sector assistance, was 21%. Clearly, government welfare helps to reduce total U.S. poverty but it does not lift all needy households above the threshold.

The figures for 1997 are not atypical of recent years, although viewed historically U.S. poverty rates have risen slightly over time. Relatively comparable data exist, using the Census Bureau criteria, starting with the early 1960s. Poverty afflicted slightly more than 20% of the population at the beginning of the time series. The percentage declined rapidly over the prosperous 1960s and early 1970s, stabilized between 11% and 12% during the 1970s, but rose thereafter. The best year of the 1980s saw a greater share of the population poor than the worst year of the 1970s. There was a slow reduction in poverty rates over the long economic upswing of the 1980s, but this was completely reversed by recession. Only gradually is the long recovery of the middle 1990s showing an effect in lower poverty rates. Systematically higher poverty is thus apparent even after matching for similar phases in the business cycle. Part of the explanation is demographic, as there are more elderly and single-parent families in the population. Yet another significant part of the explanation concerns the declining availability of government benefits, and another concerns basic changes in the U.S. economy and the paucity of adequately paying jobs. Over the past two decades, income inequality among American households has also increased and the ratio of the poverty threshold to the median income has widened.

Most poor persons in the United States are poor for very short periods. The average poverty spell is less than three years. This is true even for single mothers with young children, although a disturbing minority is persistently poor. The implication of this finding is that, seen over time, a significant share of the population encounters poverty. For example, approximately one-third of American children, and more than two-thirds of African American children, will experience at least one poverty spell.[2] Changes in household composition and changes in household earnings from work are the factors most responsible for individuals entering and leaving poverty. Work, however, even full-time work, does not automatically guarantee escape. In 1997, for example, approximately 42% of non-aged poor adults worked during the year; approximately 10% worked full time for the entire year.

Government welfare programs only partly fill the gap between market income and the poverty threshold. These programs provide a combination of cash transfers and in-kind goods and services. The American welfare state is based on the distinction between contributory programs that cover a wide range of individuals, poor and nonpoor alike, and means-tested programs that rely on general revenues and target benefits toward the poor, usually restricted to certain demographic categories within the poor. Some U.S. welfare programs are administered by the central government alone, while others rely on a mixture of central and local government finance, regulation, and management. One consequence of this intricate system is that equally destitute individuals are treated quite unequally by the American welfare state depending on their location and household characteristics.

By program type, contributory programs generally spend much more money and have higher levels of benefits, giving great assistance to the impoverished to the extent that they are included among eligible households. Means-tested programs generally spend much less money and have lower levels of benefits, so they are more efficient in delivering targeted support to the poor but with less antipoverty effect. By demographic group, the elderly do much better under the American welfare state than children and working-age adults. For example, of individuals in 1996 over sixty-five years old with inadequate market incomes, more than four-fifths were lifted above the poverty threshold by the array of government tax and transfer programs, mostly the effect of social insurance. Less than one-third of children living in households with inadequate market incomes were lifted above poverty by government programs.

Cross-nationally, the United States experiences a somewhat higher rate of poverty than most other advanced industrial countries, and U.S. welfare programs do somewhat less to guarantee basic individual health, shelter, and income security. The Luxembourg Income Study produces roughly comparable data for the United States and sixteen other advanced industrial nations. Using 50% of the median household disposable income as a standard, in the early 1990s the United States had the second-highest net poverty rate, more than eight percentage points above the cross-national average. Similarly, U.S. tax and transfer programs were the second least effective, reducing market poverty by 43% compared to 73% for the cross-national average.[3]

The complex character of the U.S. welfare state reflects the complexities of American attitudes and political structures. Ideologically, Americans have long accepted a role for the public community in poor relief, but they also strongly endorse the principles of individualism and self-help. They recognize the social and psychological damages of poverty but fear fostering dependency. They are willing to award transfer payments to the needy but are attentive to the least hint of abuse with taxpayer money. The consequence is a policy arrangement comfortable with contributory insurance against unpreventable catastrophe yet far more cautious regarding support for persons ostensibly capable of providing for themselves. Similarly, the U.S. welfare state is a product of the interest fragmentation of American society, notable for its range of organized groups but without an overarching political voice to unify the interests of all working classes. It is also a product of the institutional fragmentation of American democracy that divides obligations across separate agencies and levels of government and makes coordination of effort difficult to achieve.

Welfare in the United States experienced a somewhat liberal phase during the 1960s and early 1970s. Benefits were raised, expenditures grew, and new programs were established, especially in nutrition and health care. Reciprocally, it experienced a rather vigorous conservative reaction during the early 1980s. Popular attention recently has focused on the potential moral dysfunctions of welfare, including possible incentives to long-term dependency and illegitimate births. In addition, there has been increasing demand to expand state-level responsibilities, reflected in the 1996 reform bill that replaced AFDC with temporary family assistance (TANF) block grants. Controversies abound in American welfare politics and rhetoric usually tends toward the extreme. Underneath the ideological fervor, however, lies mounting pressure of a pragmatic sort. The financial exigencies of the federal government have come to dominate the policy agenda. We now live in an era of pervasive resource constraint. Austerity effectively deterred initiatives to expand welfare protections and gave encouragement to conservatives insisting that certain existing commitments were exorbitant or ineffectual. Welfare policy has been transformed, as the politics of subtraction has come to replace the politics of addition. Competition for scarce funds has raised the stakes of legislative politics, while programs struggle and adapt to the new era of retrenchment.[4] In American government, the budget increasingly has become the final arbiter regarding issues of distributional justice.

Budgets, Welfare, and Fiscal Constraints

In FY 1997, the federal government took in $1.579 trillion in receipts and spent $1.601.[5] Despite popular perceptions, the United States does not have an especially large or rapidly growing tax state. Federal revenues as a share of the national product have changed slightly over the past few decades, and fluctuations have been minor. For example, revenues were equal to 19.8% of GDP in 1997, approximately two cents per dollar more than 1960. Federal outlays have risen somewhat faster as a share of national product. Spending in FY 1997 was the equivalent of 20.1% of GDP compared to 17.8% in 1960, a rise of 2.3 cents per dollar over these thirty-eight years.

Comparatively across the advanced industrial nations, for all levels of government combined, the United States is among the least taxed and lowest spending countries. According to OECD data, in 1997 total U.S. government revenues equaled 32.1% of GDP, which is tied for second lowest among the twenty-five nations listed and 5.7 percentage points below the cross-national mean. Total U.S. government outlays in 1997 were 32.0% of GDP, again second lowest among the twenty-five nations and 7.1 percentage points below the cross-national mean. Nor was this particular year exceptional. The growth of relative tax and spending burdens in the United States over time had been slower than in most other industrial nations.

Thus it is true, over the final one-third of the twentieth century, both that U.S. public sector spending tended to be small compared to the other advanced industrial societies and also that federal government spending tended to be large compared to the financial resources made available, resulting in a pattern of persistent deficits. In FY 1997, the federal government ran a deficit of $21.9 billion. It was the twenty-eighth year in a row with a deficit, and as a consequence, the gross federal debt rose to $5.4 trillion, the equivalent of 67.4% of the GDP. Viewed cross-nationally, the American propensity toward financial imbalance was again not remarkable. Nevertheless, despite reformed procedures, bipartisan summit agreements, and statutory deficit reduction mandates, the federal government grappled continually with fiscal stability. Its FY 1997 deficit was the smallest since the early 1970s and represented the first time since 1982 that the ratio of federal indebtedness to GDP has declined. Preliminary projections for FY 1998 and for the five years beyond indicate a moderate surplus. Yet prospects for budget balance during the early twenty-first century will depend heavily upon sustained economic prosperity.

Economists disagree about the degree of harm caused by an extended period of deficit spending. At issue is the effect on interest rates and savings rates, on the strength of the dollar abroad and the import of capital at home. Yet the subjective, political consequences from persistent government deficits in the United States often seem more salient than the objective, economic consequences. Since the early days of the Republic, the concept of government debt has carried negative normative connotations. An unbalanced budget has symbolized political corruption, inefficiency, and irresponsibility. A balanced budget has implied order, stability, and restraint in the use of public power.[6] Politicians are expected to pay homage to the ideal, even when they violate it in practice. Thus the recent era of high deficits was accompanied by distrust in government and in its leaders. Voters became increasingly suspicious of public spending and increasingly unwilling to part with their tax dollars. They warmly endorsed candidates for office promising blithely to cut costs and to reduce waste and fraud. Ironically, a problem defined by tax revenues insufficient to finance existing government projects engendered public discontent and tax resistance, combined with limited support for specific reductions in the scope of government projects. As a result, gains in the budget battle came only after protracted and painful political struggle.

Welfare played a large part in the changing shape of the federal budget. The formal budget category "Payments for Individuals" was calculated to cost $950 billion in FY 1997. This was more than 59% of total federal outlays, up from only 26% in 1960. Included in this category are virtually all the programs ordinarily considered as welfare. Nearly one-half of FY 1997 Payments for Individuals was Social Security and other government retirement support (48.0%). Another one-third was health care, especially Medicare and Medicaid (34.1%). The remaining one-sixth was comprised of unemployment insurance (2.2%), subsidized housing, nutrition, and student assistance (7.6%), means-tested cash payments (7.3%), and special veterans, refugee, and other assistance (0.4%). Payments for Individuals expanded fastest, as a share of both the federal budget and the GDP, during the late 1960s and early 1970s when Social Security was first indexed against inflation and new health and nutrition benefits were introduced, and during the 1990s when federal health care costs soared and the population aged. Over the thirty-eight-year period fiscal years 1960–1997, defense expenditures declined dramatically as a share of the federal budget and the GDP. Outlays for government domestic purchases and services also declined, especially after 1980.

These trends have significance regarding the federal capacity for fiscal flexibility. Imagine that the government wishes to cut $100 billion from its current $1600 billion in operations, possibly to afford a tax reduction, or to improve the financial balance sheet, or merely to shift spending priorities. The interest on the national debt must be paid if the government wishes to remain solvent. If Payments for Individuals is also untouched, a cut of $100 billion, using FY 1997 as a baseline, would require a 25% net reduction in all other federal government spending, more than 50% of remaining spending if national defense were also exempted. Over time, therefore, it has become less and less possible to shelter welfare from the considerations of federal budget policy, and vice versa. America has entered an era of welfare fiscalization, in which the fortunes of the poor and the fortune of the national government are necessarily linked.

The federal budget contains one additional distinction relevant to welfare expenditure. The 1990 Budget Enforcement Act categorizes outlays either as discretionary or direct/mandatory. Discretionary spending proceeds under the authority of the appropriations committees and the amounts are thus determined by the annual appropriations acts. Mandatory spending is derived directly from program legislation, which effectively requires the commitment of federal funds. Virtually the entire sum of mandatory spending comes from interest on the debt and Payments for Individuals. Predictably, discretionary spending has declined over time while mandatory spending has risen—from approximately 30% of federal outlays in FY 1960 to over 65% in FY 1997; from 6% of GDP to more than 13%. Just as issues of welfare provision now lead inescapably to those of budget control, issues of budget control lead to entitlement.

The Nature of Entitlement

According to the Congressional Budget and Impoundment Act of 1974, an entitlement is defined by the necessity "to make payments (including loans and grants), the budget authority for which is not provided for in advance by appropriation Acts, to any person or government if, under the provisions of the law containing such authority, the United States is obligated to make such payments to persons or governments who meet the requirements established by such law." The budget act therefore establishes four basic criteria for an entitlement. First, the benefit involves payment in money or in services that could be purchased for money. Second, the benefit is vested by the statutory language and by the official regulations governing the implementation of the statute. Third, each beneficiary must be certified to receive the benefit on the basis of satisfying specified legal requirements. Fourth, the beneficiary cannot be denied and the benefit cannot be altered by discretionary budget choice. Often the annual appropriations process is bypassed completely. Yet even for those entitlements requiring enacted appropriations, such as the food stamp program, the relevant committees are obliged to provide funds adequate to meet all legitimate claims and thus they must comply via supplemental action if the initial amount proves insufficient.[7]

The question nevertheless remains, what kind of "title" does an entitlement establish. In an earlier era of U.S. history, welfare was public charity. Seen as a gift from the community to the needy, it was awarded purely at the discretion of the donor, with amounts chosen by the donor and paid to those individuals whom the donor deemed worthy. The modern welfare state has moved considerably away from this conception, although contemporary jurisprudence is uncertain what alternative principle should be instituted. The creation of legally entitled claims to benefits itself implies a shift in status, to the extent that qualified individuals cannot be denied capriciously and thus the total demand upon government resources depends simply on the number of such qualified individuals and their level of need. On the other hand, although annual outlays are mandated, the substantive rules governing program eligibility and operations remain a matter of political choice. Put in terms of the old distinction, welfare-as-right versus welfare-as-privilege, the concept of entitlement establishes recipient rights under the law, but the content of the law is a privilege and the criteria it sets forth can be specified as the representative democracy sees fit.

In recent years, court decisions have gone slightly further, invalidating blatantly unfair statutory or regulatory conditions imposed upon welfare entitlement. The argument has been that individuals cannot be refused basic constitutional rights as a consequence of their dependent status. For example, they cannot be denied due process in appealing adverse bureaucratic decisions, they cannot be denied equal protection because of ascriptive characteristics or personal lifestyle, they cannot be denied mobility within U.S. borders despite different state programs, they cannot be denied dignity when applying for welfare, and they cannot be denied ordinary privacy when the details of their applications are investigated. By such decisions, courts have to a degree limited the freedom of legislators to punish beneficiaries or decrease costs.

Some theorists have urged the courts to adopt a more sweeping notion of welfare rights. "Title," argues John Brigham, is a term of property that has long forfeited any connection to traditional definitions based on possession, use, or creation. Property, he claims, entails a reasonable expectation of legal compensation, and welfare entitlement can establish such an expectation. Thus, for example, participants in the Social Security system allegedly should have enforceable claims to appropriate future payment, despite the fact that benefits ostensibly are established by ordinary law and ostensibly are subject to change at any time by congressional action.[8] An even more extreme assertion, based on the work of Charles Reich, is that the right to adequate welfare is guaranteed by fundamental law, independent of any statutory enactment. The constitutional declaration of equal citizenship and requirement that government support the general welfare allegedly prescribe conditions that the political regime is obliged to pursue. In this view, income support is a societal imperative, not a kindness granted to the recipient. It is awarded as a matter of individual respect and community membership, and as a necessary corrective against the inequalities inherent to a capitalist economy. It cannot be compromised, and the courts must ensure that it not be compromised, based on insufficient political will. According to proponents, welfare is a standard by which one judges a successful democracy, rather than a task that a successful democracy might choose to undertake. In his 1944 State of the Union address, Franklin Roosevelt declared an "Economic Bill of Rights," but there has been little in recent political platforms or judicial decisions to suggest a movement toward constitutional entitlement in this radical sense.[9]

Entitlement, instead, is best understood primarily as a budgetary category. Welfare under a discretionary budget rule implies a philosophy of public charity in which the gift-giver does not have to yield more than desired. Welfare as entitlement entails the necessity to satisfy all legitimate claims, and thus to adapt annual spending contingent on inflation and unemployment rates, demographic shifts, and the number of qualified persons who apply for benefits. Under discretion, the authorizing legislation gives license for Congress to appropriate funds as it sees fit; for entitlement, the authorizing legislation mandates that Congress provide funds. Under discretion, the appropriations process is the initiator. For entitlements, the appropriations process, if involved at all, is the responder. Under discretion, program changes result from adjustments in spending allowances. For entitlement, spending changes result from adjustments in program requirements. Under discretion, the annual appropriation establishes a fixed limit for permissible outlays. For entitlement, the itemized appropriation is merely an estimate of projected costs, given prevailing eligibility and benefit rules. Thus expenditure levels under entitlement, as Shep Melnick commented, cannot be consciously chosen and narrowly enforced, because they "result from millions of individual eligibility determinations."[10]

The key to the special status of entitlement, compared to discretionary budgeting, concerns the abolition of the division of labor between authorization and appropriations.[11] Under ordinary conditions, authorizing legislation defines the general policy goals and the means for achieving them. Appropriations then determine the extent of activities for any given fiscal year. The division of labor separates program objectives and program operations, placing them within different committee jurisdictions in Congress. Substantive committees will tend to act as advocates; fiscal committees will exercise oversight. Entitlement, however, entails no such distinction. Spending is considered "direct" or "mandatory" because the obligation to outlay funds stems immediately from the language of the statutory authorization. As open-ended, entitlement payments do not have to be scheduled in order to prevent an end-of-the-year deficiency. As spending is required by program rules, legislation has entailed multi-year effects. Yet this places extra burdens upon legislators because of the level of technical detail which must be written into the authorizing statue, for that detail establishes the rights of various claimants and therefore the total program cost. As an alternative form of budget rule, entitlement is a plausible option for policies that are quantitative in purpose, awarding valued government cash incentives or subsidies to designated nongovernment beneficiaries, in contrast to policies that are more qualitative, producing and delivering by means of federal employees goods and services useful to the public. Yet the consequence is two contrasting budget systems that together constitute the sum of federal spending.

A program granted entitlement status does not necessarily experience faster expenditure growth than a comparable discretionary program. Entitlement does signify a commitment to maintain spending over time, but many discretionary programs also operate on the assumption of long-term obligation. Inertia in public policy, even when outcomes are completely subject to political choice, usually predominates over innovation.[12] Equally, entitlement status does not always protect a program against spending cuts, especially given the use of omnibus reconciliation bills as ordered sometimes by the congressional budget resolution. A certain degree of insulation is created for programs divorced from the budget cycle's insistence on annual inspection and review, yet entitlements must be considered only relatively uncontrollable because the laws and regulations authorizing program operations can always be revised. The designation, within official budget language, of programs commonly known as entitlements as direct, as opposed to discretionary, expenditures indicates that they are perfectly acceptable parts of the federal government repertoire, differentiated by the method through which spending is determined. The differentiation, however, leads to differences in institutional processes and actor strategies. Its importance can be seen in the controversies over program entitlement status and the frequent attempts to restrain it.

In essence, the two forms of budget rule are based on two contrasting principles. Ordinary budgeting is public-sector oriented and procedural—it is focused on the total amount and separate components of government spending, and it subjects them to annual democratic deliberation and decision making, which remains in potential even when legislators do not utilize the full range of their opportunity. Entitlement, by contrast, is private-sector oriented and substantive—it is focused on the consumption levels of needy American households, and it serves to guarantee full welfare benefits to those households eligible and enrolled, which is a valuable protection even though Congress retains the power to redefine who is needy and the extent of their need. The two different principles, in turn, foster different politics, for discretion facilitates competition for scarce fiscal resources whereas entitlement, by permitting certain programs to bypass appropriations jurisdiction, establishes a more difficult legislative road for program challengers. Moreover, the different principles promote different policy outcomes, for discretion allocates a specified dollar amount for each fiscal year independent of the level of societal need, whereas entitlement responds automatically to defined societal need independent of any predicted amount for annual program spending.

"Rights," Melnick observed, "can quickly become expensive."[13] Entitlement spending has grown enormously in America, both in absolute dollars and as a percentage of total outlays. This was caused in part by policy liberalizations during the late 1960s and early 1970s, and in part by macroeconomic instability during the late 1970s and early 1980s. Yet entitlement spending has continued to grow over the past decade, albeit at a somewhat slower pace, despite enacted statutory restrictions and generally favorable market conditions. According to the Bipartisan Commission on Entitlement and Tax Reform, current trends are "not sustainable." It forecast, assuming prevailing program rules and a reasonably prosperous economy, that entitlement spending will comprise nearly 60% of federal outlays by the year 2003. By 2012, entitlements plus interest payments will absorb the entire amount of tax revenue raised by the federal government. By 2030, entitlements alone will more than absorb all federal tax revenues. The Commission expressed concern about "the long-term imbalance between the government's entitlement promises and the funds it will have available to pay for them," which poses a threat to the solvency of the federal government and to the economic future of the nation.[14]

No two welfare entitlement programs are alike and thus it is often unfair to lump them all together. Among cash transfer programs, for example, Social Security is a contributory system with its own trust fund that supports benefits indexed to the inflation rate. Unemployment insurance similarly is a contributory program but its benefits are determined by the states individually. Supplemental Security Income is a categorical means-tested program for the elderly, blind, and disabled financed out of general revenues, with uniform national benefits indexed to inflation. Aid to Families with Dependent Children, before it was replaced by the TANF block grant, was similarly means-tested, categorical, and financed out of general revenues, but its benefits were not indexed and differed widely across the states. Among the in-kind programs, Medicare is available to all elderly individuals who contributed to the trust fund; Medicaid is means-tested and categorical; food stamps are available to virtually all poor households. The two health programs have the government directly pay the provider for the benefits supplied; the food stamp program instead issues a special form of pseudo-money, which the recipient then uses to pay the provider.

The different programs have not expanded at the same pace. According to Entitlement Commission estimates, of the $775 billion calculated increase (inflation adjusted) in entitlement spending, 1963 through 1999, 75% is derived from contributory sources. Only 11% comes from nonhealth care, means-tested entitlements. To make the same point somewhat differently, Social Security, Medicare, Medicaid, and federal retirement programs, which currently comprise more than three-quarters of entitlement spending, were projected by the Entitlement Commission to grow by $168 billion (inflation adjusted) between 1993 and 1999. Spending on all other entitlements—including most of the assistance programs targeted to the poor—was projected to decrease by more than $15 billion. Primarily from demographic causes, especially the aging of the U.S. population and the increase in average lifespan, health care costs should more than double by 2030; Social Security will have fully depleted its trust fund of assets.[15] Yet the differences in growth rates across entitlement programs are political as well as sociological in cause. The programs especially vulnerable to legislated restraint are those targeted narrowly to help the nonaged needy in society, who are most susceptible to being labeled undeserving and are least capable of mobilizing the political resources of influence.[16] Ironically, the more politically secure entitlements—i.e., those which are contributory, respected, established, and inclusive—are also the ones that cost the most and have grown the fastest. By contrast, the entitlements most often under political attack are in general less responsible for America's long-term budget dilemmas and have less capacity to help resolve them.

In the politics of public finance, wrote Austrian economist Joseph Schumpeter, one hears "the thunder" of history "stripped of all phrases."[17] Much of the thunder over American budgeting in recent years concerned the continued efforts of the federal government to effectively reconcile aggregate revenues and aggregate expenditures. Americans seem delighted with each promise for a new round of tax cuts but they seem equally defensive of program obligations, especially those that deliver tangible benefits to valued constituencies. Entitlements apparently have exacerbated the federal budget problem, commanding government spending regardless of revenues and giving priority to the claims of legally qualified beneficiaries over other uses of available funds. From the perspective of welfare advocates, the increasingly contested environment under budget constraint simply makes entitlement guarantees for the poor and vulnerable ever more valuable. From the perspective of budget regulation, the growth of entitlements is fetter to the effective management of government finances. Predictably, when fiscal discipline appears low and deficit fears run high, mainstream politicians from both political parties will wonder whether America can afford its current welfare state.

Caught in the deepening tension between budget restraint and welfare protection, American policymakers have sought greater control over the relatively uncontrollable. Their announced goal has been to maintain basic commitments to the needy yet also improve program management, contain costs, and facilitate choice among competing public priorities. The difficulty is to reestablish policy balance without harming important constituent interests, among the poor and the nonpoor alike. Yet there has been no consensus in America regarding how to achieve such a balance. When substantive issues are hard to resolve, politicians begin to experiment with institutional mechanisms. The hope is that new rules for operating procedures—governing what decisions can be made, when they are made, or how they are made—will somehow help relieve the policy tension or facilitate political accord.

Expenditure caps, which allow outlays to increase but only up to a given threshold, are an obvious attempt to reconcile specific benefit promises and aggregate fiscal management. Caps can be constructed in a number of possible variants. They might apply to all government spending, to all entitlements, to a group of entitlements, or to an individual program. They can apply to the budget authority to spend, to the expenditures forecast for the coming year, or to actual treasury payments. They can be fixed at a specified dollar amount, or they can float to accommodate changing inflation rates, poverty rates, or demography. Common to all versions, however, is the use of a fiscal trigger to force the integration of otherwise automatic spending into the budget process.

According to proponents, the cap mechanism is intended to enhance legislative oversight and responsible decision making. Cap procedures compel political attention by their crude threat of benefit reductions whenever annual program costs exceed prior expectations. However, there is usually a delay between the official prediction of funding insufficiency and the obligation to curtail outlays, which allows for a range of potential policy responses. Possibly, administrative reforms can be introduced that generate required savings yet leave benefits untouched. Possibly, legislators will decide that the priority given to welfare assistance is sufficiently high to justify cap overrides, despite the impact on debt, taxes, or competing programs. Possibly, legislators will accede to welfare benefit reductions but will try to apportion the costs equitably across recipients, altering eligibility or allotment rules rather than acquiesce to across-the-board cuts. Possibly, legislators will accept the mandatory cuts imposed by the expenditure cap. The substantive response to welfare spending that breaches the cap threshold is entirely a matter of political selection. Yet the option that will prevail if legislators fail to reach agreement is mechanistic and indiscriminate cost reduction, as dictated by the cap formula previously enacted. Proponents assert that without such a looming threat, politicians will not willingly confront difficult tradeoffs and establish a clear preference.

In a sense, spending caps occupy a middle budgetary position between entitlement and discretionary rules. Up to the cap threshold, program funding operates in entitlement fashion; all qualified recipients receive benefits at the full level of their eligibility. Above the cap threshold, program funding operates in discretionary fashion; unless legislative action occurs to override the cap, no additional funds can be expended, regardless of individual need or policy intent. On the other hand, spending caps are usually defended as an attempt to transcend the perceived limitations of both entitlement and discretionary rules. The gain from entitlement is the protection given to needy beneficiaries, but the danger is that programs then sit outside the purview of annual legislative vigilance and that spending will accelerate necessarily under changing economic conditions. The gain from discretion is greater government control and regular scrutiny of program value, but the danger is that the politically weak and vulnerable traditionally sit outside the halls of power and that benefits will not be adjusted despite changing economic conditions. In both cases, there is the assumption that problems arise—whether fiscal or social—as a result of the disregard and drift that so often characterizes American politics. The cap solution, allegedly, would force the inherent tensions of welfare budgeting onto the active agenda and thus help institutionalize deliberation and conscious choice.

Optimism need not be matched by results. Skeptics warn about the complexity and distortions that additional budget requirements might impose upon decisions. Congress might defer in the exercise of its new responsibilities rather than meet them with reason and understanding. The same intractable policy tensions that produced recourse to procedural reform might equally deadlock the caps mechanism if legislators fail to agree on a remedy when thresholds are breached. Even worse, the caps might provide an incentive to strategic manipulation or fiscal gimmicks. At issue in the debate is the direction of the effect upon politics and policy caused by the character of the institutional rules adopted. Rules can modify bargaining relations among interested actors, thereby altering the tactics adopted, the powers exercised, and the outcomes anticipated in the legislative game. Yet the impact of any institutional change can be assessed only as a consequence of empirical testing. The remainder of this chapter will present a more rigorous discussion of discretionary, entitlement, and expenditure-cap budget rules, examining their expected impact on the patterns of political decision making. This will provide a framework for the concrete analysis to follow, based on the actual experiences of the food stamp program.

The Logics of Budget Rule

From one perspective, social scientists collect data in order to evaluate models. Their interest is with the specification of abstract representations of collective behavior and with testing the validity of the empirical hypotheses derived from such representations. From another perspective, social scientists develop models in order to organize data. Models help to focus attention, distinguishing important from unimportant observations and identifying the patterns of regular relationships. Seen through the framework of a model, collective behavior appears somewhat less chaotic, conflicts less embroiled, and outcomes less random. The discussion of welfare and budgeting in this book combines both perspectives. Two formal but relatively elementary social science models will be presented to help compare the interest calculations and strategic choices under discretionary budget rule, entitlement rule, and expenditure-cap rule. Data from food stamp policy history will be used to assess the general utility of the explanatory models. Reciprocally, the models will be employed to further understand the political behavior of actual players in the food stamp arena. Although the models are analytical and the data historical, the object of this study is intentionally practical. The goal is to consider the interconnections between budget and welfare politics in the United States, and to comment upon the policy repertoire adopted by the federal government in the attempt to reconcile them.

Budgetmaking under discretionary, entitlement, and expenditure-cap rules differs critically in those situations when no political agreement is reached. The reversion point is the outcome that occurs by default. Without explicit legislation, policy reverts back to the status quo. Yet the location of that status quo is different under the three alternative types of budget rule. Under ordinary budgeting, all expenditures are discretionary. An act of Congress is required to appropriate funds for public purposes. The absence of agreement, therefore, means that no spending is permitted. The reversion point is zero. One might expect consistency with the past, maintaining the current base level of program outlays while making gradual adjustments at the margin. Yet neither the base nor the adjustment is guaranteed.

By contrast, entitlement rules legitimate expenditures independent of appropriations agreement. Qualified recipients have claim to the full allotment of benefits established by law. Spending therefore proceeds at a cost sufficient to comply with legal requirements. The reversion point is defined by the number of eligible households who apply for benefits and the level of their determined need. This implies a distinction between spending growth mandated under the practices of existing law and spending growth that exceeds the requirements under existing law. Under entitlement, the base and the former type of addition are guaranteed, whereas the latter type of addition can proceed only as a consequence of new, substantive enactment.

Finally, an expenditure cap is a combined form of rule which satisfies recipient claims and permits spending to rise accordingly, but only up to some specified maximum level. If outlays threaten to exceed that maximum, allotments must be reduced and/or enrollments curtailed unless the cap is expressly overridden by legislative action. Absent congressional agreement to change, the reversion point thus exists at the cap threshold. In essence, a further distinction is introduced regarding program spending. The base and that share of any mandated addition up to the cap limit are guaranteed; the remainder of the otherwise mandated addition plus all further cost increases from intentional policy changes are not.

Quite obviously, the different budget rules lead to very different expenditure outcomes in the absence of explicit agreement. In addition, they often lead to different strategies by political actors and to different policy outcomes even when agreement is achieved. Politicians can be expected to understand the prevailing context for collective choice and to act rationally within that context. The fact that a particular result occurs by reversion affects the kinds of compromise various players would find acceptable. This, in turn, affects the demands they would make and their abilities to realize these demands. A shift in the reversion point, through backwards induction, thus alters the logic of game bargaining and the expected solutions from play. The implication of this simple observation will be explored in two distinct ways—first with respect to actors divided institutionally and then with respect to actors divided ideologically. Although each will be introduced separately, their impact upon events is necessarily combined.

Institutional Dynamics

Regarding institutions, the U.S. Constitution gives to the legislative branch principal power over the purse. Since the Budget and Accounting Act of 1921, however, the president has become responsible for preparing and submitting to Congress each year a detailed and comprehensive budget proposal for revenues and expenditures. The consequence is a sequential process of budget decision making, based on presidential initiation and congressional response, which requires effective agreement in order for the federal government to maintain operations. The question to be asked regarding welfare spending is whether or not the actors play honestly—whether the budget proposal from the president and/or the budget approved by Congress reflect well-intentioned estimates of the expected costs from normal program implementation, or whether they are intentionally inaccurate. The incentives to honesty vary with the different forms of budget rule (see Figure 2-1).

Figure 2-1. ***Institutional Budget Game***

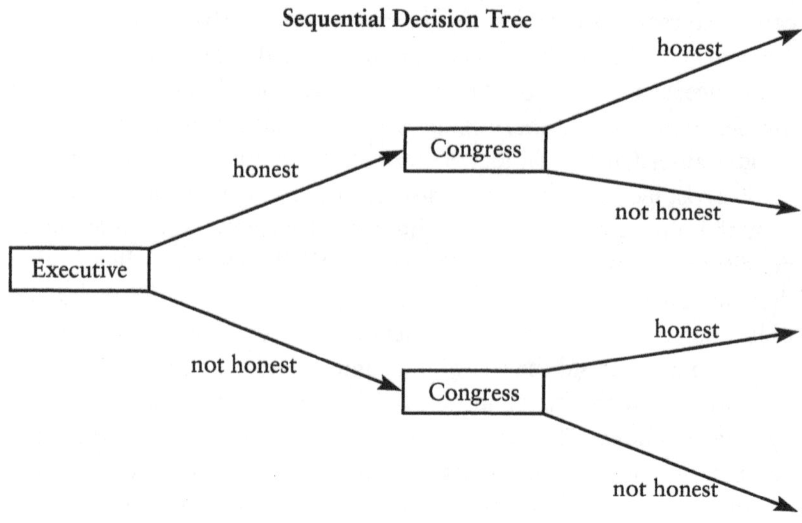

Hypothesized Political Play

Budget Rule	*Agency*	*President*	*Congress*
Discretion (FY 1965–71)	Overestimate	Overestimate	Honest
Entitlement (FY 1972–77, 1991–)	Honest	Underestimate	Honest or Underestimate
Spending Cap (FY 1978–90)	Honest	Within Cap: Underestimate Breach Cap: Honest	Underestimate

First, assume a welfare program that depends for its funds entirely on discretionary budgeting. Assume further that there is no essential ideological controversy between the president and Congress with respect to this program and there are no applicable spending or deficit limits to constrain political choice. This was roughly the situation for food stamps during the early 1970s, the latter part of its formative period. The agency administering a successful program has no incentive to underestimate entailed costs, as this might initiate harmful cuts or require a supplemental appropriation to make up the deficiency. The agency might even seek to overestimate costs, in order to finance program expansion and provide protection against unanticipated contingencies. Yet the president, acting through his budget office, would try to limit such aggressive behavior to preserve control over the executive branch and ensure sound management of fiscal policy. The congressional appropriations committees should reason similarly. They too can see unnecessary program risk from underestimation and undesirable political maneuvering in overestimation. Given generalized support for program goals, the appropriations committees should tend to be honest, striving to keep spending in line with perceived needs and allowing for reasonable growth over time.

Relative honesty in discretionary budgeting is reinforced by repetition. Although the entire program is open to appropriations review each year, the required effort and attendant uncertainty leads legislators toward abbreviated calculations. The expectation is that ordinarily a program will seek to protect its base and receive a fair share of any aggregate increase or decrease in spending. As Aaron Wildavsky has shown, budget struggles under discretion usually proceed at the margin, and thus growth under normal conditions occurs incrementally. The success of incremental budgeting, however, depends on continued confidence. An agency that systematically makes impractical requests or submits unreliable data will incur congressional retribution; a committee that appropriates imprudently invites agency deception. Ironically, the range and uncertainties of discretionary budget decision making itself facilitates strategic behavior intended to reinforce stable institutional bargaining and political accommodation.[18]

Next, assume that this same welfare program is suddenly and completely protected by entitlement rules. As before, by stipulation there is no inherent ideological controversy over program goals. Yet the structural incentives now encourage a quite different pattern of institutional play. The administering agency has no excuse to overestimate costs, because net expenditures are determined externally by the number and need of eligible recipients, as defined under the authorizing legislation. The president, for corollary reasons, has a strong incentive to underestimate costs. Whether to demonstrate apparent fiscal restraint or to find room in a tight budget for desired discretionary programs, the president can gain by adopting low spending estimates for welfare entitlements. Importantly, there are no penalties from such dishonesty. Eligible recipients are ensured full benefits and thus all obligatory costs eventually must be met.

Congressional strategy is similarly determined by the existence of entitlement protections. For those welfare programs that do not require appropriations action, Congress is free to be a complicitor in systematic cost underestimation. It will simply appear in the end-of-year accounting that expenditures far exceeded expectations. For those welfare programs that do require appropriations action, the political costs of raising the president's budget totals must be weighed against the institutional costs of making corrections later through supplemental legislation. Regarding the food stamp program under pure entitlement rules, during the middle 1970s and again during the early 1990s, Congress sometimes responded to presidential underestimation by adopting a more plausible set of outlay estimates, and sometimes it responded with part-year appropriations intended to force supplemental requests from the president. In the first case, Congress was willing to accept the political onus of honesty, while in the second it sought to shift the onus back to the administration. Either way, the dollar outcome was predetermined by the level of program utilization. Under entitlement rules, budgetary posturing and position-taking can proceed with complete safety because the reversion point establishes a fixed and fully adequate result.

Last, imagine the same popular welfare program under expenditure-cap budget rules. Here there is a strong incentive for Congress systematically to underestimate expenditures, while the executive branch faces more uncertainty. The administration still can gain by artificially making the program budget appear small, but only if the mandatory excess falls beneath the cap threshold. It would not wish to surprise the nation, deep into the fiscal year, when program spending suddenly threatens to breach the cap. Either the cap explicitly must be overridden and appropriations raised, or otherwise worthy recipients will have their benefits arbitrarily reduced. In either case, the administration should fear the political backlash. Thus the president's anticipated value from budget dishonesty depends largely on the allowance permitted any eventual overage. The higher the risk that the cap threshold might be exceeded, the greater the probability that he will play honestly. The lower the risk that the cap threshold might be exceeded, the greater the probability that the president can underestimate safely, and thus he will play as if entitlement rules still pertained.

Regardless of the president's request, Congress systematically should prefer underestimation, using the need for later corrective action to provide the grounds for program intervention. Especially during tight budget times, legislators would welcome expanded opportunities for oversight and review, enhancing control not just by the appropriations committees but by the authorizing committees as well. With the reversion point looming, Congress can hold hearings, chastise lax administrators, display its concern about profligate spending with taxpayers' money, and loudly condemn waste, fraud, and error. It can then with good conscience take the necessary emergency steps to save the program and protect the interests of legitimate beneficiaries. Allegedly compelled to respond by the cap mechanism, Congress can make a visible demonstration on behalf of efficiency and prudence, yet it can also take credit for supporting needy claimants, which is akin to having one's cake and eating it too. The result, even when there is complete ideological support for the program across institutions, should be a repetitive pattern of crisis legislation and supplemental appropriations, in which politicians intentionally respond to an initial under-allocation of funds merely by revising the total rather than by addressing its determinants.[19] This is, for example, what happened with the food stamp program during its period of tight budget caps, during the late 1970s and early 1980s. The main dangers from such a complicated procedure come from the delay of ordinary legislative business, from the appearance of uncontrollability that creates disrespect for the program, and from the expanded leverage that the prospect of an arbitrary benefit cutoff gives to players willing to use brinkmanship tactics.

The main hypothesis emerging from this brief discussion of institutional players and reversion point effects is quite clear—the fewer the consequences, the more probability of aggressive political play. Under discretionary budgeting, the consequences are substantial because the failure to reach agreement has a direct impact upon program operations; the very extent of that risk leads players to establish more stable and moderate norms of behavior. Under entitlement budgeting, the consequences from aggressive play are virtually zero; the assurance of adequate funding freely permits political maneuvers such as intentional presidential underestimates and intentional congressional part-year appropriations. Spending caps occupy a somewhat in-between budgetary position, with more consequences from political play than with entitlements but fewer than with discretionary budgeting. One might hope that it would produce the best of both worlds—regular legislative supervision over program operations to restrain unnecessary costs and promote efficiency, and conscious action to override the cap threshold and ensure recipient benefits to the degree justified by welfare need. It might equally produce the worst of both worlds—continual threats to legitimate benefits from legislatively engineered and recurrent crises, and repeated tinkering interventions into program operations alongside costly concessions to favored constituents. Advocates for budget caps loudly celebrate the opportunity for reasoned deliberation associated with the former alternative. This analytic discussion suggests that actual results might logically reflect the latter.

Ideological Dynamics

The other dynamic inherent to the character of the budget rule concerns ideological rather than institutional differences among the key actors. The previous model assumed, somewhat artificially, generalized support for the welfare program facing budget choice. The object now is to introduce intense partisan controversy into the calculation. The previous model was based on the sequence of decision-making. Here, because actor preferences differ and the location of those preferences is important, the model is based on a spatial array of possible policy positions. Imagine a one-dimensional linear map ranging from the ideological left to the ideological right. Each actor has a single preferred policy location on the map, reflecting the spending outcome desired for the welfare program under consideration. The further the distance between some given point and an actor's preferred location, the greater the actor's utility loss if that point is chosen as the ultimate policy outcome. Any two points equidistant from an actor's ideal location, by definition, involve the same net utility loss and thus lie on the same indifference curve. The actor has no preference between them but will always favor a point closer on the map to his ideal. For simplicity of presentation, this preliminary example posits only two stylized actors, a relatively liberal Congress (C) and a relatively conservative president (P), each operating rationally and with perfect information. The ideologically preferred position of Congress is determined by the conference committee report acceptable to the median voter in both chambers. The ideologically preferred position of the president is determined by the annual budget request. In the model, both C and P remain constant regardless of the budgetary rule adopted. What changes is the reversion point (Q), with implications for political play and policy outcomes (see Figure 2.2).

As before, first assume a welfare program operating under a discretionary budget rule. Normal budgeting practice creates an outcome ex-

Figure 2-2. ***Ideological Budget Game***

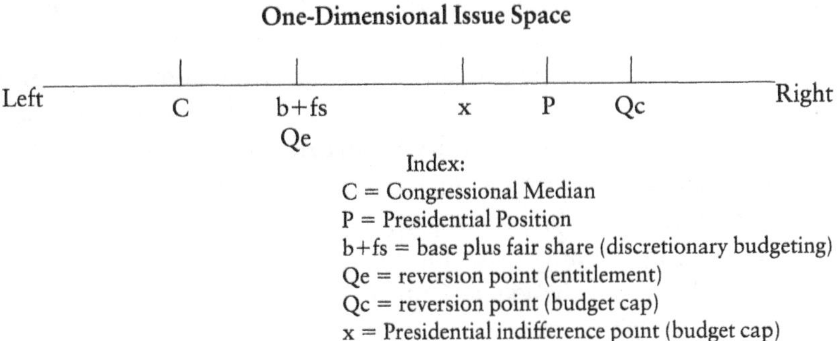

Hypothesized Political Play

Budget Rule	*Expenditure Decisions*	*Reversion Point*	*Predicted Outcome*
Discretion (FY 1965–71)	Annual	Zero (expectation is base + fair share)	C . . . P
Entitlement (FY 1972–77, 1991–)	None Required	Qe (determined by recipient need)	Qe
Spending Cap (FY 1978–90)	Only if spending breaches the cap ($Qc < Qe$)	Qc (determined by legislated limit)	Within cap: Qe Breach cap: x . . . P

pectation, founded upon the base spending level from the previous year (b) plus a fair share (fs) of any increment in total government spending. The liberal Congress prefers even more spending, an outcome to the left of expectation [$C > (b+fs)$], whereas the conservative president prefers less spending, an outcome to the right of expectation [$P < (b+fs)$]. Nevertheless, base plus fair share is not a reversion point. Under the American political system of separated institutions sharing power, the failure to reach agreement means that no spending at all occurs, a position so far to the right that it is extremely distant from the ideal location of both actors. The policy result from bargaining should occur anywhere in the space from C through P. If Congress can attach the appropriation for this welfare program to a veto-proof omnibus spending bill, it can enforce outcome C. If the president has use of a line-item veto, he can enforce outcome P. Between them is the area of potential compromise. Base plus fair share provides a convenient rule of thumb intended to minimize potential conflict, but it has no formal priority, and thus the actual outcome within the bargaining space depends entirely on relative power, commitment, and tactics. For the food stamp program, ideological controversy under discretionary budget rule prevailed in the middle 1960s, during the early stages of program establishment.

Next, assume that the program is given entitlement status. Spending is determined by statutory provision and is based on the number of qualified individuals and the extent of their need. It can be estimated for budget-making purposes from the previous year's outlay, adjusted for changing demographic and macroeconomic conditions. This establishes the reversion point for entitlement spending (Qe), which prevails, given fixed program regulations, independently of actor budget preferences. For ease of comparison, assume that the location of Qe under the entitlement budget rule is identical to the location of expectation (b+fs) had the discretionary budget rule been maintained. Congress is again to the left and thus would prefer granting a somewhat higher level of payments to a somewhat larger pool of recipients, reforming the authorizing legislation to raise spending above Qe. The president is again to the right, and thus would prefer legislative reforms to contract the program and reduce spending below Qe. However, unlike before, there is only one rational outcome for the entitlement case, exactly at the reversion point. Congress would refuse to cooperate with proposed legislative changes to the right of Qe because it can obtain a preferable outcome simply by default. The president, conversely, would veto any proposed legislative change to the left of Qe because he equally can obtain a preferable outcome by default. Consequently, there is no room for negotiation. In fact, because the reversion point occurs automatically under situations of noncooperation, each side is free to trumpet loudly its own ideal ideological position without the least hint of concession or compromise. The equilibrium outcome, maximizing under the circumstances to both parties, will be enforced regardless of political intransigence. This was the situation for the food stamp program under entitlement rules during the Ford administration.

Finally, assume the imposition of a budget cap at a spending level below that which would occur under entitlement rules alone, ensuring that the cap will be breached if no remedial action is taken. The cap establishes a new reversion point (Qc) to the right of Qe and even further to the right of C. The president in this illustration, although resolutely opposed to the current level of guaranteed benefits, is not completely antagonistic to welfare spending and thus would not necessarily welcome sudden and across-the-board benefit reductions to otherwise qualified claimants if during the course of the fiscal year outlays threatened to exceed previously specified limits [C > Qe > P > Qc]. Because of the cap rule, the more liberal Congress can no longer enforce Qe simply by noncooperation, but rather faces Qc, which is far from its preferred position. The conservative president is in a more advantageous spot. By definition, there is a point (x) an equal distance from P as Qc, lying on the same indifference curve. The president would allow the reversion point, Qc, to occur by default rather than agree to an outcome to the left of x, yet he would instead prefer any point on the line segment between x and Qc, whether to the left or the right of P. This determines the space for strategic bargaining, since Congress would accept any outcome to the left of Qc and the president would reject any outcome to the left of x. Within that space, Congress would strive for a result as close to x as possible, which is its maximizing point under existing conditions; the president would strive for a result closer to P. Unlike under entitlement rules, there is a high probability that the budget-cap game will be solved by an explicit agreement, as there are many potential cooperative outcomes that dominate the reversion point occurring by noncooperation. This pattern of strategic interaction is most relevant to the food stamp program during the early years of the Reagan administration.

The deductive conclusion from this excursion into social science modeling is that, whether the key division among actors is institutional or ideological, a change in budget rule entailing a shift in the locus of the reversion point affects both the rational strategies of the players and the predicted outcome from political play. The critical institutional dynamic concerns the honesty of appropriations estimates. The critical ideological dynamic concerns the security of the status quo and the inherent advantage or disadvantage this gives to the contending sides. Under a discretionary rule, there is no security to the status quo and thus no inherent advantage; outcomes fluctuate with the shifting balance of power. Under an entitlement rule, the status quo is secure and thus political advantage goes to its defenders; outcomes will reflect stalemate to the extent that both the right and left prefer the status quo compared to the options advocated by the opponent. Under an expenditure cap rule, the status quo is insecure given emergency conditions, conveying inherent advantage to conservatives who can threaten to enforce the caps rather than to override them. The three contrasting forms of budget rule, as a consequence, have different practical implications regarding the provision of welfare benefits and the government's ability to assert fiscal control. The main inference, as before, is that rules predictably affect results, but possibly in ways less than completely satisfying to the proponents of rational policy deliberation.

It should be noted that the models introduced above are not intended to be comprehensive for all possible versions of budget rule, including all the forms of expenditure cap considered in the contemporary American debate. Most other variants can be understood by extension. For example, it can be shown that the more expenditure caps are grounded on fixed dollar amounts, the more they permit enforceable threats upon beneficiaries when costs suddenly rise due to unexpected economic fluctuations; the more caps are flexible upon changing economic conditions, the better they protect welfare benefits against the danger of deficit constraint. Similarly, caps that apply to a single program face the potential grievance that some particular constituency is vulnerable to an unjust penalty; caps that apply broadly to a group of programs leave the allocation of restraint more subject to interest bargaining. Equally, the models presented above are not comprehensive for all potential political situations. Most obviously, they are based on an ideological division in which the median voter in Congress is liberal relative to the reversion point and the president is conservative. The models easily can be reformulated to reflect the opposite situation.

The model variants developed here were selected because of their direct relevance to the food stamp case. They are quite simple yet provide clear hypotheses to be tested by the empirical account to follow. At the same time, they effectively illustrate the contrasts across the different forms of budget rule, so that the lessons learned can be used to help guide future U.S. policy reforms. Despite the possible variations, the basic framework remains consistent, as does the essential political tension it reflects.

Conclusion

"Budgeting and entitlement," wrote Aaron Wildavsky, "are incompatible concepts."[20] The object of budgeting is the collective allocation of scarce public resources among competing programs. Discretionary rules therefore facilitate the exercise of democratic choice, reflecting the vagaries of power inherent to such choice. The object of entitlement is the segregation of resources earmarked for a particular set of vulnerable claimants. Entitlement rules therefore entail some loss of legislative control over the government's purse strings as a consequence of the extraordinary funding protections granted to a segment of the population. Over time, an increasing percentage of the U.S. budget has been exempted from annual appropriations review and restriction. As the federal government's policy responsibilities have risen, the political capacity to manage its own affairs—especially fiscal affairs—has fallen. On the other hand, the American public has shown a reluctance to award extensive welfare benefits and seems content to permit relatively high levels of domestic poverty compared to other advanced industrial nations. This is a country remarkable for the fragmentation of power, the extent of political influence by organized interest groups, and a civic culture of individualism, factors not especially conducive to income transfers in aid of the poor. Special budget protection can be a useful instrument in support of basic social equity.

Welfare budgeting therefore represents an essential moral dilemma for American society, between the indeterminacy of democratic choice and the obligations of distributive justice. Both are important values that are not abandoned easily. In the effort to reconcile them, policymakers recently have begun experimenting with new procedural mechanisms. Fixed budget caps, which allow spending to proceed automatically but only up to a given threshold unless deliberately overridden, are an attempt to manage more consciously the ostensibly unplanned and upward drift of government outlays. They are advertised to improve policy oversight, placing on the budget agenda programs that otherwise would be relatively uncontrollable. They require politicians, if those programs ever breach given spending limits, to make explicit decisions regarding the level of acceptable support. A change in budget rule, specifically one that alters the location of the reversion point, can affect the character of budget politics and policies. As the deductive models show, spending caps imposed on welfare entitlements can have both intended and unintended but predictable consequences. Evaluation of their usefulness as a policy tool depends on the empirical study of how these are combined in actual practice.

Notes—Chapter 2

1. Unless otherwise noted, the data for this section come from the U.S. Bureau of the Census, Current Population Reports, Series P60–201, *Poverty in the United States, 1997* (Washington, D.C.: U. S. Government Printing Office, 1998); and U.S. House of Representatives, Committee on Ways and Means, *1998 Green Book,* WMCP 105–7, 105th Cong., 2nd sess., 1998.

2. Mary E. Corcoran and Ajay Chaudy, "The Dynamics of Childhood Poverty," in *The Future of Children,* vol. 7, no. 2 (1997): 45–47.

3. Luxembourg Income Study, "Low Income Measures Based on the LIS Data," computed by K. Vleminckx (August 1998): http://lissy.ceps.lu/lim.htm.

4. Paul Pierson, *Dismantling the Welfare State?* (New York: Cambridge University Press, 1994).

5. The data for this section come from the Executive Office of the President of the United States, *Budget of the United States Government, Historical Tables, Fiscal Year 1999* (1998); and Organization for Economic Cooperation and Development, *OECD Economic Outlook,* vol. 63 (June 1998).

6. James D. Savage, *Balanced Budgets and American Politics* (Ithaca: Cornell University Press, 1988).

7. *United States Statutes At Large,* 93rd Cong., 2nd sess., 1974, 88: 318; Robert Giamo, letter to Thomas Foley, House *Report* 96–264, 4.

8. John Brigham, *Property and the Politics of Entitlement* (Philadelphia: Temple University Press, 1990).

9. Charles Reich, "The New Property," *Yale Law Journal* 73 (1964): 733–87; Charles Reich, "Individual Rights and Social Welfare: The Emerging Legal Issues," *Yale Law Journal* 74 (1965): 1245–57; Rand E. Rosenblatt, "Legal Entitlement and Welfare Benefits," in *The Politics of Law,* ed. David Kairys (New York: Pantheon, 1982): 262–78.

10. R. Shep Melnick, *Between the Lines: Interpreting Welfare Rights* (Washington, D.C.: Brookings Institution, 1994): 42.

11. Joseph White, "Entitlement Budgeting vs. Bureau Budgeting," *Public Administration Review* 58 (1998): 510–21. The argument in this paragraph is deeply indebted to White's insight.

12. Richard Rose and Phillip L. Davies, *Inheritance in Public Policy* (New Haven, CT: Yale University Press, 1994).

13. Melnick, *Between the Lines,* 278.

14. Bipartisan Commission on Entitlement and Tax Reform, *Interim Report to the President,* August 1994.

15. Bipartisan Commission on Entitlement and Tax Reform, "Entitlement Reform Discussion Document," June 7, 1994.

16. R. Kent Weaver, "Controlling Entitlements," in *The New Directions in* American Politics, eds. John E. Chubb and Paul E. Peterson (Washington, D.C.: Brookings Institution, 1985): 307–41.

17. Joseph A. Schumpeter, "The Crisis of the Tax State," trans. W.P. Stolper and R.A. Musgrave, *International Economic Papers,* no. 4 (1954): 7.

18. For the classic statement of this perspective, see Aaron Wildavsky, *The Politics of the Budgetary Process* (Boston: Little, Brown, 1964); and revised to reflect subsequent changes in budget procedure, Aaron Wildavsky, *The New Politics of the Budgetary Process* (Glenview, IL: Scott, Foresman, 1988).

19. Christopher Wlezien, "The Political Economy of Supplemental Appropriations," *Legislative Studies Quarterly* 18 (1993): 51–76.

20. Wildavsky, *The New Politics of the Budgetary Process* (1988): 260.

THREE

Stamping In: Discretionary Budgeting and the Origins of the Food Stamp Program, 1964–1973

The Food Stamp Act of 1964 authorized the secretary of agriculture "to formulate and administer" a program under which "eligible households within the State shall be provided with an opportunity more nearly to obtain a nutritionally adequate diet through the issuance to them of a coupon allotment which shall have a greater monetary value than their normal expenditures for food."[1] The food stamp program is intended to increase the food purchasing power of low-income households to the point where they can afford the "Thrifty Food Plan," the least expensive of the food purchasing plans developed by the U.S. Department of Agriculture. The Thrifty Food Plan is intended to be adequate for household members to obtain the recommended daily allowances of key nutrients, as specified by the National Academy of Sciences. It is adapted for size of the consuming household and is adjusted annually for the rate of inflation.

The basic unit for food stamp benefits is the household, which is defined as a group of individuals living together who customarily purchase food and prepare meals in common.[2] The program assumes that a participating household will spend 30% of its net income on food. It therefore provides a subsidy sufficient to make up the difference between a household's expected contribution and the cost of the Thrifty Food Plan. The stamps, whether awarded through booklets of coupons in dollar denominations or by an Electronic Benefit Transfer card, can be used by designated program recipients in approved grocery stores to buy food items intended for home preparation and consumption (although the elderly and disabled can use stamps for meals in approved communal dining programs or delivered to the home).

For purposes of benefit calculation, a household's net income is defined as gross ordinary cash income minus a series of specified deductions. As the law currently stands, these include a standard deduction for household necessities of $134 per month; a work incentive equal to 20% of any earned income; dependent care expenses up to $175 per month ($200 if the child is younger than age two); a special deduction for households with shelter expenditures that exceed 50% of net income, up to a ceiling currently set at $250 per month (except for households with an elderly or disabled member); and a special deduction for elderly and disabled household members with out-of-pocket medical expenses exceeding $35 per month. (Some of these deduction amounts are higher for food stamp programs operating outside of the forty-eight contiguous states.)

A family with zero net income receives stamps equal in value to the cost of the Thrifty Food Plan. For example, for the typical one-person household in FY 1998 with no net income, this maximum monthly stamp benefit was $122; for a four-person household, the maximum monthly stamp benefit was $408. Families have their benefit levels reduced by 30 cents for every dollar of net income. About 25% of food stamp recipients have income from non-governmental sources, and thus the average monthly per person benefit is somewhat below the specified maximum level.

Households entirely comprised of welfare recipients are automatically eligible for food stamp benefits. Otherwise, eligibility is limited to households with monthly net incomes that do not exceed the federal poverty threshold, and monthly gross incomes (except for elderly and disabled recipients) that do not exceed 130% of that poverty threshold. Households also cannot possess liquid assets worth more than $2000 ($3000 if elderly); the portion of any owned vehicle's fair market value in excess of $4650 is counted as a liquid asset. Unless exempt, adult applicants must register for work or work training and must accept a suitable job if offered. Striking workers, most noncitizens, college students, and individuals living in institutional settings are categorically ineligible for food stamps. Recipients who violate the work requirements, who traffic in stamps, or who file fraudulent claims can be disqualified from benefits. Yet food stamps explicitly cannot be denied because a household has no permanent address. Moreover, benefits are not limited by the length of time a household has resided in a particular jurisdiction or by the length of time a household has been on welfare—with the exception of able-bodied poor adults between 18 and 50 with no dependents, who must work an average of twenty hours per week or else receive a maximum of three months of food stamp eligibility out of every three years (although this rule can be waived for areas with high unemployment or an insufficient number of available jobs, and the states can at their own discretion exempt another 15% of individuals).

The food stamp program operates in all fifty states, the District of Columbia, Guam, and the Virgin Islands. A companion program exists for Puerto Rico. The federal government, through the Food and Consumer Service (formerly the Food and Nutrition Service) of the U.S. Department of Agriculture, is responsible for program regulations, coupon printing and redemption, and general oversight. The states, through their local welfare offices, are responsible for day-to-day operations, including certifying applicants, determining benefit levels, and issuing coupons to individuals. States can also apply for special waivers from USDA regulations for demonstration projects intended to improve efficiency or coordinate with other welfare programs. Food stamp benefits are fully financed by the federal government out of general revenues. The federal government is also financially responsible for its own administrative costs and generally for half of state welfare agency administrative costs. This federal share can vary because of sanctions or rewards assessed on the basis of a state's benefit error rate, as determined by random checks by the quality control system.

In FY 1998, the federal government expenditure for the food stamp program was $20.1 billion. On average, the program serves approximately twenty-five million people monthly, more than 9% of the total U.S. resident population. Nevertheless, nearly a third of potentially eligible households do not receive food stamp benefits, whether from ignorance regarding eligibility, conscious choice, or barriers against application. Participation rates are greatest among poor single-parent households; they are smallest among the elderly. Qualifying households with lower net incomes and thus higher scheduled allotments participate at a greater rate than qualifying households with relatively higher net incomes and thus lower scheduled allotments. A sizable majority of food stamp participants also receive benefits from other government assistance efforts. Yet the food stamp program is the only U.S. welfare program available to virtually all impoverished households, imposing few categorical restrictions.

As an income supplement, food stamps contribute to reducing poverty in the United States. As an earmarked subsidy, it has a positive effect upon the aggregate level of food purchases and upon the nutrient intake by low-income individuals.[3] The relevance of the food stamp program to this study, however, is budgetary. The program at different times in its history has experienced all three forms of budget rule—discretionary, pure entitlement, and expenditure cap. The fiscal history of the food stamp program is thus intrinsically interesting. It provides a useful case study, allowing us to investigate the reasons why a cap was placed on this particular welfare entitlement and the practical effects the cap had on politics and policy. Each federal welfare program is atypical in its own special way. Yet, given the recent return of welfare budget caps to the active policy agenda, there is cause to consider the experience of the food stamp program and much to learn from its lessons.

Food Stamps and Budget Rules

Food stamps were introduced as an experimental program late in the New Deal era and were revived as a pilot program intended for recession relief during the early 1960s. More permanent enactment began in 1964. During its formative years, the food stamp program operated under the control of the congressional appropriations process, which determined the amount of annual funding and thus the pace of expansion. As is customary under discretionary budgeting, program legislation expressly limited the authority of the appropriations committees to allocate funds, specifying both the maximum amount and the number of years covered. Within these strictures, the appropriations committees were free to dictate as they saw fit the number of dollars that actually could be distributed from treasury funds during any given fiscal year. The annual appropriation did not have to correspond to the sum of recipient need and did not have to be adjusted for changing economic conditions. Discretionary budgeting was a consequence of the initial small scope of the food stamp program and its high political insecurity. Yet the political climate soon changed, reflecting a conscious campaign by nutrition advocates. In the early 1970s, Congress transformed food stamps into an entitlement, establishing the open-ended budget authority necessary to ensure all individual claims under the law. The appropriations committees became responsible for providing the funds sufficient to cover the costs of awarding fully entitled benefits to qualified food stamp recipients. As Senator Edmund Muskie noted, appropriation is "a completely perfunctory action, for Congress must provide whatever funds are required for the obligation." Since a legal requirement existed to meet all legitimate demand, an insufficient initial appropriation did not entail reduced agency expenditures, but instead compelled a supplemental appropriation to make up the deficiency.[4]

It was quite reasonable for food stamps to be budgeted in this manner. With open-ended authority, Congress could accommodate the increasing numbers of qualified poor individuals enrolled as program coverage expanded and regulations were liberalized. Between FY 1970 and FY 1977, participation rose from 4.3 million to 17.1 million individuals; outlays rose from $577 million to $5.4 billion. Moreover, open-ended authority permitted quick budgetary adjustment because utilization and expenditures proved highly sensitive to macroeconomic fluctuations, especially to unemployment rates and food price inflation. Despite the best efforts by agriculture department and congressional forecasters, five supplemental appropriations were required for the fiscal years 1974–1977.

In 1977, however, Congress removed open-ended budget authority from the food stamp program. For the next thirteen years, through FY 1990, program legislation imposed a strict cap on permissible expenditures. Unlike discretion, the appropriations committees were not free to restrict annual spending below the cap threshold. Unlike entitlement, total outlays had to be contained within the cap, regardless of recipient numbers or need, unless it was overridden by explicit enactment. Introduced first as a House floor motion by Congressman Dawson Mathis (D-GA), the new arrangement restored congressional budget control over the food stamp program by making payment "subject to the availability of funds." The secretary of agriculture was ordered to "limit the value of those allotments issued" to an amount not in excess of the established ceiling and was instructed to reduce the value of allotments to eligible households if he determined that ordinary funding requirements during the fiscal year would exceed that ceiling.[5]

Under the provisions of the Lugar amendment of 1979, the secretary was instructed to report to Congress by the middle of each month whether there was any reason to anticipate excess spending for the remainder of the fiscal year. Not less than sixty days after the issuance of a monthly report indicating a predicted insufficiency of funds, the secretary was to notify the states to reduce household allotments by the requisite amounts. Within seven days of taking such action, he was to submit a statement to the congressional agriculture committees explaining the basis for his determination and the manner by which allotments would be reduced.[6]

Food stamps were intended to help ensure that Americans could achieve minimum nutritional sufficiency. Spending caps were intended to help the government manage costs, regardless of nutritional need. The Mathis plan held outlays for otherwise deserving households, in cases of budget misestimation or unexpected contingencies, hostage to a set of dollar limits specified by legislation that had been passed a number of years before. Congress could always raise the cap to permit additional spending, yet any such revision required three separate bills—budget, appropriations, and authorizing legislation—and at least six separate committees. Food stamp budgeting under the Mathis provision thus imposed additional costs in political time and struggle, impeding program adaptability and threatening material harm to the most vulnerable in society. Yet there is usually a reason when an overworked body deliberately opts to complicate its tasks. In this case, Congress explicitly was responding to the tension between entitlement protection and budget control, seeking a procedural means that would improve the balance between these two competing ideals. The object of this study is to examine the operation of the food stamp program under all three forms of budget rule, and in particular to see whether the promise of budget caps was fulfilled in practice. Although the caps were allowed to expire in 1990, proposals to reimpose food stamp expenditure ceilings and to modify recipient entitlement status surfaced again during the welfare reform debate of the middle 1990s. In fact, they were on the verge of legislative reinstatement as part of the Personal Responsibility Act of 1996. The findings from this study are not merely historical but have contemporary relevance.

Discretionary Origins

The story regarding the creation of the food stamp program in the early 1960s, its rapid growth over the next decade, and its establishment as a central component in the repertoire of the U.S. welfare state has been told often, usually from the perspective of the triumph of social justice over entrenched opposition and public apathy.[7] This chapter will emphasize just one element in this story of fundamental policy innovation—during the initial phase of the food stamp program, it functioned under ordinary discretionary budget rules. It was not initially intended as an entitlement. Counties did not have to participate. Eligible individuals did not have a legal right to benefits. The pace of program expansion was constrained by the amount of money provided. Authorizing legislation legitimated appropriations for only a few years at a time and placed low limits on the total amount that could be appropriated. Annual appropriations legislation then fixed the level of yearly spending, usually below the maximum permissible amount. The consequence of discretionary budgeting during the formative period for the food stamp program was slow growth and intense political conflict. Despite the announced goal of improving nutrition among poor Americans, the funding principle adopted for food stamp policymaking at first helped to deter its achievement. Change came only during the Nixon administration era.

A New Deal food stamp program had existed from 1939 through early 1943. In operation, it was a complex system largely because it was intended primarily to supplement the distribution of surplus foods from federal storage. Recipients would buy orange coupons usable for all foods and would receive free a number of blue coupons, usually fifty cents worth for every dollar of the orange ones purchased, usable to obtain just those commodities officially listed in surplus at the time. The plan was financed by "Section 32" funds, which designated 30% of all U.S. customs receipts to programs that encourage the domestic consumption or foreign export of agricultural commodities for the purpose of helping stabilize the farm economy. At its height, the New Deal plan was functioning in 1700 counties and was assisting four million individuals. With the coming of World War II, however, the unemployment rate decreased and the market demand for food commodities increased. The program generally was viewed as a success, but without agricultural sector need it was deemed unnecessary and was terminated in March 1943.

A few legislators—particularly George Aiken in the Senate and Leonor Sullivan in the House—called repeatedly for a revival of the food stamp plan during the post-World War II era. The Eisenhower administration was not interested. Surplus food stocks held in federal warehouses were sometimes distributed to the poor, but this was based on local availability and not inadequate recipient nutrition. The agriculture committees in Congress were focused on distributional politics, delivering benefits to farm constituency interests and avoiding divisive controversies that might erode internal unity and lead to challenges on the floor. The committees were dominated by southern Democrats, ideologically conservative and wary of the intrusion of federal welfare into regional race and labor relations. Southern producers, especially of cotton and tobacco, would not benefit from general government subsidies to food consumption. The Department of Agriculture was composed primarily of clientele agencies whose primary goal was to protect farmer incomes and ensure economic health to the nation's agricultural sector. It had little experience with income supplement programs and little enthusiasm for operating one. In addition, there was virtually no grass roots pressure demanding a major initiative to improve nutrition among poor Americans. Thus, aside from a handful of policy entrepreneurs, political leaders saw little gain from the issue and did not place food support high among their legislative priorities.

As an aspect of the partisan positioning typical during an economic downturn, the Democratic Congress in 1959 passed legislation permitting, not mandating, the USDA through 1961 to set up a limited food stamp program along New Deal lines. As anticipated, the Eisenhower administration did not implement the provision. John Kennedy, while campaigning in West Virginia, allegedly observed both hunger and the limits of the surplus commodity distribution program. In his February 2, 1961, special message to Congress, Kennedy announced the establishment of a pilot food stamp program. Because the 1959 authority was soon due to expire, he created the program by executive order using Section 32 funding. The pilot program began with eight projects and later expanded to forty-three. Sites were selected for their previous experience with food distribution and for Democratic political advantage. The two-tiered stamp system of the New Deal was replaced by a one-stamp arrangement, in which recipients were expected to pay a sum equal to their usual level of food expenditures, receiving in return stamps of greater value to use for obtaining food commodities. Whereas the agricultural interests in Congress apparently preferred supplemental stamps earmarked merely for those particular commodities in surplus, the Kennedy administration wished to include subsidies for perishable goods that could not be stored, and it also expected a positive antirecession effect from increased demand across the entire farm economy.

"From the beginning," writes Ardith Maney, "the principal limitation holding down food aid program activity was budgetary."[8] As part of his January 1963 budget presentation, President Kennedy requested $51.5 million in food stamp funding for FY 1964, approximately the same level as for FY 1963, indicating no planned growth within the pilot project framework. The House appropriations bill cut the amount by nearly 25%, well below the previous year's level. The conference finally agreed to $45 million. In the meantime, the administration proceeded with preparations for a permanent food stamp program, to be based on legislated authorization and general revenues for support. Much of the impetus was financial, as Section 32 funding would severely limit further development. The USDA estimated that a nationwide food stamp program would cost about $360 million annually, which easily would exhaust all the money provided under Section 32. Moreover, neither the department nor its political constituency would accept a simple exchange, establishing somewhat larger aggregate demand for farm goods in general to replace targeted relief for those specific commodities that happened to be in surplus. The secretary of agriculture, Orville Freeman, enjoyed the budget flexibility provided by Section 32 funds and was intent on keeping the apparent cost of agricultural support programs from rising too fast. Producer groups wanted to ensure that a sufficient reserve remained available for emergency farm assistance. The consensus was, if additional food and nutrition benefits were to be provided, it would have to be through a new program financed from a source less threatening to established interests.

In mid-1963, the Kennedy administration requested Congress to authorize the creation of a national food stamp program. In February 1964, the House Agriculture Committee tabled the matter. Apparently, the majority coalition of southern Democrats and conservative Republicans was bothered by the idea of uniting welfare with agricultural assistance and was afraid that it would deflect the USDA from its established mission. The bill was saved only as the product of "mutual hostage taking" among Democratic factions in Congress.[9] Nutrition advocates delayed a tobacco research bill in the Rules Committee until Agriculture reported the food stamp bill. They then traded votes on cotton and wheat price supports for guaranteed passage on the House floor and protection in conference. This pattern of legislative logrolling dominated food stamp politics during its early period.[10]

The Food Stamp Act of 1964 explicitly was given a dual justification, to "help achieve a fuller and more effective use of food abundance," and to "raise the levels of nutrition among low-income households."[11] This reflected the two, very different sets of interests concerned with its provisions. The act permitted—not required—food stamp programs to be established in all communities upon request, in lieu of direct commodity distribution. Eligibility requirements were determined by the states but all allotment costs were borne by the federal government. Participating households would purchase stamps greater in value than their price, implying a clear distinction between the base amount equivalent to a household's normal food expenditure and a supplemental amount provided by the government. Regarding funding, the 1964 bill permanently established the food stamp program but authorized spending for three years only, limited to maximum amounts of $75 million in FY 1965, $100 million in FY 1966, and $200 million in FY 1967. This was less than the administration and congressional reformers had wanted, yet they were content in defeating committee amendments designed to impose on the states a major share of the program costs.

Within the legal spending authority, as Secretary Freeman noted, the scope of program operations "would be governed by the size of the annual appropriation."[12] That appropriation was always subject to contention. The short authorization period and the discretionary budget rule implied that control over the pace of food stamp expansion remained within the domain of hostile agricultural interests in Congress.[13] There would be, by necessity, yearly battles over the program budget and periodic battles over program provisions that affect the budget. Despite a long list of counties wishing to join, limited funding led to gradual growth during the middle 1960s. Moreover, the entire fate of the food stamp experiment depended on legislative renewal in 1967.

Regarding annual appropriations, funding games began immediately. The FY 1965 supplemental appropriation, to add funds consistent with the new program legislation, approved food stamp spending up to $60 million, which nevertheless was 20% less than the maximum permissible amount. Moreover, the House sought to use only Section 32 funds as a signal that future costs must be severely limited, whereas the Senate insisted that food stamps as a welfare program should be financed from general revenues rather than money especially designated for food price support. The final compromise sided with the Senate in the use of general revenues but deleted explicit language forever prohibiting the use of Section 32 funds. For FY 1966, the House Appropriations Committee initially proposed $75 million, 25% less than the maximum permissible amount. According to Leonor Sullivan, this "would have meant either cancelling the start of projects in 25 new areas scheduled to come into the program in the coming fiscal year, or else a cutback in the 110 projects in operation during this fiscal year."[14] Yet a farm bill was still pending at the time and thus, as part of a logroll for urban votes, the committee agreed to introduce a friendly amendment appropriating the full amount permissible, and this was accepted on the floor and later by the Senate. For FY 1967, without similar pressure, House Appropriations was back to its tricks, recommending annual spending much less than the maximum amount, to be financed largely out of Section 32 funds. The Senate again insisted upon the use of general revenues, and it again prevailed in conference. This dynamic was repeated for FY 1968, with the appropriation approved contingent upon the enactment of renewed program authorizing legislation.

Regarding legislative reauthorization, Secretary Freeman asked for no substantive modification of the food stamp program, just for extended authority without a maximum spending limitation to allow operations to continue in FY 1968 and beyond. "The principles and operating guidelines . . . incorporated into the Food Stamp Act of 1964 have stood the test of time," he told the congressional hearings. Administrators should now be granted the flexibility to expand and adapt the program as local conditions warranted.[15] The House Agriculture Committee, however, reported merely a one-year extension limited to $195 million. Expressing concern over possible fraud and abuse, the committee majority argued that it was necessary to "maintain surveillance" through "periodic legislative review, adjustment and refinement." Congresswoman Sullivan, the most prominent of the food stamp advocates, had a different interpretation. The Agriculture Committee, she said, unsympathetic to policies combating domestic hunger and malnutrition, intentionally imposed budgetary restrictions on expansion and "undoubtedly" would use the one-year extension to "try once again next year to add further limitations and restrictions which could only have the result of damaging the effectiveness of the program."[16] A House floor amendment to insert three-year budget authority, similar to the provision approved by the Senate, failed in a teller vote. It took three months of conference committee deadlock and the threat by reformers against a peanut acreage bill to produce a viable compromise. The final legislation extended food stamp authorization for two further years, with appropriations limited to a maximum of $200 million in FY 1968 and $225 million in FY 1969. It also included language specifying that spending must be financed out of general treasury sources, ending the danger that program growth might be constrained by the amount of available Section 32 funds or that it would have to compete for money directly against agricultural crop supports with their active and entrenched clientele groups.

A major ideological change occurred in late 1967 and early 1968. Food stamp politics had previously taken place among Washington insiders with little public awareness or concern. Now food stamp politics became the focus of vigorous outsider pressure and intense media publicity. The origin of this activism can be found in the civil rights movement and the war on poverty. Nutrition policy reform combined an attack against Southern oligarchy with a regard for the welfare of its victims. The movement began with hearings by a subcommittee of the Senate Labor and Public Welfare Committee, led by Robert Kennedy and Joseph Clark, that traveled to rural Mississippi and reported the minimal social impact of federal food relief programs. The Field Foundation sent a team of doctors into the region to investigate the extent of hunger and malnutrition. A Citizens Board of Inquiry issued a widely publicized study, *Hunger U.S.A.*, which characterized federal food assistance as inadequate. Nick Kotz won a Pulitzer Prize for his newspaper stories critical of USDA secretary Freeman and of the agriculture potentates in Congress. CBS News televised a documentary, "Hunger in America," that presented graphic if over-dramatized proof of malnutrition and its effects. Within Washington, the Senate established a Select Committee on Nutrition and Human Needs, chaired by George McGovern, to institutionalize attention to the issue separate from the domain of the traditional agriculture committees. The Poor People's Campaign, organized under the aegis of the Southern Christian Leadership Conference, set up a tent city on the mall near the Lincoln Memorial (not far from the Department of Agriculture) and lobbied for expanded food assistance.

As quiescence turned into activism, Secretary Freeman was caught in a bind. The secretary had been proud of the incremental expansion of the food stamp program, achieved without angering powerful southern conservatives, without threatening regional racial or labor relations, and without disturbing agriculture department support for producer interests. This had won him no friends from the ideological right. Yet he now also faced strident criticism from the left, complaining that he was more concerned with political accommodation than with ensuring nutritional sufficiency for all Americans. Critics pointed to the slow reduction in the backlog of communities with applications for inclusion within the food stamp program, and they condemned department inattention to the fact that individual participation often declined in counties that had switched from commodity distribution to food stamps. Much of the blame centered upon the purchase requirement, which forced beneficiaries to pay in cash the amount they otherwise would have spent on food in order to receive a higher value in stamps.

Secretary Freeman asked Senators Kennedy and Clark not to pursue reforms until the 1967 program reauthorization and FY 1968 appropriations bill were enacted. He then personally traveled to Mississippi to announce a reduction in the purchase price for the poorest of households, from two dollars to fifty cents per month, and a restructuring of the purchase price system so that no household was expected to spend more than 30% of its income to obtain the recommended food diet. This action still brought him no favor. On the one hand, it was done unilaterally, without the support of the Agriculture Committee leadership. On the other hand, it was insufficient to appease activists demanding faster program expansion, greater supervision over local implementation, higher benefits, and no purchase requirement for the poorest households.

Freeman's political tightrope was complicated by the Johnson administration's budget tightrope, in which it had to maintain a careful balance between guns and butter so as to win votes from Democratic conservatives for the Vietnam tax surcharge while deflecting attacks from Democratic liberals challenging for the party's presidential nomination. Throughout late 1967 and early 1968, President Johnson refused to consider further food stamp reforms because of their cost. This did not earn him escape from the issue. The small scheduled reduction in the purchase requirement plus a slight acceleration in the pace of food stamp program expansion into low-income counties resulted in the need for a FY 1969 supplemental appropriation that could not proceed through Congress unless the maximum spending authority was raised by special legislative enactment. The resulting conflicts exemplify perfectly the difficulties of welfare provision under ideological division and discretionary budget rule.

In February 1968, the president reluctantly requested another $20 million in spending authority, raising the FY 1969 maximum to $245 million. The Senate granted this amount without controversy, but in the House Leonor Sullivan seized the opportunity to propose far more costly changes in program provisions. Moreover, she sought open-ended budget authority for the food stamp program, to last until FY 1972. This way, expansion would not be unnecessarily constrained by fixed appropriations and subject to control by hostile legislative committees. Supported by 129 co-sponsors in the House, Sullivan bluntly told the Agriculture Committee, "If we have to have another fight, let's have it."[17]

Administration aides were certain that Johnson ultimately would accept some form of food stamp liberalization. While the president hesitated, Secretary Freeman publicly endorsed the proposal for open-ended budget authority. Johnson was furious and banned all executive branch staff from further efforts that might assist Congresswoman Sullivan's revolt. As expected, the House Agriculture Committee rejected all proposed liberalization provisions, and instead it reported the simple $20 million increase in funding authority, as was originally requested by the Johnson administration. According to chairman W. R. Poague and his allies, it would be wrong to turn the food stamp program loose without limits or restraints. Rather, Congress should assure that it be properly administered and grow at a reasonable pace, especially given prevailing concerns regarding overall government spending. Sullivan and her allies took the matter to the House floor, where they triumphed 227–172. Yet the measure was represented by its opponents in conference committee. The conference thus rejected open-ended food stamp budgeting and merely raised the ceiling for FY 1969 from $225 to $315 million, established a ceiling of $340 million for FY 1970 and $170 million for the first half of FY 1971. It meant that food stamp funding authority would expire on December 31, 1970, to coincide with the expiration of farm subsidy legislation and ensure a vote-trade linking the two policies together.

This completed only half of the requisite action. Permission to spend more money in FY 1969 for the food stamp program had been approved, but the level of actual expenditures within that permissible amount was still contingent upon the dollar figure specified in the supplemental appropriations bill. The majority in the House Appropriations subcommittee on agriculture, led by Congressman Jamie Whitten of Mississippi, proved relatively uncooperative. In a show of support for its colleagues on the Agriculture Committee, House Appropriations reported only $20 million in additional funding for FY 1969, returning yet again to the figure originally requested before the attendant controversy. The total was raised to $40 million in a compromise negotiated on the House floor and $55 million by the conference, but this remained $35 million below the newly legislated maximum authority.

Discretionary budget rules for the food stamp program meant annual limits on permissible spending and decision making located within the legislative domain of those interests least sympathetic to its aims. Although the balance of political power slowly shifted in favor of greater liberalization, the budgetary base was never quite secure and every increment required a pitched battle. Discretion therefore placed serious constraints upon the early growth and development of the food stamp program, despite increasingly apparent need and the best strategic efforts of its advocates.

Escape from Political Discretion

The new Republican administration of Richard Nixon was far more sympathetic to nutrition issues and more willing to advance a costly policy initiative than the outgoing Democratic administration of Lyndon Johnson. Soon after the inauguration, a task force of the Urban Affairs Council recommended a significant food stamp reform package, designed to cost an additional $1.7 billion. "This is the hottest item on the domestic front," said Agriculture Secretary Clifford Hardin, "and we must take the leadership ourselves."[18] When the administration's budget advisers opposed the plan and President Nixon vacillated, Senate activists decided to push the matter. George McGovern scheduled an appearance for Secretary Hardin before his Select Committee on Hunger and Human Needs and then leaked a copy of the Urban Affairs task force report to the press. Facing potential embarrassment, the president decided to seize the agenda. On May 6, 1969, he delivered a special message to Congress proposing "to put an end to hunger in America." Using dramatic language, Nixon declared "there can be no doubt" that hunger and malnutrition are problems not solely confined to less fortunate nations. They also exist in the United States, affecting millions of individuals. He called the situation "intolerable" and announced that "the honor of American democracy is at stake."[19] Proposed reforms included a nationally defined stamp allotment level sufficient to meet the USDA standard for a low-cost nutritious diet, annual cost-of-living indexing to compensate for inflation, national eligibility criteria, no purchase requirement for very poor families, a purchase price limitation so that no recipient household would spend more than 30% of its income for food stamps, and a guarantee that the food stamp program would soon operate in every county in the United States that requested it.

The Senate Agriculture Committee moved quickly and reported a slightly more moderate bill. In a pattern that would be repeated often during the 1970s, Senator McGovern challenged the committee with a more liberal version and prevailed on the floor. The McGovern substitute called for $2.5 billion in food stamp spending authority by FY 1972. "The very least we can do is fund the new program at a level commensurate with the problem it is designed to solve."[20] By contrast, the House Agriculture Committee held hearings on food stamp revision and reauthorization during 1969 but postponed mark-up sessions to ensure logrolling with the forthcoming farm legislation. Again, the threat of political embarrassment forced the administration's hand. A White House Conference on Food, Nutrition, and Health was scheduled for December 1969. To forestall potential criticism, the USDA implemented most of the planned food stamp reforms by bureaucratic regulation.

Whereas the legal capacity to take such action most likely existed, the budget justification was implausible. Acting unilaterally while the food stamp reauthorization bill was still pending, it was not certain whether Congress would grant the funding capacity necessary for the Nixon administration's reforms to proceed. Earlier in the year, Congress had raised food stamp spending authority just for FY 1970 to $610 billion to permit faster program expansion under existing rules. Although the leadership had promised that this was just a first installment, the budget move was certainly not intended to finance yet-to-be-enacted substantive changes. The Nixon administration, however, claimed this minor spending adjustment as fiscal permission for its administrative liberalization of program rules. In essence, the administration was declaring that it would not willingly yield to discretionary budget politics. Premature commitment therefore put pressure on Congress to accept extensive program growth as part of the new reauthorization bill and to accommodate its costs. The period of conservative opponents using spending allowances as a means of limiting food stamp expansion was coming to an end.

Bowing before the inevitable, the House Agriculture Committee eventually reported a food stamp bill, although it was more restrictive than the Senate version. The House committee first delayed floor consideration to help ensure liberal votes for the pending farm bill and then it delayed conference negotiations until the deadline for program expiration loomed, improving its leverage over the final compromise. Regarding spending authority, the House committee report somewhat disingenuously sought to avoid blame and shift responsibility. It explicitly denied any past or present disposition to refuse funds needed to supplement the food purchasing capacity of poor households. Moreover, it promised for the future that legislated ceilings on permissible appropriations would no longer limit the amount of nutritional assistance awarded. The committee thus proposed completely open budget authority for three years, fiscal years 1971–1973.

The House Agriculture Committee majority, in response to political pressure, thus altered its position in a critical way. On the one hand, it conceded apparent control over food stamp program development by abandoning strict dollar restraints imposed through the appropriations process. On the other hand, it sought to contain expenditures quite severely by means of program changes, rejecting free stamps to low income households, proposing cost-sharing with the states, and removing nutritional specifications from the national benefit standard. Abandoning oversight via finance, it would instead exercise substantive command by means of policy rules and regulations. According to chairman Poague, the committee bill "would leave the matter of financing to the Appropriations Committee, but it would require no more than $1.5 billion to fund this bill. While this is about twice what the program has been costing, it is only about one-quarter of what the other body proposes to spend."[21]

The food stamp reform adopted eventually by the conference committee was located ideologically between the Senate and House bills, which placed the final outcome reasonably close to the initial proposal by the Nixon administration. Legislative enactment therefore gave reinforcement to the program changes previously advanced by regulatory decree. Regarding funding, the conference set the budget ceiling generously for FY 1971 at $1.75 billion, and it accepted open-ended authorizations for FY 1972 and FY 1973, justified in order to remove all artificial hindrance upon program expansion.

Food stamp politics calmed down considerably in the following years, largely because of broad acceptance, whether ideological or tactical, that the program was becoming an integral part of the American welfare system. There was some ambiguity during this period caused by the Nixon administration's predisposition to cash-out the food stamp program as part of the comprehensive welfare reform proposal slowly being prepared for congressional submission. Food advocates successfully insisted on autonomy for nutrition assistance, and the welfare reform never truly approached enactment. Thereafter, liberals pressured the Nixon administration, rapidly shifting rightward in policy orientation, to maintain its commitment to food stamps as an essential ingredient in the campaign against hunger. A supplemental appropriation was approved without controversy for FY 1971. The Nixon administration requested and Congress scheduled incremental spending increases for FY 1972 and FY 1973. Conservatives tried to find an angle by which to embarrass the program, focusing upon potential eligibility for strikers and college students. The liberal Senate raised food stamp appropriations above both the administration's request and the House recommendation, in an effort to facilitate even faster program expansion into new counties. Both sides watched carefully when actual costs differed from prediction.

Yet fundamental controversy had diminished enormously, which became obvious in 1973 when it was again time for the food stamp program to be reauthorized. Included as part of the Omnibus Farm Bill, the only major revision in food stamp rules eliminated community request as a condition for participation. No longer optional, a food stamp program now had to be established in every county in every state, thereby completing the move toward full national coverage. The bill extended the authority of the program to expend money through FY 1977, retaining the open-ended provision that imposed no fixed ceiling on the amount of permissible spending. There was a remarkable absence of dispute, in both chambers, regarding this section of the bill.

Appearing before the Senate Select Committee on Nutrition and Human Needs, Assistant Secretary of Agriculture Richard Lyng explained why food stamp outlays in FY 1972 had fallen short of appropriations, resulting in impoundment of the excess. There are two features of Lyng's testimony worth noting. First was his insistence that the administration was playing honestly and that it had no incentive to do otherwise. Ordinary incremental budgeting depends heavily upon relatively stable and predictable bargaining patterns among the various actors playing within an inherently complex process. An actor who proves unreliable or practices deception can sacrifice goodwill and invites political retribution. As the food stamp program gradually gained legitimacy, the ideological manipulation of predicted costs decreased and was replaced by more technical spending estimates, based on predicted utilization rates and allotment levels under existing program rules. Thus Lyng was quick to assert that the impoundment entailed no deliberate withholding of funds. Rather, there was difficulty in accurately forecasting program needs. Complicating factors included the fluctuating economy, the implementation of new regulations, and the uncertain pace of program expansion into new communities. Under those circumstances, even the best forecasts would contain errors. The mistake in estimation should thus not become a cause for distrust.

The second essential feature of Lyng's testimony concerned his assumption that it was the task of program administrators to accommodate every household qualified within existing rules up to the level of its determined need. The job before USDA budgeters estimating food stamp costs for the coming fiscal year was econometric rather than substantive. Lyng explicitly told the committee that the food stamp program did not operate as a fixed federal grant, with some limited sum of money allocated and assigned to the states for a specified purpose. The program instead guaranteed to the 2100 participating counties that all eligible households would receive "the full benefits of food assistance—all eligible, regardless of how many that might be. There are no constraints on total numbers of dollars or total numbers of needy people a county or a State may serve."[22] Ten years earlier, food stamps had been an experimental pilot program available to a handful of communities. Now the USDA was telling Congress that the food stamp program was becoming a budget entitlement. It soon would exist throughout the United States, ensuring the ability to purchase a nutritionally adequate diet by all qualified households, with benefits based upon income, with eligibility specified by law, and with no fiscal limitations imposed by the entailed price upon the treasury and the taxpayer.

Budget management and welfare entitlement do not necessarily fit well together. Legislative discretion meant that the amount of funds available to the food stamp program in any fiscal year was uncertain. Given a policy goal to supplement food purchasing power and ensure adequate nutrition to every American, it made sense to abandon annual control in favor of security and predictability. The goal was self-evident to food stamp advocates during the 1960s and early 1970s. Once they prevailed over the opposition of agricultural interests and conservative opponents, they quickly sought the added budgetary protection of entitlement status. Ideological controversies had begun to die down during the Nixon era and a more routinized pattern of incremental budgeting was in the process of becoming established. Gradually, the technical task of estimating spending needs came to dominate over agricultural sector efforts at forestallment, and the level of budget honesty increased. Yet the structure of discretionary budgeting does not prevent vulnerability to hostile interests competing for funds through the annual appropriations process, and it does not escape the limitation upon annual spending established by the dollar allocation determined by that appropriations process. In retrospect, the strategic pursuit of entitlement appears quite wise, as the coalition that succeeded in promoting food stamp program development despite discretionary rules proved transitory and its superiority temporary.[23] The attack on uncontrollable spending was about to begin.

Conclusion

The political logic of discretionary budgeting is founded upon base and increment. For a growing program, the expectation is that spending will equal last year's total plus an additional amount to pursue reasonable expansion. Given general policy consensus, routinization helps to promote actor honesty and incremental growth. Yet there is no strict formula for budget growth, no guarantee that the base will be protected or a sufficient increment granted. The program is completely subject to the authorizing legislation if Congress wishes to place a limit on the maximum amount available in any fiscal year, and it is completely subject to appropriations legislation for the allocation of funds that actually can be spent during that year. Moreover, in the absence of policy consensus, discretionary spending becomes liable to the dynamic of power and influence. With respect to the food stamp program during its formative period, the fundamental conflict was between entrenched agriculture interests with institutionalized advantage and an insurgent food lobby aggressively using media exposure and grass roots mobilization. Often caught between the two sides were the president and the U.S. Department of Agriculture, responsive to its traditional constituency of organized producer groups but also sensitive to mounting pressures from public opinion.

Powerful farm interests sought to protect budget funds for their own subsidy programs and prevent the expansion of welfare assistance operating within the domain of agricultural policy. Yet there was a strong emotional appeal to the campaign against domestic hunger and malnutrition, and the civil rights movement had weakened the standing of the southern Democratic leadership in Congress. Moreover, legislators ordinarily favor programs that distribute funds within their districts, and thus the extension of food stamps geographically made it attractive to more and more politicians wishing to claim credit for the benefits awarded. As the balance of power shifted, agricultural forces began holding the food stamp program hostage to gain votes for commodity support bills while working to slow the pace of program growth through their control over key committee positions. The procedural wrangling and ideological intensity of the fight gave to the food stamp program a special place in the agenda of its advocates. Their victories gradually nationalized the program and liberalized its benefits. More important, they progressively removed political discretion over program provisions. The household food allotment was indexed to inflation; participation was required from all U.S. counties; and funding eventually was made open-ended. Often the best victories are those that alter the rules of political play.

Politics is structured by the institutional rules of play, but it also helps structure those rules. Discretionary budgeting can be risky for program advocates in search of funds, who perceive threats from competing program claimants, aggregate spending managers, and hostile interests. It is often desirable to escape from micro-budgeting controls, obtaining favorable standing through changes in policy design or decision-making procedures.[24] Entitlement budgeting for food stamps shifted the burden of initiation. Spending was guaranteed, sufficient to cover all entailed program costs, and no longer had to depend on explicit and recurrent legislative permission. The status quo protected program operations, and thus inaction was no longer a weapon available to opponents. One can imagine a program so strong in political support that it prefers the uncertainties of discretionary budgeting, believing that its policy mission can be fulfilled and expansion achieved more effectively by continued success within direct budget competition. This was certainly not the situation facing the food stamp program. Advocates were probably at the peak of their power during the early 1970s, benefiting from adjustments within the Democratic party constituency and a general mood of public concern. Under the circumstances, it was logical to be risk averse and to lock in, through special entitlement protection, the gains that had been made. Over the next period in its history, the food stamp program would operate under open-ended budget authority. The politics of food stamp budgeting would, as a consequence, also be transformed.

Notes—Chapter 3

1. *United States Statutes At Large,* 88th Cong., 2nd sess., 1964, 78: 704.

2. The data and details regarding food stamp program operations discussed in this section come from the U.S. House of Representatives, Committee on Ways and Means, *1998 Green Book,* WMCP 105–7, 105th Cong., 2nd sess. 1998, 923–49.

3. Regarding program design issues and effects, see Peter H. Rossi, *Feeding the Poor* (Washington, D.C.: American Enterprise Institute Press, 1998); Peter H. Eisenger, *Toward an End to Hunger in America* (Washington, D.C.: Brookings Institution, 1998); James C. Ohls and Harold Beebout, *The Food Stamp Program* (Washington, D.C.: Urban Institute Press, 1993); Maurice Macdonald, *Food, Stamps, and Income Maintenance* (New York: Academic Press, 1977).

4. *Congressional Record* 120: S 7662. This interpretation was reinforced by court opinion, by statements of legislators during debates over both the Budget Act and various food stamp amendments, and by legislative practice between FY 1972 and FY 1977. For a complete discussion, see House *Report* 96–264, 2–8.

5. *Congressional Record* 123: H 25218.

6. Senate *Report* 96–236, 19.

7. Ardith L. Maney, *Still Hungry After All These Years: Food Assistance Policy from Kennedy to Reagan* (New York: Greenwood Press, 1989); Kenneth Finegold, "Agriculture and the Politics of U.S. Social Provision: Social Insurance and Food Stamps," in *The Politics of Social Policy in the United States,* eds. Margaret Weir, Ann Shola Orloff, and Theda Skocpol (Princeton: Princeton University Press, 1988): 199–234; Jeffrey M. Berry, *Feeding Hungry People: Rulemaking in the Food Stamp Program* (New Brunswick, NJ: Rutgers University Press, 1984); Maurice MacDonald, "Food Stamps: An Analytical History," *Social Service Review* 51 (1977): 642–58; Gilbert Steiner, "Stamps for the Hungry," in *The State of Welfare* (Washington, D.C.: Brookings Institution, 1971): 191–236; Nick Kotz, *Let Them Eat Promises* (New York: Anchor Books, 1971).

8. Maney, *Still Hungry,* 32.

9. R. Kent Weaver, *Automatic Government: The Politics of Indexation* (Washington, D.C.: Brookings Institution, 1988): 101.

10. For two views of the vote trading arrangement, see Randall B. Ripley, "Legislative Bargaining and the Food Stamp Act, 1964," in *Congress and Urban Problems,* ed. Frederic N. Cleaveland (Washington, D.C.: Brookings Institution, 1969): 279–310; John Ferejohn, "Logrolling in an Institutional

Context: A Case Study of Food Stamp Legislation," in *Congress and Policy Change,* eds. Gerald Wright, Leroy Rieselbach, and Lawrence Dodd (New York: Agathon, 1986): 223–53.

11. *United States Statutes At Large,* 88th Cong., 2nd sess., 1964, 78: 703.

12. U.S. House of Representatives, Committee on Agriculture, *Food Stamp Plan,* 88th Cong., 1st sess., 1963, 16.

13. Berry, *Feeding Hungry People,* 36–37; Maney, *Still Hungry,* 59–60.

14. *Congressional Record* 111: H 11652.

15. U.S. House of Representatives, Committee on Agriculture, *Extend the Food Stamp Act of 1964 and Amend the Child Nutrition Act of 1966,* 90th Cong., 1st sess., 1967, 11–12.

16. House *Report* 90–189, 2; *Congressional Record* 113: H 15142.

17. U.S. House of Representatives, Committee on Agriculture, *Amend the Food Stamp Act of 1964,* 90th Cong., 2nd sess., 1968, 13.

18. Daniel P. Moynihan, *The Politics of a Guaranteed Income* (New York: Vintage, 1973): 121; Berry, *Feeding Hungry People,* 61.

19. Richard M. Nixon, "Special Message to the Congress Recommending a Program to End Hunger in America," May 6, 1969, *Public Papers of the Presidents of the United States, Richard M. Nixon, 1969,* 350–54.

20. Senate *Report* 91–292, 27.

21. *Congressional Record* 116: H 41981.

22. U.S. Senate, Select Committee on Nutrition and Human Needs, *Nutrition and Human Needs, 1972,* 92nd Cong., 2nd sess., 1972, 619–20.

23. John Mark Hansen, *Gaining Access: Congress and the Farm Lobby, 1919–1981* (Chicago: University of Chicago Press, 1991): 164–213.

24. Roy T. Meyers, *Strategic Budgeting* (Ann Arbor: University of Michigan Press, 1994).

FOUR

Caps On: Entitlement Budgeting and the Politics of Uncontrollable Food Stamp Spending, 1974–1977

From FY 1974 to FY 1977, corresponding roughly to the Ford administration era, food stamp expenditures rose by nearly 90%, from $2.8 billion to $5.4 billion. From FY 1977 to FY 1981, corresponding to the Carter administration era, expenditures rose by nearly 110%, up to $11.3 billion. Part of this growth was caused by factors internal to the food stamp program, including liberalized rules and expanded utilization as the program achieved national scope. Much of the growth, however, came from external factors beyond the control of program managers, especially high unemployment rates and high food price inflation. Hypothetically, Americans might have welcomed the steep rise in food stamp costs. It could have been interpreted as a sign of success—that the program was reaching an increasing number of poor households across the country, was delivering benefits sufficient to cushion them against the shocks of recession, and was helping to guarantee adequate nutrition despite the rising price of food. Rapidly increasing expenditures imaginably could have been a cause for satisfaction; instead, they were most often seen as a symptom of disease.

Americans are deeply ambivalent about welfare spending. Food stamps are generally popular to the extent that they are viewed as targeted assistance to supplement the diet of the deserving yet needy. It is admitted, across virtually all political persuasions, that hunger and malnutrition are an embarrassment in a nation of affluence. Nutritional assistance thus becomes part of organized public generosity, which most citizens support as long as the costs do not strain the budget framework. By contrast, food stamps are unpopular to the extent that taxpayers fear that funds are being squandered through waste and fraud, that stamps are not being used for nutritional purposes, or that many recipients are undeserving of aid, either because they already earn an adequate income or because they are not interested in ever earning an adequate income. Suspicions of this sort usually intensify during times of precipitous cost increases, when citizens have more temptation to believe that a purge of the welfare rolls can save money while simultaneously protecting truly justifiable benefits.

During the period of initial establishment for the food stamp program, the former concerns predominated. During the subsequent period of secure operations, the latter concerns predominated. In the ideological battle over how the program was portrayed politically, during the mid-1970s advantage shifted toward the conservatives. Yet spending continued its upward pace without restraint, largely because of the presence of entitlement budget rules. In 1977, a fixed cap was placed on the amount of annual food stamp spending.

A number of factors contributed to the more conservative mood regarding food stamps. One piece of the explanation concerns the life cycle of a public policy. Enthusiasm for the program mission is highest during the adoption phase. The passion for reform carries the program over the hurdles of inertia and leads to legislative enactment. Once a new program is in place, however, policy attention shifts to the details of implementation, the complications of efficient design, and the mid-course corrections necessary given the inevitable gap between fine intentions and actual effects.

Another explanatory factor is public perception. Ordinary achievements are not especially newsworthy. Thus stories in the press about the food stamp program centered on a few dramatic cases of fraud or illegal trafficking. Moreover, as the program grew, shoppers were more likely to see recipients in line in the supermarket, identified by their peculiar form of payment, and there was resentment whenever taxpayer money was perceived to be used for the purchase of items normally considered luxuries.

A further piece of the explanation is political. Congress became more liberal in the aftermath of Watergate, and the enlarged Democratic majority adopted procedural reforms that led to a significant turnover in the leadership and composition of the agriculture committees. The Republican presidency, however, became more conservative, and the result was a period of increasingly strident partisan conflict across the branches of the federal government. The food stamp program was one of the battlegrounds of ideological warfare. Opponents could no longer be dismissed simply as intransigent Southerners and plantation farm interests. The president of the United States, in a State of the Union address, now labeled the program "scandal-ridden" and publicly blamed its rapid growth on "too many abuses."[1]

Finally, American public opinion was becoming cautious about domestic policy initiatives. Added to the sweeping distrust of government from war and Watergate was the fear of declining living standards caused by the 1973 oil shock followed by economic stagflation. Individuals are less amenable to welfare concessions when their own, personal conditions are deteriorating. If hard work no longer brings the expectation of increasing reward, there is less willingness to yield benefits to those viewed as unwilling or unable to work for themselves. Therefore, compared to the 1960s, voters were somewhat more suspect regarding the political uses of tax dollars and somewhat more reluctant to part with them. They were more susceptible to complaints about food stamp program abuses and more likely to be disturbed by them.

This chapter is concerned primarily with the effect of budget rules. The argument is that the form of budget rule was itself a contributing factor to the intensifying politics over food stamp expenditures. The Ford era, remarkable for operational concerns and ideological controversy, was also a period in food stamp history of budgeting under pure entitlement conditions. Spending authority was open-ended. The appropriations committees were obliged to provide funds adequate to ensure that all eligible households received their full allotment for food assistance. In a sense, entitlement rules worked exactly as their authors designed them to do, adapting program spending to the fluctuations of the U.S. economy while insulating it against the fluctuations of U.S. politics. Regardless of popular complaints or politician attacks, benefits to qualified households were determined entirely by the provisions of prevailing law. Under discretion, given divided party government, the political compromise necessary to enact annual appropriations bills would most probably have resulted in expenditure restraint, limiting the ability of the food stamp program to respond to changing needs. Under entitlement, the program was now shielded from appropriations dominion and also from the necessity of political compromise in order to continue annual outlays. Spending would proceed automatically unless altered by substantive law, and the conditions of divided partisan government would help forestall such substantive changes, further protecting the entitled and their benefits.

Yet, in another sense, the entitlement rules functioning to safeguard the food stamp program equally encouraged the conservative reaction. From the institutional-centered model presented in chapter 2, we predict that the president systematically would underestimate food stamp spending requirements so as to enhance the appearance of fiscal restraint. Because the entitlement reversion point mandates that sufficient funds eventually must be provided, the result would be a repetitive series of annual food stamp supplemental appropriations. It would thus seem to the casual onlooker as if program costs were growing out of control and had defeated reasonable government attempts at management. From the ideology-centered model in chapter 2, we predict that partisan opponents would have little impetus to bridle their attacks upon the food stamp program. Because the entitlement reversion point protects program operations even in the face of no political agreement, partisan critics would be free to issue scurrilous condemnations and to refuse all attempts at accommodation. It would thus seem to the casual observer that food stamps were mired in controversy and represented an insolvable political problem.

This chapter will focus on these two predicted consequences from the political game of entitlement budgeting. Ironically, the budget mechanism that effectively privileged the food stamp program against fiscal short-run pressure during the Ford administration subtly helped to increase the intensity of those pressures over the longer run. It is therefore a story of gradually mounting policy strain that ends with the imposition of strict caps upon the maximum amount that could be expended on food stamps during any specified fiscal year.

The Reversion Point and Budget Honesty

During the four years of open-ended budget authority established by the food stamp reauthorization of 1973, five different supplemental appropriations were required. This was a difficult period for budget estimation, given the extent of macroeconomic instability. Inflation soared after the removal of wage-price controls and under the shock of the OPEC oil embargo. The nation then experienced the deepest recession since the

Second World War, with unemployment climbing from 4.3% in 1973 to 7.5% in 1975. Recovery proceeded at an uneven pace while inflationary pressures proved resistant to the accepted fiscal and monetary techniques of control. These movements had dramatic consequences for food stamp program costs. From FY 1973 to FY 1977, the number of persons participating in the program increased by 40%; the average per person monthly allotment increased by 48%. It was impossible to anticipate such major changes in utilization and benefits. Outlay predictions in the federal budget regularly fell short of program needs.

Furthermore, there is evidence that the Republican administrations of the era did not always submit plausible spending estimates to Congress. Nor did they always respond quickly and accurately as soon as these estimates proved to be in error. The behavior was quite deliberate. It is in the interest of incumbent politicians to predict that the future will represent an improvement over the present. This led to excess optimism regarding economic conditions and a tendency to underestimate entitlement costs, forcing later corrections during the fiscal year. Similarly, it is to the advantage of presidents to present a seemingly tight budget to Congress. Presidents Nixon and Ford found that the attack on runaway food entitlements fit well with the economic campaign to reduce inflationary deficits and the political campaign to castigate big-spending liberals. In the pattern of sequential decision making, the onus then moved to Congress, which usually chose to accede to food stamp underfunding rather than face blame for raising welfare appropriations above the amount requested. There was always a hope that the economy would improve sufficiently to avert supplemental action. If not, there remained the mandatory second stage for supplemental redress. Although the sequential budgeting game was in equilibrium, it was not particularly satisfying to the actors involved. To food stamp advocates, the game placed them in a defensive position, forcing them to endure attacks against outlay levels considered necessary for combating hunger and worrying them that, some day, required supplemental relief might not be forthcoming. To food stamp critics, the game placed them in a powerless position, allowing them the freedom to condemn but not to limit outlays believed contributing to swollen government, welfare abuse, and further inflationary pressures.

The appropriation for FY 1974 was $2.5 billion, the same as 1973. The mandatory semiannual inflationary adjustment in January 1974 made the amount inadequate and another $500 million was provided, without conflict, by supplemental action. The justification offered by Edward Hekman, administrator for the Food and Nutrition Service of the USDA, was purely technical. Higher retail food costs had caused a $26 increase in the monthly allotment for a family of four with no net income. Entitlement rules required that funds be provided to cover the extra cost. The request for an additional $500 million was derived from estimates of program participation and recipient characteristics. Asked about the reliability of his statistics, Hekman merely replied that the basic data were submitted to the federal government by the individual states, and that it was cross-checked for "internal consistency and comparability with known facts."[2] The House committee recommended $450 million, commenting that the administration's estimates might be a bit high. The Senate restored the $500 million figure to guarantee spending leeway, and this amount was accepted in conference.

Benign politics did not carry over into FY 1975. The Nixon administration's budget request for approximately $4 billion was 25% higher than the previous year, but it intentionally used cost estimates based on food prices at the time of submission. Quite explicitly, no allowance was made for further inflationary adjustments during the fiscal year itself, although the prevailing law mandated semiannual corrections. Given economic optimism and the declared intention to improve program implementation, the administration preferred to wait and see. Congress, already facing a veto fight over the entire agriculture appropriations bill, acceded to the president's total. What in fact occurred was recession. Program participation soared by more than four million persons between November 1974 and April 1975. Yet the incoming Ford administration delayed asking for a supplemental appropriation. Instead it attempted to control costs.

The president in late November announced $4.6 billion in proposed budget cuts, choosing to orient aggregate fiscal policy against perceived inflationary demand. Food stamps were designated as a prime target. Ford explicitly directed the secretary of agriculture "to come up with a plan for controlling the spiraling cost of the Food Stamp Program."[3] The decision was to save $325 million from projected FY 1975 outlays, and more than $650 million in future years, by fixing the purchase requirement for coupons at 30% of net income for all households except the very poorest, tightening work registration requirements, disqualifying students, and improving bureaucratic procedures. White House officials recognized that increasing the purchase requirement for most households would be "very controversial" and would "meet stiff opposition."[4] Thus the administration chose to sidestep Congress and implement the changes directly by regulatory decree.

"We decided," Edward Hekman told the House Agriculture Committee, "it was fair and proper to ask program participants to share with the general taxpayer in paying the rising costs of the food stamp program." There was an "urgent need" to control the growth of federal expenditures in the face of mounting budget deficits. The regulations would help keep FY 1975 food stamp spending within the original appropriation. It was "one element" in the president's overall economic package intended to "turn the American economy around and assure a more stable financial picture for all our citizens."[5] Yet the concept of a welfare entitlement means that the recipients are not expected to share fairly with others the costs of general fiscal restraint nor to depend on a generally improved economic picture for their material protection.

Congress was naturally defensive of its decision-making authority. Citing adverse effects upon the needy, it moved in early 1975 to prohibit the regulations from taking effect. The vote was 374–38 in the House, 76–8 in the Senate—margins high enough to deter a veto and convince President Ford to let the bill become law without his signature. A large supplemental appropriation was now inevitable. Even had the program cuts been accepted, they would have only partially offset the higher demand for entitled benefits caused by the recession. The Democratic leadership in Congress was not about to take the initiative and risk partisan condemnation for its allegedly profligate ways. The onus thus shifted back to the president, who waited until May and the Senate hearings on the FY 1975 supplemental appropriations bill to request an additional $885 million for the food stamp program. This amount was accepted by the Senate and the conference. Both executive and legislative branch actors with complete safety thus played dishonestly in round one of the FY 1975 budgeting game because they knew that the entitlement reversion point ultimately dictated an honest round two outcome.

With the relevant actors more experienced in the dynamic of entitlement budget politics, appropriations fights intensified for FY 1976. The president's request was for merely $3.5 billion, nearly 30% less than FY 1975, plus another $1 billion for the Transition Quarter inserted artificially to facilitate a change in fiscal year accounting dates. The budget estimate assumed higher purchase requirements and the imposition of a five percent annual limit on inflation adjustments, despite the fact that these would not be accepted by Congress. Conscious underfunding served a useful partisan purpose for President Ford—narrowly, it directed attention toward his preferred program revisions; more broadly, it connected the entitlement spending supported by congressional Democrats with the budget deficits and inflationary pressures said to be afflicting the nation. Administration spokesmen asserted the need to gain control over food assistance costs. In response, Jamie Whitten, chairman of the House Appropriations Agriculture Subcommittee, noted that the budget request was about $2 billion short of the amount evidently necessary. "We would be spinning our wheels to just go through the motions of a hearing, if you are tied down to defending the budget before us."[6] The House committee postponed consideration for more than a month but the administration declined to offer a revised estimate. Both the House and Senate committee reports termed the request "grossly and obviously inadequate," criticized the administration for its lack of cooperation, and noted the legal obligation to fund projected costs. "While this action has the outward appearance of holding down bill totals, it will not have any real effect on total federal spending."[7]

Appearances, however, can be dangerous, and the congressional leadership was reluctant to take any initiative that would give President Ford an excuse for rhetorical condemnation. The solution was inventive. Since the administration's request would cover approximately seven months of food stamp spending, Congress granted the request without revision but limited the appropriation to seven months in duration, forcing the administration to return with a supplemental request. The president's July 1975 special message requesting the funds was aggressive rather than conciliatory in tone. Ford refused to accept the notion of relatively uncontrollable programs and inevitable cost increases, and he blamed Congress for lacking the backbone to act. Nevertheless, administrator Hekman had to go to the appropriations committees that fall to seek $3.1 billion more for FY 1976 and nearly $800 million more for the Transition Quarter in order to ensure the availability of funds to meet mandatory payments. One can even detect a certain degree of pleasure from appropriations committee members when they cut that request by over forty percent for FY 1976 and rejected any additional funding for the Transition Quarter, claiming that the administration's estimates were overstated due to a recent improvement in economic conditions and a decline in program participation.

There was a second supplemental bill in the spring of 1976. Although neither sought by the administration nor considered by the House, the Senate Appropriations Committee added $400 million for the Transition Quarter because the economic recovery was hesitant, placing "projected requirements for the Food Stamp Program . . . in a state of flux and uncertainty."[8] The conference accepted a $200 million addition, which was enacted into law. Yet whether Congress decided to initiate honestly as it did here, or whether it sought politically to force the president to make the first concession as it did previously, program rules protected, despite soaring food stamp costs and fiscal policy concerns, the privileged budgetary status of the entitled. Thus, for example, when supply-side conservative Representative John Rousselot [R-CA] proposed across-the-board cuts in food stamp appropriations, he was reminded by Frank Evans [D-CO], "as a matter of fact under the law . . . we will have to foot the bills and we will have to pay them, either here or elsewhere. . . . The program will not operate by my rules or by the rules of the gentleman from California. The bills will come due and they will have to be paid."[9]

Institutional sparring continued over the FY 1977 budget, as both parties prepared for the coming elections. The Ford administration sought major cuts in agriculture spending, especially targeting nutritional assistance. Congress, led by Jamie Whitten, strongly resisted. The official request for food stamps was $4.8 billion, less than the amount appropriated for FY 1976. Again, the administration consciously chose underfunding, predicting significant program revisions to contain costs. As agriculture secretary Earl Butz told Congress, any attempt to bring USDA spending under control "inevitably leads to food programs."[10] The House and Senate appropriations committees merely accepted the administration's budget figure, although clearly inadequate, rather than commence discussion about the likely need for higher spending, mandatory under entitlement rules. Strategically, the committees directed the Food and Nutrition Service to reassess spending obligations and submit a supplemental request if required by subsequent cost estimates. It was soon apparent that macroeconomic forecasts were overly optimistic regarding unemployment and that controversial reform legislation would not be advanced prior to the deadline, approaching next year, for food and farm program reauthorization. The FY 1977 supplemental appropriation, signed by President Carter in May, added $720 million for necessary food stamp spending.

Repeatedly during this period, there was a sequential game of initial underfunding and supplemental corrections, with intense institutional conflict and political attempts to shift responsibility. Yet despite the gimmickry, benefits were paid without constraint to all eligible food stamp recipients. Entitlement rules granted nutrition assistance for the poor at a spending level hardly predictable had discretionary budgeting been maintained. Equally, however, those same entitlement rules permitted budget posturing that might have seemed risky had expenditures actually depended on explicit agreement. In the process, budget controversy and recurrent supplemental bills gave the appearance that food stamp spending was completely out of control, that it exceeded all government attempts at management, and that flagrant cost overruns diverted resources from other public projects. To the casual observer unschooled in the politics of entitlement, it might not seem obvious that the greatest proportion of the food stamp spending increase over these years occurred because the program was succeeding at the task intended—accommodating outlays to unforeseen economic fluctuations while protecting the nutritional benefits guaranteed to qualified poor households against arbitrary manipulation—albeit in a political context that easily could make it look otherwise.

The Reversion Point and Budget Ideology

The ideological dynamic of entitlement budgeting is structured by an equilibrium outcome at the reversion point, regardless of the preferred expenditure position of the contending sides. The exact location of that reversion point, however, was the subject of dispute, as were the proposals by political actors consciously seeking to shift it toward their desired direction. Regarding location, both liberals and conservatives complained that bureaucratic operations for the food stamp program artificially moved the reversion point away from its "natural" position, thereby making spending too low or too high relative to where it ought to be. Regarding conscious shifts, both liberals and conservatives sought legislative reforms intended to alter food stamp program content and thereby entailed program costs. The partisan division of government institutions ensured deadlock. There was no substantive accord during this period, while political tensions intensified. In fact, the protections established by entitlement status to maintain program integrity despite the lack of consensus only helped encourage ideological actors to become more intransigent.

Food stamp advocates complained that the Ford administration, having failed to impose its will by regulation, was trying to cut food stamp costs by means of managerial practices. Based upon data showing that as many as half of all potentially qualified beneficiaries were not enrolled in the program, they criticized the USDA for not expanding operations fast enough to all 3100 local jurisdictions, and then for accepting complicated application procedures and for neglecting outreach efforts. The main strategy of attack was judicial. The goal was to involve the courts, the third branch of government, by suing the administrative branch for not upholding standards established by the legislative branch. The main player in this effort was the Food Research and Action Center (FRAC), and there were some notable successes. For example, a minor provision of the 1970 act required the states to undertake "effective action" to inform low-income households about the food stamp program and to achieve high participation rates. The matter had largely been neglected until FRAC filed suit in more than twenty jurisdictions challenging existing outreach efforts. In *Bennett v. Butz,* a Minnesota court found USDA implementation of the provision ineffective, leading to a series of consent agreements with the states and new outreach requirements from the department. Similarly, FRAC successfully challenged the USDA's economy food plan for failing to guarantee a nutritionally adequate diet, forcing the department to undertake a new analysis of the plan. Ford administration officials were distressed by such legal orders given rising food stamp costs, but had no option other than to accede.[11]

Simultaneously with efforts to better ensure the "natural" entitlement reversion point under existing law, food stamp advocates also sought new legislation that would shift the reversion point further to the left. Nothing came of these efforts during the Ford era. Sometimes the advocates were frustrated by the separation of powers. For example, in 1975, the Senate approved an amendment by Senator Robert Dole proposing automatic eligibility to new program applicants for a maximum of thirty days, rather than requiring them to wait for the completion of the certification process. President Ford indicated that he would veto any bill that included self-certification. Although the House Agriculture Committee reported a similar provision, it did not bring the futile measure to the floor for a vote.

Sometimes program advocates were restrained by the need to promote congressional unity in the political wars against the president. For example, in 1976, Senators Dole and McGovern proposed the elimination of the purchase requirement, that amount eligible households with positive net incomes had to pay in cash in order to receive their monthly allotment of food stamps. Under the prevailing law, qualifying households received coupons in the full value of the Thrifty Food Budget and in exchange had to pay in dollars to local administrative offices the value of their calculated household cash contribution. The alternative proposed was that the USDA provide stamps only for the marginal increment by which any specified household's food budget was to be supplemented above its calculated cash contribution. Households, it was argued, voluntarily would use the money currently required for purchasing stamps to obtain the remainder of their food diet. According to proponents, elimination of the purchase requirement would have a negligible impact on household nutrition but would remove a major deterrent against participation by legitimate beneficiaries who could not each month come up with the lump-sum cash advance necessary to buy their stamps. According to opponents, elimination would substantially weaken the link forcibly connecting recipient status to household food purchases, thereby transforming the program more into a general income maintenance arrangement. Dole and McGovern lost in the Agriculture Committee by a 7–7 tie. Despite probably having enough support on the Senate floor to overturn the committee, they instead chose to compromise with moderates, and thus the final amendment adopted by the entire Senate simply lowered the purchase threshold to 25%, in contrast to the committee's 27.5% and the president's insistence that the purchase requirement be 30%.

Ideological conservatives, like ideological liberals, were similarly not content with equilibrium at the reversion point. They also argued that the reversion point had been shifted bureaucratically away from its natural position under prevailing law. Whereas liberals charged that food stamp officials were admitting too few deserving households, conservatives charged that those same officials were admitting too many undeserving ones. Whereas liberals claimed that the consequence was food stamp spending that was artificially too low, conservatives claimed that spending was artificially too high. Their argument was that entitlement rules guaranteed nutritional benefits to qualified recipients by guaranteeing almost the entire cost of program operations. Allegedly, this led to a neglect of management efficiency and reasonable oversight. Moreover, food stamp program implementation was the responsibility of state welfare offices, whereas the fiscal burden for all benefits paid was borne by the national government, further reducing incentives for strict compliance.

The initial conservative attack was on the improper certification of strikers and college students, which was said to undermine the integrity of the food stamp program. This was soon replaced by a general condemnation of widespread waste, fraud, and abuse. Preliminary quality control data indicated that approximately 9% of food stamp households (apart from those AFDC and other public assistance households automatically qualified for benefits) were in fact ineligible; 6% of denied or terminated cases were in fact eligible. Nearly 20% of nonpublic assistance food stamp households were overpaid—either charged too little for their stamps or given too many stamps—while nearly 7% were underpaid.[12] The error rate was a matter of concern, especially given the president's denunciation of high food stamp costs and rising anti-welfare sentiment, and it severely damaged overall program legitimacy.

Public discontent was exacerbated by sensational accounts in the press. The *Washington Star* did a three-part exposé of food stamp mismanagement, reporting that 54% of all food stamp applications contained some sort of error that resulted in overpayments of approximately $800 million per year. *Reader's Digest* published a story claiming that food stamps was "a program that has literally run amok." A paid advertisement appearing in *Parade Magazine,* a Sunday supplement found in more than one hundred local newspapers, promoted the sale of a booklet showing how middle-income families could qualify for food stamp coupons. Reports on program mismanagement were commissioned from the USDA, the Census Bureau, and the General Accounting Office. Hearings were scheduled in both the House and Senate. The Ford administration participated aggressively in the condemnation. Treasury secretary William Simon said that the food stamp program was "spinning out of control" and claimed that it had become "a well-known haven for chiselers and rip-off artists." The president instructed his Domestic Council that "the top priority . . . right now is to find ways to tighten up on the Food Stamp Program," and he repeatedly demanded action, in both public and private statements, to curb abuse and reduce costs.[13] The attacks, while often exaggerated, made it seem axiomatic that something soon had to be done "to restore credibility to the food stamp program"—eliminating those factors "which have brought it into disrepute," and "to ensure the continued viability" of the program by better guaranteeing that "its benefits are directed at those who really need them."[14]

Program critics saw in the credibility issue an opportunity for new legislation. Although some proposals were intended to help protect the natural reversion point against wasteful abuses, these were usually combined with policy initiatives consciously designed to shift that reversion point further to the right. The problem for conservatives preaching cost restraint was that most of the increase had come from external economic factors, for which program administrators were blameless. According to Senate Resolution 58, the secretary of agriculture was instructed to study the food stamp program and recommend by June 30, 1975, changes that would disqualify families deemed non-needy, reduce administrative complexity, tighten accountability, and increase penalties for abuse. The USDA investigation concluded that the enormous growth in food stamp costs over time "can be attributed mostly to factors which appear to be totally within the law." It conceded that the error rate was large compared to other income support programs but found that the primary cause was local caseworkers making too many mistakes when applying complex rules to determine applicant eligibility rather than from any widespread fraud or abuse.[15]

Consequently, the department proposed a package of technical reforms, the most important of which would replace the complex array of special deductions from gross income with a single standard deduction applicable to most households. These would not have had a dramatic effect upon food stamp costs. Thus Ford administration officials, parallel to liberal advocates, also focused upon the purchase requirement. Their recommendation to save additional food stamp money—contrary to eliminating the requirement—was to increase it from an average 25% to a fixed level at 30% of net income for all participating households. Yet, because such a proposal would spark an immediate adverse reaction from Congress, the president decided merely to announce a long list of minor items, which "by themselves . . . will not provide significant reform." At the same time, he established an inter-agency task force to undertake a comprehensive review of food stamp operations and to consider a much wider agenda for change.[16] Between May and late October, White House experts debated fundamental issues of philosophy—the value of in-kind benefits, the effect of the purchase requirement, the role of work incentives, the causes of caseworker error—and slowly prepared a major policy initiative for later presidential consideration.

While the administration deliberated, other conservative forces mobilized to fill the political vacuum. In Congress, 120 Republican House members co-sponsored a bill, drafted by a former Reagan welfare official from California, to cut $2 billion from the food stamp program and reduce participation by more than one-third. The measure would dramatically raise eligibility thresholds and place greater fiscal burdens on the states. Technically, USDA analysts advised, the conservative bill contained many flaws and had little chance of passage, but politically it was an embarrassment to the administration. "The President says that we've got to get ahead or at least get even on this issue. He wants to have something on Congress' doorstep as soon as they return."[17] Finally, after considerable revision and a firm presidential instruction to make the package more conservative and reduce costs further, the administration's food stamp proposal was announced on October 20. Less extreme than the House Republican bill, it sought to save $1.2 billion by restricting participation to households with net incomes below the poverty line, denying automatic eligibility to welfare recipients, defining need in terms of previous earnings, reducing and simplifying allowable deductions from gross income, establishing effective work requirements, revising the penalties for fraud, and imposing a 30% purchase requirement. Predictably, President Ford justified his proposal by the "need to control the growth and abuse of the Food Stamp program."[18] It was promptly ignored by Congress.

There was no reason for partisan politicians, in the context of divided party government, to pursue new legislation when they knew that the status quo would be preferable to any outcome acceptable to the other side.[19] Compromise would require that the Democrats negotiate unity among their various factions and that the Republicans moderate their rhetorical attacks against wasteful welfare spending. But there was no obligation to pursue such compromise and no possible policy gain to compensate for the political costs incurred. Even President Ford seemed content with appearances over action, given the legislative stalemate, until challenged from the right by Ronald Reagan. Four days before the 1976 New Hampshire primary, Ford announced that the USDA would implement most of his food stamp reform proposals by regulatory dictate. For the second time in his brief administration, Gerald Ford sought escape from distasteful equilibrium at the reversion point by the assertion of executive authority. Congress now would have to either bow before Ford's decree or fashion a legislative package acceptable to him.

The strategy was inventive, but it did not survive court challenge. The Food Research and Action Center filed suit claiming that the proposed regulations illegally reduced or eliminated benefits by preempting congressional prerogative. A U.S. district court agreed and granted a temporary injunction, effectively enjoining the USDA from implementing the directives.[20] Legislative wrangling continued, over the somewhat liberal measure passed by the Senate in April and then over an enormously complex bill reported—with a minimal majority and pages of dissenting views—by the House Agriculture Committee in September. Yet there was little time and even less inclination to consider such a controversial matter on the floor before the adjournment for elections. After November, it was decided to await the new Congress and the new Democratic president.

All legislative efforts at cost containment and program reform were left in abeyance until 1977, when the entire food stamp program had to be reauthorized to permit expenditures for FY 1978 and beyond. As a result of logical stalemate, both program advocates and program critics freely played the political game of rhetoric, symbols, and public posturing. In the process, the credibility of the food stamp program came under intense and unrestrained attack. Impossible to change and impossible to escape, the entitlement reversion point dominated food stamp politics and policy over the entire Ford presidency.

Reauthorization, Reform, and Budget Caps

The Carter administration hurried to prepare a balanced food stamp reauthorization proposal, more generous to the poor than that of President Ford while at the same time restraining costs and giving even greater emphasis to management efficiency. The centerpiece of the proposal was the total elimination of the purchase requirement. Instead of requiring recipient households to outlay cash in order to receive a full allotment of stamps, the USDA would assume that they actually had paid 30% of net income for food, and thus it merely would supplement this amount with bonus coupons up to the standard of the Thrifty Food Budget. The main justification was increased participation by eligible individuals who had been deterred by the necessity for upfront cash at the beginning of each month. Yet eliminating the purchase requirement was also publicly defended as an efficiency move, for it would eliminate over $3 billion per year in payments "to 15,000 check cashing firms, banks, post offices, welfare offices, town clerks, churches, and even fire stations and corner stores who sell food stamps," and it meant "that over $3 billion less in stamps would be printed, shipped, stored, issued, redeemed, and reconciled each year."[21] On the other hand, the Carter proposal sought compensating cost reductions—denying eligibility to households with net income above the poverty threshold; ending automatic eligibility for welfare recipients; and imposing a single standard deduction from gross income with extra allowances for working families—and it introduced a series of incentives and penalties to encourage improved state compliance. Congress tinkered with the details and by September, before the beginning of the fiscal year, had approved a bill that in its essentials was quite similar to the Carter request. The legislative package was enacted in conjunction with the farm bill reauthorization, ensuring yet again a political bargain linking rural support for the food stamp revisions with urban support for commodity subsidies.[22] The intensity of the ideological contest seems to have waned considerably by the time of eventual passage.

Nevertheless, President Carter initially was ambivalent about the food stamp proposal. His first concern was financial. Despite a recommendation from his domestic policy staff that the food stamp bill should include full elimination of the purchase requirement, Carter's inclination was to wait for the comprehensive welfare reform measure then in the process of formulation. Carter had received memoranda from Chairman Herman Talmidge of the Senate Agriculture Committee predicting that the provision would add more than $1 billion to annual food stamp costs, far more than administration analysts had estimated. In a handwritten note to agriculture secretary Bob Bergland, Carter wrote, "I'm worried about the proposal to eliminate the purchase requirement for food stamps. It could cost us $400 to $1000 million if we fail to implement the cost control proposals (a strong likelihood)."[23] Secretary Bergland immediately sought a personal meeting with Carter, at which he defended the original cost estimate, about $450 million minus administrative savings of $25–$50 million. There was a margin of error because it was impossible to predict accurately the increase in program participation caused by purchase requirement repeal, yet the consensus allegedly had Talmidge's figure "well beyond the range of possibility." As a consequence, Bergland reiterated, the entire food stamp package "would have little added cost" compared to current policy.[24] Carter yielded on the matter.

Cost concerns also predominated in Congress. The CBO estimate, prepared by Bill Hoagland, showed that elimination of the purchase requirement would be quite expensive but that the price tag could be reduced by compensating adjustments in other aspects of the overall food stamp program. This notion of a balanced package was seized upon by John Kramer, counsel to the House Agriculture Committee. Legislative negotiations thereafter primarily concerned the tradeoffs needed to finance purchase requirement repeal.[25] Advocates eventually accepted new restrictions upon eligibility and a relatively low standard deduction. Moderates, despite remaining fears about excessive cost, then accepted removal of the purchase requirement. In this form, the package won approval by considerable margins in both the Senate and House agriculture committees.

President Carter's second concern was the length of the food stamp reauthorization period. Agriculture had recommended a four-year period, the same as the other provisions in the farm bill. Joseph Califano, secretary of the Department of Health, Education, and Welfare, objected. It was important "that the extension of the food stamp program not be perceived as precluding consideration of additional changes in that program in the context of welfare reform, including the option of a complete cash-out to eliminate the indignity of using stamps and the duplicative administrative structure." Califano, in order to emphasize the administration's commitment to comprehensive welfare reform, favored a two-year extension, and he was supported in this view by the OMB, the Council of Economic Advisers, and the domestic policy staff.[26] The president agreed, and thus his eventual proposal sought open-ended food stamp spending authority for FY 1978 and 1979 only.

Yet food stamp advocates in Congress, who had battled hard to establish the program, were not willing to concede on reauthorization or to consider abandoning the principle of special welfare assistance targeted to improve nutrition and food consumption by the poor.[27] Supporters argued politically that it was wise to maintain firm linkage to the farm bill timetable, procedurally that it was foolish to reopen the program for reexamination in just two years after having worked so long to reform it, and pragmatically that it would take the states months to implement the new regulations and they needed the promise of future stability to ensure cooperation. In the Senate, George McGovern's amendment for five-year reauthorization lost in committee by a tie vote and on the Senate floor by only three votes. In the House, chairman Thomas Foley succeeded in getting the Agriculture Committee to approve a four-year open-ended reauthorization.

It was in this context—of pervasive cost concerns and uncertainty regarding the length of the reauthorization period—that Congressman Dawson Mathis [D-GA] introduced an amendment on the House floor to permit food stamp spending for four years, fiscal years 1978–1981, but with a cap limiting the amount of funds available for annual appropriations. "The obvious reason for this cap that is being offered today," Mathis stated," is because without it we have absolutely no handle or authority in the food stamp program." Expenditures, he asserted, had grown at an extraordinary pace and there was much worry over possible waste, inefficiency, and fraud. Some increases in food stamp costs were the natural effect of economic changes, but some were attributable "to the professional regulators who write the program within the broad parameters of eligibility set in the Act. Not answerable to the public and subject to no spending limitation by Congress, the regulators can be expected to use their independence . . . to administratively repeal, rewrite, or simply ignore those provisions in the Act they do not like." To cede responsibility to program managers meant "the final abrogation by Congress of any fiscal responsibility for the food stamp program." The issue was how to better manage welfare spending in order to target benefits to the truly needy, control administrative costs, and prevent overpayment. A mechanism had to be invented to "bring some fiscal responsibility" to food stamps, "in order to keep some kind of control on this program."[28]

According to Mathis, ample provision would be made at the time of periodic legislative reauthorization for ordinary program growth, based on prevailing eligibility standards, observed recipient needs, and anticipated macroeconomic conditions. The administration could always return to Congress and ask for spending authority in excess of the prevailing cap, but Congress would retain the right to approve, reject, or amend the request, or even to enact compensating changes in rules and regulations to help reduce total costs. Mathis was quite explicit in denying that his amendment represented a thinly disguised effort to limit all cost increases or expel deserving individuals from the food stamp program. "You will hear arguments," he told the House, "made by those who oppose the amendment that what we have done is to lock in the expenditures and that there is no way we could secure an increase in authorizations under this cap. In order to refute that argument in the beginning, let me say that it would be very simple if the Department of Agriculture spends in excess of its anticipated goal, or anticipates spending in excess of the amount that is covered in the legislation, to come back to the Committee on Agriculture and ask for a change in the authorization. We could then report the authorization bill to the floor and then the Committee on Appropriations could report a bill on the floor, that we could pass for such additional funds as might be necessary to finish out the fiscal year."[29] Yet the implication was that the committees would carefully review any department request, and that they would exercise the right of refusal if fiscal irresponsibility was suspected. As such, it was a creative attempt to use a procedural mechanism to force improved management and control.

The cap provision imposed no changes in the basic structure of the food stamp program. Eligibility criteria and benefit rates remained unaltered. As long as spending stayed within the cap threshold, normal operations would not be affected, qualified households would have legal claims for payment, and the program would function exactly as it had under entitlement rules. When spending threatened to exceed the cap, however, otherwise existing benefit obligations would be canceled. Allotments could be reduced and individuals dismissed from the rolls, unless the dollar threshold was overridden. Under entitlement, in cases of unanticipated cost increases, recipient rights dominate over declared aggregate spending limits. Under the cap, spending limits would dominate over recipient rights. Mathis himself did not expect the cap to be especially burdensome. His announced intention was to place greater incentives on bureaucrats to keep administrative costs down and to curtail error and abuse. Yet program outlays could also grow for reasons beyond bureaucratic control, because of changes in household participation rates or changes in the macroeconomy. The elimination of the purchase requirement and the economic instability of the 1970s necessitated that some margin for error was built into the cost estimates. Mathis thus proposed that the cap for FY 1978 be set $300 million above USDA projections to provide a cushion against contingencies, and that the ceiling on expenditures rise by 10% for each of the three subsequent years. After a short debate, his amendment was approved on the House floor. It was accepted by the conference committee and enacted into law.

The Mathis amendment was passed by a center-right coalition in Congress. It found favor among legislators worried by rising food stamp costs and suspicious of experts with their obscure and highly technical methods for estimating future utilization rates. For example, Senator Bellman announced that the reform bill "opened a Pandora's box . . . and that the budgetary impact of this change in the food stamp program is far more than anyone is able to anticipate today."[30] Even the chief estimator, Bill Hoagland, conceded that the cost projections contained a great deal of uncertainty because they sought to model how people would react to an entirely new series of program incentives. The House Agriculture Committee majority had rejected Mathis's proposal largely because it represented the primacy of fiscal over substantive provisions. This is exactly what made the proposal attractive on the House floor. There, it received an "extra push" from key members of the Budget Committee who believed it was consistent with "their role as budget watchdogs to promote spending controls wherever possible."[31]

The Mathis amendment had another dimension, less visible but very political in intent. For years, logrolling had characterized the relationship between nutrition advocates and agriculture interests. The advocates had recently enjoyed the upper hand, threatening crop subsidies until food stamp liberalizations had been approved. In 1977, the focus was peanuts. According to John Kramer, Mathis sought to turn the tables, using budget concerns to help place the liberals on the defensive. The probability of needing agriculture representatives to protect food stamp funding in cases of cap excess would make its supporters somewhat more reluctant to challenge commodity benefits.[32]

Republicans provided more than half the votes for the Mathis amendment on the House floor, as a means of constraining runaway food stamp spending. They proposed an even more restrictive motion, to eliminate the $300 million cushion and keep program outlays strictly within the CBO budget estimate. This was defeated on the floor by a center-left coalition, with Mathis's help. Northern Democrats provided more than three-quarters of the votes against the Mathis amendment. Food stamp advocates argued to no avail that entitlement status was necessary to protect the needy, that other programs in the omnibus farm bill were not similarly capped, that it was wrong to practice budgetary economy at the expense of the poor, that unemployment and inflation had proved impervious to fiscal manipulation, and that the requisite legislative flexibility and responsiveness by Congress would not be forthcoming. If budget restraint was unavoidable, the cap should fluctuate, rising or falling with the price of food and the rate of unemployment. This would allow for program oversight in the case of abnormal cost increases without risking the fortunes of needy recipients suffering unavoidably from macroeconomic shocks. To Mathis and his allies, however, a floating cap demanded too great a concession, as it would reintroduce budget uncontrollability in place of a rigid cap threshold, and they successfully defeated the proposal when it was offered in conference.

Nevertheless, liberal Democrats did not protest the food stamp budget caps too strenuously. The general belief was that it was a small price to pay for the repeal of the purchase requirement. The chairmen in both the House and the Senate agriculture committees were not especially enthusiastic about repeal. The president's support was known to be hesitant. It was necessary to provide solid reassurances against high future costs to prevent defections by moderates on the floor. Even liberals had to admit that outlay forecasts were highly uncertain. In fact, as a corollary to the argument that the purchase requirement had artificially constrained food stamp utilization, they expected repeal to spark significant program growth. Kramer advised that the cap was less of a barrier than it appeared. Having beaten back the challenge from the right, the cap formula retained a certain degree of budget leeway over current spending estimates. If outlays ever truly threatened to exceed the cap threshold, legislators would be somewhat loath to "cut back a program that affects 19 million people, many of them in my district, many of whom rely on this for food."[33] Yet the food stamp budget caps did shift the focus of attention from program adequacy to budget capacity. And the imposition of new procedures carried a potential danger, for procedures are never neutral in their political effect and are rarely simple in their application.

In 1977, Dawson Mathis represented the views of the median voter in Congress. After two years of intense debate, Congress had finally enacted a series of reforms promising to impose greater efficiency on the food stamp program. Moderates felt the need to expand program oversight and accountability to ensure effective administrative management and to protect against waste and fraud. Similarly, Congress had finished the long process of food stamp policy reform to expand participation by all eligible households. Yet the majority of legislators remained concerned about program costs and were resolved not to let them drift out of control. They therefore sought a mechanism between the strict spending constraints of discretionary budgeting and the absent constraints of entitlement budgeting. The Mathis amendment was intended to restore to Congress a role in food stamp funding, escaping from open-ended expenditure authority at the sacrifice of automatic, full protection to needy recipients. Equally, however, there was little desire to return to complete congressional prerogative over food stamp budgeting, placing recipient allotments entirely at the mercy of annual appropriations politics.

The cap was designed to operate only in cases of exceptional expenditure growth. It would not set limitations so tightly as to threaten program benefits upon the slightest deviation from predicted outlays. Yet it would not set limitations so loosely as to disregard all cost increases resulting from extraneous, economic conditions. Mathis's assumption was that legislators would act responsibly, given their greater opportunity for program supervision and policy intervention. Confidently, he believed that Congress would distinguish justifiable from unjustifiable cost overruns. Optimistically, he predicted that Congress would devise budget solutions to improve food stamp management without unduly penalizing poor households in need of nutritional assistance. Instead, however, the next few years saw the regular occurrence of procedural logjams, budget gimmicks, excess policy tinkering, and partisan political stratagems.

Conclusion

Food stamp politics and policy during the Ford era were dominated by the presence of entitlement rule. As hypothesized, there were repeated food stamp supplemental appropriations because the legislated guarantee of adequate program funding at the reversion point permitted political games over cost estimates to proceed without policy consequences. As hypothesized, there were fierce ideological battles regarding food stamp operations because the guarantee of program maintenance at the reversion point permitted electoral position-taking and rhetorical posturing to proceed unconstrained by the necessity of compromise. The play of food stamp entitlement politics during this era can be portrayed quite easily using the one-dimensional issue space outlined in chapter 2. Program advocates were situated to the left of the congressional median voter, who was somewhat to the left of the entitlement reversion point, Qe. Ronald Reagan and his allies in the conservative insurgency were situated to the right of President Ford, who was somewhat to the right

Figure 4-1. *Ideological Budget Game, Fiscal Years 1974–1977*

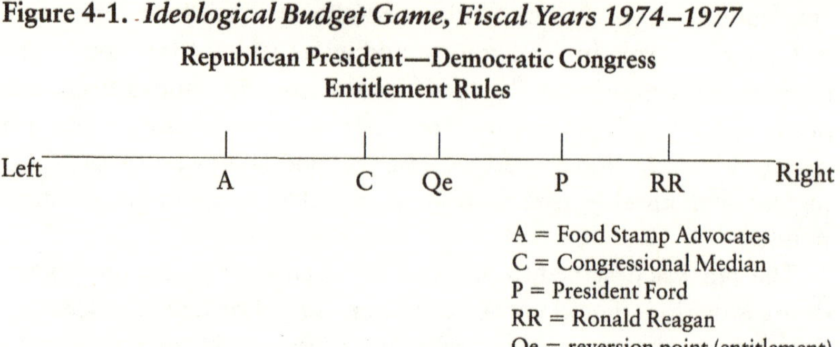

of the entitlement reversion point. Nevertheless, the policy outcome remained at Qe, since neither side had anything to gain from cooperation while each could lose if it played for less than intransigent opposition. The game was in equilibrium, although it was not an equilibrium satisfying to the individual players (see Figure 4-1).

Compared to the previous experience with discretionary rules, entitlement budgeting seems to have served the food stamp program well. During this period, the program spread geographically to include every locality in the nation. Deep recession drove poverty rates up and real incomes down, yet the resulting increase in food stamp obligations was accommodated relatively smoothly. Eligible households received the stamp allotments guaranteed to them by law and total spending grew in response. No longer was a disjunction possible between the determination of individual need and the aggregate level of nutritional assistance provided. Budget allowance was not subjected to a political decision separate from substantive intent. Program demand and program capacity expanded together, as entitlement proponents intended they should.

Ironically, however, the budgetary success of the food stamp program helped engender the reaction against it. Advocates have the advantage when the focus of public attention is upon overcoming hunger and malnutrition. Conservatives have the advantage when the focus of attention is alleged runaway costs and program waste. It is a fact of political life that concern eventually shifts from initiation to implementation, and then the promise of achievement becomes deflected by the problems of effective management. The logic of entitlement budgeting helped encourage popular suspicions regarding the food stamp program. Fully protected participant benefits alongside unanticipated rapid expenditure growth made food stamps susceptible to the complaint that undeserving individuals had betrayed the generosity of taxpayers. Guaranteed program outlays made it vulnerable to the charge that bureaucratic fraud, error, and inefficiency were squandering government money. The political bickering safely unleashed within entitlement rules further encouraged such suspicions. Repeated supplemental appropriations gave the impression of spending out of control. Unconstrained partisan attacks gave license to specious allegations and exaggerated protests.

As the public perception became less favorable to food stamp spending, politicians sought escape from equilibrium at the reversion point. President Ford, for example, twice asserted regulatory authority but was stymied by the courts. Congressman Mathis succeeded through the imposition of a fixed expenditure cap. Provision would be made for reasonable annual growth. Outlays that exceeded that threshold would be permitted only after explicit congressional approval. Entitlement status had provided food stamps with an escape from microbudgeting supervision. The Mathis caps were a countermove intended to restore some degree of legislative prerogative regarding program operations and expenditures. To the moderates in Congress who backed the measure, the Mathis amendment was primarily a symbolic expression of concern regarding growing costs, with some potential budgetary effectiveness at the margin. There was no anticipation that, given extraordinary economic circumstances, needed food stamp outlays would be refused and allotments to deserving households consequently reduced. However, the threat of funding denial was welcomed as a desirable weapon, useful for affecting program management and for giving politicians an added measure of control, both of which were felt to be lacking under entitlement rule.

Budget caps on the food stamp program lasted from FY 1978 through FY 1990. They existed first during a period of unified partisan governance in which the president and Congress were favorably predisposed toward program goals, and then during a period of divided partisan governance in which a conservative president revived the attack on program legitimacy and sought substantial spending cuts. The following chapters will examine the actual effects upon policy and politics resulting from the food stamp budget caps, which were often quite different from those intended by Congressman Mathis and his allies.

Notes—Chapter 4

1. Gerald R. Ford, "Address Before a Joint Session of Congress Reporting on the State of the Union," January 19, 1976, *Public Papers of the Presidents of the United States, Gerald R. Ford, 1976–77*, 38; Gerald R. Ford, "The President's News Conference," October 10, 1975, *Public Papers of the Presidents of the United States, Gerald R. Ford, 1975*, 1669.

2. U.S. House of Representatives, Committee on Appropriations, *Second Supplemental Appropriation Bill, 1974*, 93rd Cong., 2nd sess., 1974, 771.

3. Mike Duval, Memorandum for Norm Ross, "Food Stamp Program," September 10, 1974, WE 10–4, Box 26, White House Central Files, Gerald R. Ford Presidential Library.

4. Dennis H. Wood, Memorandum for Dean Burch et al., "Possible Reforms in USDA Food Assistance Programs," September 23, 1974, William E. Timmons papers, Congressional Relations Office, Subject File, Food Stamp Folders, Box 3, Ford Presidential Library.

5. U.S. House of Representatives, Committee on Agriculture, *Food Stamp Regulation Proposals*, 94th Cong., 1st sess., 1974, 13.

6. U.S. House of Representatives, Committee on Appropriations, Subcommittee on Agriculture and Related Agencies, *Agriculture and Related Agencies Appropriations for 1976*, Part 4, 94th Cong., 1st. sess., 1975, 907.

7. House *Report* 94–346, 67; Senate *Report* 94–293, 5, 75.

8. Senate *Report* 94–802, 18.

9. *Congressional Record* 122: H 18670–71.

10. U.S. House of Representatives, Committee on Appropriations, Subcommittee on Agriculture and Related Agencies, *Agriculture and Related Agencies Appropriations for 1977*, Part 1, 94th Cong., 2nd. sess., 1976, 7.

11. Jim Cannon, Memorandum for Phil Buchen, March 7, 1975; and Ken Lazarus, Memorandum for Jim Cannon, March 20, 1975, both in Arthur Quern papers, Domestic Council, Subject File, Food Stamp Folders, Box 3, Ford Presidential Library. For a detailed account of food stamp litigation, see R. Shep Melnick, *Between the Lines: Interpreting Welfare Rights* (Washington, D.C.: Brookings Institution, 1994): 202–32.

12. House *Report* 94–1460, 36–38.

13. Jerry H. Jones, Memorandum for Jim Cannon, March 4, 1975, WE 10–4, Box 27, White House Central Files, Ford Presidential Library; James Cannon, Memorandum for the President, "Food Stamp Reform Proposals," March 6, 1975, Arthur Quern papers, Domestic Council, Subject File, Food Stamp Folders, Box 3, Ford Presidential Library; Jim Cannon, Memorandum for Mike Duval, "Food Stamps," April 23, 1975, WE 10–4, Box 27, White House Central Files, Ford Presidential Library; Jeffrey M. Berry, *Feeding Hungry People* (New Brunswick: Rutgers University Press, 1984): 80–84.

14. Senate *Report* 94–697, 3.

15. Edward J. Hekman, Memorandum for the Secretary, February 8, 1975, WE 10–4, Box 27, White House Central Files, Ford Presidential Library; Jim Cannon, Memorandum for the President, "Food Stamps," May 22, 1975, James Cannon papers, Domestic Council, Issues File, Food Stamp Folders, Box 15, Ford Presidential Library.

16. Jim Cannon, Memorandum for the President, "Food Stamps," June 17, 1975; Jim Connor, Memorandum for Jim Cannon, "Food Stamps," June 20, 1975, both in James Cannon papers, Domestic Council, Issues File, Food Stamp Folders, Box 15, Ford Presidential Library; Jim Cannon, Memorandum for the Secretary of the Treasury et al., "Review of Food Stamp Program," June 24, 1975, Arthur Quern papers, Domestic Council, Subject File, Food Stamp Folders, Box 4, Ford Presidential Library.

17. James Cannon, Memorandum to Art Quern, July 2, 1975, Arthur Quern papers, Domestic Council, Subject File, Food Stamp Folders, Box 4, Ford Presidential Library. Similarly, Edward Hekman of the Food and Nutrition Service wrote that "it would be suicidal" to appear before Congress without a detailed proposal on food stamps. Earlier in the year, "we got burned" before the agriculture committees with the reform package that was "neither positive, substantive, or even controversial." To appear again without a developed program "would be to abdicate Administration leadership, encouraging (and tacitly approving) the Congress to legislate whatever it wishes." Edward Hekman, letter to L. William Seidman, September 26, 1975, William Seidman papers, Economic Policy Board, Name File, Hekman folder, Box 186, Ford Presidential Library. It should be noted that the administration closely monitored Ronald Reagan's public statements on food stamps. Jim Cavanaugh, Memorandum for Jim Cannon, "Reagan Column," July 7, 1975, James Cannon papers, Domestic Council, Issues File, Food Stamp Folders, Box 15, Ford Presidential Library.

18. Gerald R. Ford, "Special Message to the Congress Proposing Food Stamp Reform Legislation," October 20, 1975, *Public Papers, 1975*, 1715.

19. "Our bottom line assessment on our current situation," observed one staff memo to the president "is that we want reform of the food stamp program, while our friends on the Hill would prefer to have the issue." Jim Cannon, Memorandum for the President, "Meeting on Food Stamps," October 16, 1975, WE 10–4, Box 27, White House Central Files, Ford Presidential Library.

20. For an analysis and criticism of the court decision, see Melnick, *Between the Lines*, 217–21.

21. Agriculture Secretary Bob Bergland, in U.S. House of Representatives, Committee on Agriculture, *Food Stamp Program*, 95th Cong., 1st sess., 1977, 893.

22. John G. Peters, "The 1977 Farm Bill: Coalitions in Congress," in *The New Politics of Food*, eds. Don F. Hadwiger and William P. Browne (Lexington, MA: Lexington Books, 1978): 23–35.

23. Jimmy Carter, handwritten memorandum to Bob Bergland, April 1, 1977; Stu Eizenstat and Frank Raines, Memorandum for the President, "Department of Agriculture Food Stamp Program," March 31, 1977 (including marginal notes by the president); Herman E. Talmidge, Memorandum for the President, "Eliminating the Purchase Requirement in the Food Stamp Program," April 1, 1977. All in Stuart Eizenstat papers, Domestic Policy Staff, Subject File, Food Stamp Folders, Box 207, Jimmy Carter Presidential Library.

24. Bob Bergland, Memorandum for the President, April 2, 1977; Stu Eizenstat, Memorandum for the President, "Meeting with Secretary Bergland," April 4, 1977. Both in Stuart Eizenstat papers, Domestic Policy Staff, Subject File, Food Stamp Folders, Box 207, Carter Presidential Library.

25. Elisabeth Rhyne, "The Congressional Budget Office and Food Stamps Reform," Kennedy School of Government Case Program, C14-80-278 (1980): 8–13.

26. Joseph A. Califano, Jr., Memorandum to Bert Lance, March 28, 1977; Bert Lance, Memorandum for the President, "Food Stamp Legislation," 1977; Bruce Gardner, Memorandum for Frank Raines, "Agriculture's Food Stamp Proposal," March 28, 1977; Stu Eizenstat and Frank Raines, Memorandum for the President, "Department of Agriculture Food Stamp Program," March 31, 1977. All in Stuart Eizenstat papers, Domestic Policy Staff, Subject File, Food Stamp Folders, Box 207, Carter Presidential Library.

27. Laurence E. Lynn, Jr. and David deF. Whitman, *The President as Policymaker: Jimmy Carter and Welfare Reform* (Philadelphia: Temple University Press, 1981).

28. *Congressional Record* 123: H 25218–19; House *Report* 95–464, 824.

29. *Congressional Record* 123: H 25218.

30. *Congressional Record* 123: S 8389.

31. Rhyne, "The Congressional Budget Office," 14.

32. John Kramer, personal interview, New Orleans, May 13, 1996.

33. Rhyne, "The Congressional Budget Office," 25.

FIVE

Cap Sizes: Food Stamp Budget Caps under Unified Partisan Control, 1978–1980

The Mathis food stamp budget caps imposed expenditure authority limitations for four fiscal years, 1978–1981. They were intended to be adequate for normal program growth over this period, based on the income characteristics of recipient households, expected food price inflation, and trends in utilization rates. The spending limit for FY 1978 was $5.8 billion, slightly greater than the USDA estimate of program need, and it rose by approximately 6.6% over the next three years to a limit of $6.2 billion for FY 1981. These legislated budget constraints lasted just one year. By the middle of FY 1979, they were obsolete and irrelevant. Food stamp outlays more than doubled between FY 1978 and FY 1981, the consequence of macroeconomic shocks and a misestimation of the effects of purchase requirement repeal. The budget caps had to be raised concomitantly, for the consequence of inaction would have been severe, arbitrary, and across-the-board reductions in allotment benefits to deserving households. The tension between fiscal restraint and welfare provision quickly became inescapable. The inability of forecasters to predict food stamp costs placed the program in financial crisis. Representative Mathis had expressed optimism that Congress would be able to reconcile managerial oversight and spending control with legislative flexibility and compassion for the nutritional needs of the poor. The test of this optimism came almost immediately.

Ostensibly, there should have been little danger. As depicted in Figure 5-1, the reversion point under the budget caps (Qc) was far to the right

Figure 5-1. ***Ideological Budget Game, Fiscal Years 1978–1981***

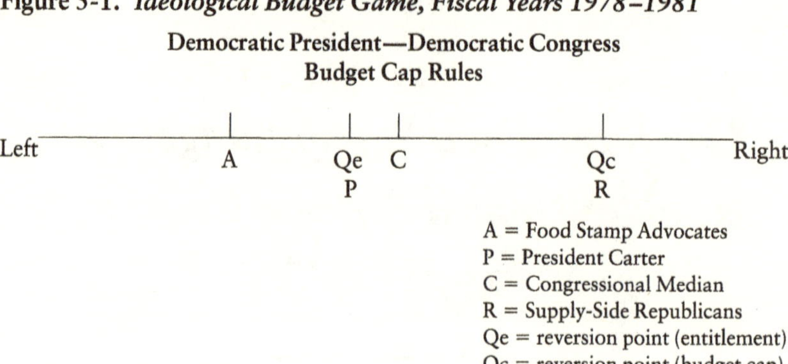

of the reversion point had entitlement rules been maintained (Qe). There were a handful of conservative Republicans insisting that the cap not be adjusted in order to prevent rising program costs. Yet President Carter was committed to full funding for all qualified recipients, and the Democratic majority in Congress, although not insisting that every dollar be protected, was equally intent upon avoiding arbitrary benefit reductions to poor households. The president and Congress belonged to the same party and had recently cooperated to reform the basic food stamp law. There were no great ideological wars to fight, no partisan reasons for posture and blame regarding the causes why entailed costs had exceeded the cap threshold, and no political barriers to prevent agreement for remedial action. With food stamp supporters relatively entrenched in power and with food stamp administrators relatively guiltless for exceptional cost pressures, there was little doubt that the caps would be overridden and adequate funding restored. Therefore, one might expect, budget caps during the Carter era should have imposed minor complications but not much of a fetter upon food stamp program operations.

There are three reasons why the actual outcome was not quite this simple. First, regarding the pace of legislation, initial underfunding created the need for three separate bills—budget, authorization, and appropriations—and at least six committees all acting under strict deadlines in order to raise the cap and approve increased expenditures. These procedural hurdles, combined with the necessity to adjust food stamp spending totals during the middle of an ongoing fiscal year, led to emergency legislation passed under crisis conditions. Yet Congress was not willing to lift the budget caps nor to revise them for future years based on re-estimated cost projections. Rather, in order to preserve its new instrument of oversight and control, Congress chose to maintain systematic underfunding and to override the caps one step at a time. The result were repeated fiscal crises avoided only at the last possible moment.

Second, regarding the bias of political debate, welfare programs tend to generate support when they tap citizen sympathy toward the hungry and destitute; they tend to be on the defensive on management and eligibility issues, for "it is always possible to find cases of abuse, and policymakers do not wish to be seen as defending welfare cheaters or maladministration."[1] Inherent to any expenditure-cap override is the question, how much of the extra expenditure can be considered unnecessary or illegitimate and thus should be refused. Even among program friends, an instinctive reaction arises that there must be some percentage of the unanticipated cost that could have been avoided. Congress therefore had a policy predisposition just slightly to the right of Qe. The cap would always be overridden and the painful cap reversion point, Qc, would be escaped. Yet at the same time, Congress found it impossible to resist the temptation to tinker repeatedly with food stamp rules and regulations, defended in terms of cutting costs while protecting the truly needy.

Third, regarding political manipulation, the existence of multiple legislative hurdles and the strict deadlines to avoid arbitrary benefit reductions gave power to those capable of enforcing delay. The budget caps provided extensive opportunity for brinkmanship. Politicians soon learned that they could play within the cap-override game for personal aggrandizement and factional advantage. Strategic maneuvers became more commonplace, and essential welfare benefits became hostage to nonwelfare purposes. As a consequence, the politics of ensuring a minimal nutritional diet to deserving poor households was excessively complicated and food stamp allotments were sometimes inappropriately threatened.

This chapter tells the story of the food stamp budget cap politics and policy during the Carter era—under conditions of systematic underestimation and repeated crisis overrides, compounded inherently by procedural complexity, policy tinkering, and political maneuvering. None of these factors were dramatic in their effect. All of them, however, reflected a divergence from the comfortable image of responsible policymaking predicted by Congressman Mathis, and all of them were logical products of the budget cap mechanism. This pattern occurred during a period of unified party government, in which policymakers were generally supportive of food stamp program provisions and aspirations. Yet the repetition of fiscal crises and emergency correctives could easily give the impression that something was fundamentally wrong with the program. Over time, critics became more vociferous in their challenges and public opinion became more suspect. The next presidential administration, of Ronald Reagan, would not be so favorably disposed toward the food stamp program. The effectiveness of budget caps would then receive a different kind of test, under the divided partisan control of government institutions.

FY 1978 and FY 1979 Budget Requests—Estimation Problems

The four-year period covered by the Mathis expenditure cap amendment began relatively calmly. The appropriations committees in both chambers accepted the president's food stamp budget recommendation for FY 1978, which was approximately $200 million over estimated need and $200 million below the cap threshold. The House committee, expressing concern about widespread irregularities and abuse, placed 7% of appropriated funds in reserve, to be released only if absolutely necessary. The Senate committee established a separate budget account for Food and Nutrition Service administrative costs, in order to more clearly distinguish operating expenses from individual benefits. In contrast to these minor adjustments, conservative Republicans challenged the food stamp budget proposals on the floor. Complaining about skyrocketing costs and arguing that bureaucrats needed a strong incentive to trim "excess fat, or slush," Representative Rousselot moved to cut $678 million from the FY 1978 appropriation. The motion was essentially symbolic, as it was generally assumed that adequate funding would have to be provided up to the cap threshold, but symbols often convey a powerful message. "By enacting my amendment," Rousselot contended, "we will say to the program's administrators, 'Do a better job—cut out the waste and direct the program to the truly poor and the truly needy, including the elderly. The Congress is saying make the program work the way it was originally intended.'"[2] The majority, however, was convinced that the budget caps themselves provided sufficient incentive for cost control and thus Rousselot's motion failed by more than 100 votes. In fact, FY 1978 was the first year since the food stamp program began its rapid expansion that a supplemental appropriation was avoided.

Similarly, the appropriations committees accepted the president's food stamp budget recommendations for FY 1979. There was some question why entailed program costs were expected to rise given that the 1977 reform act had promised fiscal balance between policy liberalizations and regulatory contractions. Noting the slow pace of implementation for the new regulations, the Senate committee warned that it "would not be favorably impressed by an increase in the error rates at a substantially higher administrative cost," and that it would carefully review any request for reprogramming funds.[3] Again for FY 1979, conservatives in the House moved to cut the budget request by $290 billion to keep appropriations equal to the previous year. The need to finance inflation-induced increases in individual benefits allegedly would provide a great incentive for administrators to curtail fraud and error. This time, possibly as a reaction to the Proposition 13 tax revolt in California, the conservative motion failed by only seven votes, 194–201. The Democratic leadership argued that food stamp budget submissions were calculated carefully using the best available technical forecasts, and that any lower amount risked a funding crisis. Yet a funding crisis came anyhow, even without the added impetus from Republican-instigated appropriations restraint.

There was little doubt that the Carter administration would recommend overriding the budget caps in response to increasing FY 1979 food stamp costs. There was little doubt that the Democratic majority in Congress would respond favorably. Neither had any wish to enforce the cap reversion point (Qc) or to use the threat of the reversion point to bargain for programmatic changes. Neither expressed general ideological opposition to taxpayer-supported nutritional assistance to the poor, nor a desire to impose a lesson in fiscal restraint at the expense of reduced welfare benefits. Food stamps were not a matter of intrinsic interest to President Carter, as they had been to Ford. They commanded presidential attention only when a funding crisis threatened, and then the reaction was to support the legislation necessary to avert disaster. Equally, the leadership of the relevant congressional committees had changed over the past decade and could now be considered among the proponents of adequate food stamp financing sufficient to meet all legitimate demand. The only issue at the moment was the amount needed.

The president in his January 1979 budget presentation notified Congress that a FY 1979 supplemental appropriation would be necessary to maintain full food stamp benefits to qualified recipients, although there was uncertainty regarding the size of the forthcoming request. He asked Congress to remove all dollar limits from the authorizing legislation and in exchange offered a new management system in which the states would be liable for errors above a specified threshold. During the winter and spring, a debate raged over cost estimates and expenditure needs. At first, both the OMB and CBO believed that the supplemental request could be kept to $245 million, within the boundaries of the cap. This was the total reported by the House and Senate budget committees for the Third Budget Resolution. Yet food stamp outlays for the first quarter of the fiscal year were much higher than anticipated. In early May, the administration announced that the cap most certainly would be exceeded and that the program would be denied needed money by September unless corrective action was taken. James McIntyre, director of the OMB, had sent to the president a "major alert" in which he noted, "We are in deep trouble whether or not the 1979 cap is removed: If the cap is raised, 1979 and 1980 outlays will run up. . . . If the 1979 cap is not raised, USDA may have to act quite soon to cut food stamp benefits to stay within the 1979 ceiling. The human and political consequences of this are substantial and disturbing."[4] The CBO, emphasizing uncertainty in the data, predicted a supplemental appropriation between $600 million and $1 billion, exceeding the cap by $220 to $620 million. The administration argued that these estimates erred toward the low side and were based on the assumption that participation would diminish later in the year. The USDA's official request, submitted on May 23, 1979, was for $1.038 billion in additional funding, which would require overriding the cap by nearly $660 million.

All parties to the funding debate were genuinely surprised by the escalating food stamp costs. According to the USDA analysis, two-thirds of the supplemental amount was caused by food price inflation. In the two years since the caps were written, food prices rose by 22%, as compared to the 6% to 8% originally estimated. Each 1% increase in food prices added approximately $58 million to program costs. Most of the remainder came as a consequence of the purchase requirement repeal. More households entered the program than was predicted; they entered earlier in the fiscal year, requiring payment for more months; and these new entrants were poorer than expected, requiring higher than average household allotments.[5]

The real problem, however, was inherent more than accidental. Expenditure predictions are uncertain even when moving from one fiscal year to the next. Yet the Mathis cap formula fixed maximum outlays authoritatively across a number of fiscal years. Under conditions of program reform and macroeconomic instability, it is not surprising that underestimation occurred. Moreover, the procedural and political dangers from such underestimation were great. President Carter was reminded regularly by his advisers that his administration had not supported the original cap proposal and had called for its repeal. In the meantime, to protect FY 1979 food stamp spending, three different legislative hurdles had to be surpassed—budget, appropriations, and authorization—each requiring hearings, mark-up sessions, committee reports, floor debate, and recorded votes. As USDA secretary Bergland wrote to House Appropriations Committee chairman Jamie Whitten, "the alternatives that face us are stark indeed. If insufficient funds are provided, we will need to cut benefits on a pro rata basis for all food stamp recipients. We have already directed all States to reprogram their computers so that these pro rata reductions can be instituted if necessary. I am sure you understand the consequences in terms of human suffering that could accompany such an action."[6]

The FY 1979 Cap Override—Multiple Hurdles

The initial experience with overriding the food stamp budget cap would teach legislators the procedural complexities inherent to the effort. First, the budget resolution had to be amended to allow for higher spending. Since no provision was made in the committee reports, friendly amendments had to be offered on the floor in both the House and the Senate. The main reason for the change, it was explained, was that food price inflation had been much higher than expected, requiring an increase in allotment benefits to qualified households. Yet Republican critics complained that it was improper to appear "at the 11th hour . . . and ask for a half-billion dollars to bail out a program that our own Comptroller General is saying is wasting that much money every year."[7] Moreover, critics charged that the cost increase was not simply a natural consequence of economic instability, because the administration had failed to implement the tougher eligibility regulations of the 1977 act in a timely fashion. These challenges failed largely because the Democratic leadership pleaded for flexibility. In addition, Dawson Mathis took to the floor, claiming that he did not know whether the USDA could make a plausible case for additional funds, but that the Agriculture Committee should be given the ability to hold oversight hearings and make its recommendation. As the author of the cap amendment, he was in favor of a process by which Congress would determine for itself whether or not excessive food stamp costs should be permitted. That process could not proceed unless leeway were granted in the budget resolution. The House motion allowed for $400 billion in additional spending; the Senate motion allowed for $625 billion; the conference split the difference. However, as Appropriations chairman Whitten observed, this figure supplied only a general guideline and not a target or ceiling for other committee decisions.

The second hurdle was appropriations, where the money had to be allocated for possible food stamp outlay. Whitten's committee in the House expressed its concern about runaway entitlements and the desire of the American people to slow the growth of government spending. Ignoring the administration's request, it approved only $379.7 million in additional food stamp expenditures, the maximum allowed under the cap. The committee could claim, technically, that it had no legal justification to go further at that time. In addition, by adopting such a low dollar amount, it also escaped any potential challenge on the floor. The Senate Appropriations Committee was not so restrained. It asked for $988.8 million in additional funds, on the condition that the requisite permission to exceed the cap would soon be forthcoming from the authorizing committees. For symbolic reasons, the request was $50 million below the administration's amount but toward the higher end of the range of estimates considered. As expected, there was a conservative floor revolt, from Senator Helms to reduce the supplemental appropriation to $660 million and from Senator Hayakawa to reduce it to $800 million. Their announced purpose was to transform fiscal responsibility from a public posture into a policy reality by limiting the allegedly insatiable appetite of the Food and Nutrition Service. Yet legislator support was more secure in the Senate than the House, and the two motions were defeated easily. The conference cut the Senate recommendation to $900 million, which was still $520 million over the cap.

The third hurdle was the authorizing legislation necessary to amend the cap. The House and Senate agriculture committees conducted detailed hearings into the causes of food stamp overspending, the administration's efforts to reduce waste, and the probable effects of insufficient funding on nutrition and poverty. Both committees, in lengthy reports, held that the funding crisis could not be blamed on USDA administrative practices, but instead was caused largely by food price inflation. Both recommended $620 million in additional budget authority, which was $100 million more than the supplemental appropriation but still almost $40 million less than the Carter administration had requested. According to the CBO, the amount would be sufficient to cover all expected costs with a degree of protection. A substitute motion by Republican conservatives to retain the funding cap unaltered was defeated decisively in the House. Had the new authority not been granted and the budget cap reversion point been maintained, either food stamp benefits to qualified recipients would have been cut in half for the months of August and September, or they would have been terminated completely for September. Yet there was little joy in the legislative victory. Complicated procedural steps had been required merely to supply the funds sufficient to maintain individual recipient benefits at a level that Congress had already decided to be adequate. Congressman Frederick Richmond of the House Agriculture Committee stated bluntly, "what we are trying to do is just to keep the program alive until the end of this fiscal year." While conceding the need for emergency legislation, Representative Leon Panetta commented, "It is not pleasant when we deal with a program that, very frankly, is not being run very efficiently or very effectively." "Believe me," said Agriculture Committee chairman Thomas Foley, revising the food stamp authorization "is not a pleasant duty in these last two months of the fiscal year."[8]

Although the emergency funding measure was accompanied by demands for a clean and relatively uncontroversial bill capable of quick passage, it also provided the justification and opportunity for policy tinkering. Some of the impetus came from self-interested groups seeking advantage. For example, lobbyists for the elderly pushed for a special deduction from gross income for households with especially high medical expenses and an expansion of the existing deduction for high shelter expenses. The administration opposed these benefit liberalizations on the grounds of cost, administrative complexity, and equity, and it succeeded in limiting the amount of change. Yet it was politically hard for legislators to refuse benefits for the elderly, particularly given the evidence that certain households had been made materially worse off by the standard deduction system introduced in 1977. Most of the impetus for policy tinkering, however, came from the desire to cut program costs and thus to reduce the chances for an emergency situation to recur. As expected, the focus was on fraud and abuse. For example, the final bill included provisions requiring Social Security numbers from all food stamp beneficiaries, denying re-enrollment to individuals previously disqualified for fraud unless they agreed to reimburse the government for the fraudulently obtained stamps, and allowing the states to keep half of any amount recovered from fraudulent claims as an incentive for improved enforcement. The Agriculture Committee leadership sought to limit the number of reform proposals attached to the budget cap override because of the severe social consequences from legislative delay. Yet it was difficult to refuse minor policy adjustments useful for promoting efficiency and denying benefits to unqualified households, particularly when these adjustments promised to save money for a program currently in fiscal crisis. The crisis, artificially induced by a legislated cap inflexible despite changing recipient needs and unstable macroeconomic conditions, gave ostensible support to complaints about runaway outlays and encouraged critics to prepare for future challenges.

On the other hand, program supporters argued that the best escape from emergency conditions was to remove the barrier that created them, deleting specific dollar amounts from the food stamp authorization. The president had requested cap removal because of the uncertainty of economic forecasts. In the Senate, George McGovern fashioned a successful substitute motion which, alongside the additional funding for FY 1979, repealed all spending limits for FY 1980 and FY 1981. As Senator Talmidge noted, the budget caps did not appear capable of exerting binding control over food stamp spending. Instead, to maintain benefits for needy recipients, "We wind up voting on the same issue two, three, and conceivably four times a year. This is not the most productive use of our time and efforts."[9] The repeal of dollar limits upon food stamp spending authority did not survive in conference. Republicans and House moderates were unwilling to abandon their new instrument of oversight and control. Although the process of budget cap adjustment might be complicated, return to entitlement rules would leave legislators without the ability to manage annual food stamp expenditure levels. Similarly, the conference refused to revise and update the caps for the remaining years of food stamp authorization, despite the fact that they obviously had become irrelevant given projected spending needs. The conference majority chose consciously to underestimate future benefit obligations in order to maintain an active role during each of the coming fiscal years. Funding crisis was thus avoided for FY 1979 but would loom again in FY 1980 and FY 1981.

The FY 1980 Cap Override—Hurdles Plus Tinkering

The complicated legislative exercise that was unpleasant the first time around was far more annoying when repeated, under even tighter calendar deadlines. Moreover, under repetition, the impetus to tinker with program rules and regulations was far greater. While overriding the food stamp cap for FY 1979, Congress was preparing its budget for FY 1980. The administration initially had asked for $6.9 billion in food stamp spending. The House and Senate appropriations committees agreed on $6.2 billion, the maximum expenditure allowable under the law. The committees knew that the amount was entirely insufficient, but they preferred to wait for revised spending authority and for more accurate cost estimates along with administration proposals for further savings. The First and Second Concurrent Budget Resolutions, in April and November 1979, provided more than $1 billion above the cap. Although not binding, the resolutions indicated the desire to avoid any reduction in food stamp benefits to needy individuals. The fiscal year thus began with the certainty that emergency supplemental action would be forthcoming.

In the president's January 1980 budget presentation, the Carter administration estimated FY 1980 food stamp spending needs at $8.7 billion, nearly 2.6 billion (41%) above the cap; FY 1981 spending needs at $9.7 billion, more than $3.5 billion (56%) above the cap. The CBO's estimate was slightly lower for the former year and slightly higher for the latter. On February 12, budget director McIntyre sent to the president an "early warning" memorandum, noting that all necessary legislative action had to be completed by May 15 in order to avoid program interruption. The USDA claimed that Congress was moving too slowly and that the May 15 deadline was critical "because of the lead time that is required to notify the States to reduce or terminate benefits to avoid overspending in the event that additional funding is not forthcoming." At a White House meeting two days later, the decision was made to take an aggressive stance. As part of his monthly report on estimated food stamp spending, USDA deputy secretary Jim Williams formally notified Congress, "If no additional funding is provided for FY 1980, substantial benefit reductions will have to occur." The funding situation was described as "grave," threatening "serious and harmful consequences for millions of low-income Americans." The current appropriation would last through May. Therefore the states would be ordered "to issue no benefits for June, unless and until supplemental appropriations are provided."[10]

There was a certain political astuteness to the May 15 deadline and the threat of total benefit terminations beginning in June. The USDA could have responded earlier in the fiscal year. Such action would have led to partial benefit cuts over a longer period of time. The administration had long known that program funding was insufficient, and ostensibly it was under instruction to act as soon as such information was available. Yet May 15 corresponded to the normal congressional timetable for supplemental appropriations. In addition, there would be a managerial problem for the states in moving from full to partial benefits and then back to full benefits if and when Congress supplied the additional amounts. Finally, there was great political leverage inherent to the notion of an emergency funding crisis. The prospect of partial food stamp allotment reduction spread over many months appears less dramatic than the prospect of a sudden and complete cessation of benefits late into the fiscal year. Proportionate reductions might even seem acceptable to certain ideological factions. The USDA therefore seems to have waited until crisis loomed, using it as an incentive to push Congress to respond in a time frame and a policy direction to which it was thought amenable. In the meantime, the administration readied a public strategy of media events, legislative testimony, and impassioned speeches intended to keep the pressure on. For the override to succeed, the policy process would have to move quickly.

Attention then shifted to the agriculture committees, which had to provide greater spending authority under the cap. The task was made easier in the Senate because of a shrewd move by George McGovern and his allies the previous year. They had arranged to pass the substitute package for the FY 1979 override twice, one of which went to conference while the House left the other still active for the duration of the 96th Congress. As that substitute package also proposed removing all cap limits for FY 1980 and FY 1981, there was no need for further Senate action. Although conservatives complained that they had been left without a voice, the Senate was thus ready to go to conference with a proposal to delete all dollar constraints from the food stamp authorization.

The administration openly endorsed the cap suspension for FY 1980 and FY 1981. The House was not so accommodating. Rejecting a subcommittee recommendation to concur, the Agriculture Committee instead offered a series of further cost-cutting measures and an inventive scheme for an expenditure cap with a cushion.

According to the committee report, the goal was a bill "targeted at both the needy and the greedy."[11] There was no desire to inflict further misery upon food stamp recipients, 90% of whom already lived under the poverty threshold. Simultaneous high unemployment and inflation had swollen the rolls and raised the cost of the average stamp allotment. The poor could hardly be blamed for the explosion in program outlays and should not be held fully liable for its consequences. Yet there was also general agreement about the need for fiscal restraint and a belief that the poor would have to suffer at least some of the burdens of budget austerity. Budget officials recommended and the House accepted a move from semi-annual to annual indexing of the Thrifty Food Plan, the basis upon which food stamp benefits were calculated. The indexing delay would produce a small cut in average household benefits but would save an estimated $300 million and, it was hoped, would contribute to an overall macroeconomic environment in which large inflationary adjustments were no longer required.

Equally, although most of the additional program cost could be explained and justified, it was always true that some portion of the increment could be attributed to improper management or undeserving recipients. There would always be someone less needy than others, some benefit paid in excess of the proper amount, some individual with an application intentionally or unintentionally in error, some administrative procedure improperly followed. Finding useful things to cut was a primary reason why legislative oversight had been introduced for annual spending in excess of the cap. Evidence that Congress was doing its job would be found in the fact that it did not simply give the USDA a blank check to spend, nor a revised check equal to whatever sum was asked of it. Thus there was an irresistible impulse for legislators to tinker with program rules. None of the reforms adopted were major. However, they allowed representatives gains, both fiscal and symbolic, from showing visible concern with reducing unnecessary expenditures and from insisting that the program be run as efficiently and error-free as possible.

In addition to a long list of reforms proposed by committee, a flood of proposals were offered once the measure was exposed to amendment on the floor, although most of these failed. The final House bill added fifteen new regulatory provisions to improve program administration, including better computer matching of records, photo identification cards for recipients, a more efficient hearing structure for potential fraud cases, an option for states to use retrospective accounting and periodic reviews, a new system of penalties and incentives for states to reduce their error rates, and more intensive financial audits. In addition, the final bill altered the asset limit for potential recipients and tightened prohibitions concerning students and resident aliens. On the other hand, it provided yet another opportunity to award marginally improved benefits to favored constituencies, granting additional special deductions for the elderly, blind, and disabled and for households with high child care expenses, although these were postponed until 1982 to prevent additional concurrent costs.

The net savings was estimated at $700 million, which was just a fraction of the necessary supplemental request. It was doubtful that any of these tinkering adjustments would have been approved had the food stamp authorizing legislation not been placed on the agenda through the vehicle of revised expenditure caps. Although most of the individual items seem sensible, it was not even certain that the result would be beneficial. As the Agriculture Committee noted, each small legislative change in program rules is inevitably accompanied by a "plethora of new regulations which must be incorporated in handbooks, manuals, and most troublesome of all, instilled in the conduct of tens of thousands of State and local certification workers."[12] It therefore expressed a hope that once the changes for FY 1980 and FY 1981 were fully in place, the turbulent years of congressional action would end and the program would become more stable.

Regarding the expenditure cap, the House Agriculture Committee did not want to abandon its oversight role, as the Senate had recommended, but at the same time it realized that the caps imposed in 1977 operated as "an inflexible corset, unreasonably and rigidly restraining appropriate program growth based on unanticipated economic factors."[13] The compromise solution, proposed by Congressman Glickman, was a cap plus a cushion, in which budget authority would be raised for FY 1980 to $8.7 billion, but with an extra 5% that could be added if the secretary of agriculture determined that the limit would be exceeded because of macroeconomic conditions beyond his control. The cap for FY 1981 would be $9.7 billion, with an extra 10% cushion. The justification was that it was foolish to replace one inflexible constraint by another, especially when the economy remained volatile and even the best short-run predictions quickly could become obsolete. The cushion scheme thus provided a safety valve against possible future emergencies, allegedly establishing a middle ground that preserved congressional control against limitless growth without requiring complicated last-minute enactments for every minor mis-estimation.

Critics responded that the cushions represented no oversight at all. The broad language merely delegated to the secretary of agriculture the right to spend more money—$425 million extra for FY 1980; $975 million extra for FY 1981—without having to gain legislative approval. In essence, the cushions were a mechanism for Congress to raise expenditure limits without explicitly saying so and without having to take responsibility for the decision. Disguised as flexibility, argued the critics, they represented the abdication of Agriculture Committee responsibility to review spending overruns and they reduced incentives for managerial control over program costs.

The cap override authority bill reached the House floor eight days before the May 15 deadline set for UDSA notification to the states to prepare for food stamp benefit terminations. Rather than risk a controversial roll call vote on the cap-plus-cushion proposal, both sides accepted an alternative advanced by Dawson Mathis simply to raise the cap and ignore the cushion. The House amendment lifted FY 1980 spending authority to $9.19 billion, equal to the latest cost estimate by the CBO. Because of future uncertainties, it left the total for FY 1981 at $9.74 billion. In conference, under the constraint of the approaching funding deadline, the Senate receded from its plan to abandon all dollar specifications for food stamp spending authority.

Finally, with the clock running out, the appropriations committees could begin formal processing of the food stamp spending request. Even here, there were problems. First, because of the threat of benefit terminations, a special supplemental appropriations bill was required for food stamps only, apart from the ordinary supplemental bill already under consideration. In its report, the House Appropriations Committee continued to express concern over "lax handling and outright fraud," and thus it recommended only $2.6 billion extra, below the revised cap maximum, with 5% of that total held in a reserve fund available only if absolutely necessary. The Senate Appropriations Committee requested slightly more than $3 billion.[14] Second, there was no time to revise the budget resolution for FY 1980. The House could introduce floor consideration of the spending bill on May 13 only after voting to waive certain provisions of the Budget Act. Without the waiver, the food stamp supplemental bill would have been subject to a point of order. Yet the waiver was an unusual procedural move, and the leadership explained, quite explicitly, that it was done under emergency circumstances, that it was consistent with the clear sentiments of the House, and that it established no precedent for the future. Budget resolution permission for higher food stamp outlays in FY 1980 was incorporated within the First Budget Resolution for FY 1981, which was still in conference over unrelated matters. The House then passed the appropriation, while many expressed fears that it might have to consider further funding later in the session. The Senate approved the measure on May 14, also after voting to waive provisions of the Budget Act. A series of substantive, cost-saving amendments were offered on the Senate floor, most of which failed. The main one that succeeded would have counted student loans as income when determining eligibility.

The conference met on May 15, the day of the funding deadline, and deleted or eroded most of the extraneous provisions. Yet the House would not recede from its appropriations amount, arguing that a higher appropriation would upset the fiscal targets for the FY 1980 supplemental appropriation taken as a whole. Meanwhile, based on the latest cost estimates, USDA officials became very concerned that the additional food stamp figure would still be insufficient to cover program needs. In an "urgent call" to the White House, Robert Greenstein reported that the pending appropriation might be as much as a half-billion dollars too small. The OMB and the White House staff cautioned patience, afraid that any request for more funds to combat further cost overruns might jeopardize the pending bill.[15] The conference thus agreed to $2.6 billion in additional spending but with the proviso that the secretary of agriculture should not proceed with food stamp benefit reductions, despite insufficient appropriations, unless expenditures were expected to exceed the newly revised cap threshold. The conference report was approved by both chambers that same day. Later in the summer, as part of the general supplemental appropriation for FY 1980, another $446 million was allocated for food stamps, $203 by additional appropriation and $243 by transfer from child nutrition programs. This brought the total budget to $9.19 billion, equal to the maximum allowed by the cap. It was just barely enough to finance food stamp spending for the fiscal year.

The FY 1981 Cap Override—Hurdles Plus Political Maneuvers

The entire override process would be repeated the next fiscal year. This was virtually assured when Congress consciously made only a partial revision in the food stamp spending cap for FY 1981. "I would like to note, however," Agriculture chairman Foley had told the House, "that our refusal today to increase the $9.74 billion level is not intended to suggest that we will not do so in the future. In fact, it represents the opposite conclusion—that we will attempt to expand it later in 1981 should the need arise and when the need arises . . . $9.74 billion is not a final figure. Both the House and the Senate intend to review its validity in the course of reauthorizing the program during the spring of 1981."[16] Complicating the override process was the absorbing presence of presidential politics. The entire budget for FY 1981 was formulated and debated in the context of electoral concerns and partisan bickering. The House initially appropriated $9.7 billion for the food stamp program, the maximum allowable under the cap, making a small share of this amount available only after the secretary of agriculture had used his regulatory powers to curb fraud, waste, and abuse. The Senate concurred with the total amount, expecting the president to propose later adjustments. Yet the political desire to avoid public blame for high spending meant that the vote on the agriculture appropriations bill was delayed by extraneous controversy until after the November recess and thus after the election of a Republican president and a Republican Senate.

Wishing to set a positive precedent for the incoming administration and the incoming Congress, Senator Robert Dole, a food stamp advocate, moved to raise the appropriation to $10.7 billion, although he knew the amount could not be accepted in conference because it exceeded the prevailing cap. Jesse Helms, scheduled to become the new chair of the Senate Agriculture Committee, then moved to amend the Dole amendment, reducing the total to $10.2 billion while stipulating "that there shall be no further appropriations for purposes of this program and that the Secretary act accordingly." Senator Helms also intended to send a political signal. Whereas Dole wished to indicate a continuation of past food stamp budgeting practice, Helms sought a change in basic orientation. He would not hesitate to use the threat of cap-induced benefit reductions to force the USDA to restrict costs. Helms argued that administrators needed to know exactly how much money was coming to them, and should not expect further bailouts for their incompetence. There was plenty of regulatory discretion and plenty of opportunity, he said, for money-saving reform, cutting off the "parasites who have infested the food stamp program."[17] Following an angry floor exchange between Senators Helms and Eagleton over the meaning of compassion, Dole withdrew his motion. Tactically, he feared that the symbolic cost if Helms's amendment succeeded was greater than the symbolic gain from a vote for the record demonstrating the Senate's general willingness to spend in excess of a cap threshold that was obviously inadequate. The problem would be left for President Reagan to solve.

As fiscal conservatives who had campaigned against the size of government, the Reagan administration did not wish to take political responsibility for a supplemental appropriation that raised total federal outlays. The final Carter budget had called explicitly for additional food stamp spending and a rise in the cap threshold. Reagan hesitated making the cap override one of his first fiscal policy decisions. Finally, on March 10, 1981, he requested an additional $1.2 billion for the food stamp program, $124 million less than was recommended by Carter. The House approved this amount, and the Appropriations Committee expressed the hope that any future cost re-estimate would be offset by program savings from reduced fraud and abuse. The Senate Appropriations Committee also reported this amount, although it noted that the USDA now forecast that higher household participation rates and delays in legislated reforms had made the total insufficient by more than a half-billion dollars. The Senate floor accepted an amendment increasing the supplemental appropriation by $538 million, so that the food stamp program would not run out of money by August 1. Cautious about its ideological vulnerability, the Reagan administration quietly lobbied for this adjustment on the Senate floor yet neglected to issue a formal request for the extra funds. Carefully watching his words, Agriculture secretary John Block merely wrote to Senator Cochran, "We are committed to the principle of full funding in fiscal year 1981. I want to assure you that the Administration will request the amount we feel will be required to prevent a benefit reduction from becoming necessary."[18] The conference accepted the Senate's higher supplemental amount, $1.74 billion, but it refused to accept the political onus. Food stamp funds would become available only on the condition that the president specifically asked for the additional money. The dancing between legislative and executive branches ended on June 18, when the formal request was submitted to Congress.

These funds could not actually be distributed unless the expenditure cap for FY 1981 was raised concurrently. The real issue was not whether it would be done, but how. The entire food stamp program required legislative reauthorization or else it would expire after the end of the fiscal year. The Senate Agriculture Committee, with its Republican majority, preferred using the cap deadline to force rapid passage of a four-year reauthorization joined to extensive cost-cutting reforms. The House Agriculture Committee, with its Democratic majority, preferred attaching the food stamp reauthorization package to an omnibus agriculture bill, consistent with previous logrolling practice. The delay caused yet another emergency because, under the Lugar rules governing the application of the cap, additional spending had to be authorized by July 1, 1981, to prevent the USDA from instructing the states to drastically reduce food stamp benefits for August and September. The House on June 23, acting under time constraints, suspended its rules to pass the FY 1981 cap adjustment, separated from all other provisions. "It seems to me," commented one congressional representative, "that we are being asked to approve a very, very unusual procedure. We are being asked first of all to accept the unanimous-consent request to take the bill up. Then we are being asked, without notice, to debate this bill for one-half hour on each side. As a result, some of us are totally unprepared as we come to the floor to discuss the issue."[19]

In the Senate, Agriculture chairman Helms used the sense of emergency for conservative political gain. He held up the measure until the final vote on the administration's budget reconciliation bill, to which he had attached a series of food stamp cost-cutting provisions. He eventually brought the cap revision to the floor past midnight on June 25, as the Senate was preparing to recess for a few weeks of rest. Even then, he attempted a last-minute maneuver. The cap override would have stripped Helms of some of the leverage he wanted in order to prompt further food stamp cuts. Thus he proposed only $1 billion in extra FY 1981 authority, sufficient for August expenditures, with the remainder to be approved later in the session. Senator Eagleton learned of this stratagem from a legislative aide in the cloakroom. Angered, he marched to the floor and demanded a roll call vote, which would have required that the departing members be rounded up and returned to their seats.

Helms called Eagleton an obstructionist. Eagleton replied, "There has been no more premeditated obstructionist of the food stamp program than the Senator from North Carolina." If Congress failed to act within the deadline and termination notices went out from the USDA, he continued, the cause would be a single individual who refused adequate funding in order to obtain "another lie-in-wait opportunity to take another cut, slice, slash, sledgehammer blow at the food stamp program."[20] Helms backed down and FY 1981 spending authority at $11.48 billion—equal to appropriations but 84% higher than the cap enacted originally in 1977—was approved quickly and by voice vote.

Conclusion

Evaluation of the food stamp budget caps, based on the four years of experience, fiscal years 1978–1981, cannot be favorable. Despite the fact that, for most of this time, the president and Congress were not far apart ideologically, that both had a strong aversion to the cap-induced benefit reductions, and that both accepted the program as a valuable component of the American welfare state, useful for reducing hunger and supplementing incomes among the very poor, the budgetary politics of food stamps was remarkable for recurrent crisis.

During this period, annual food stamp costs substantially exceeded projections. Yet higher than anticipated program costs do not always engender a political reaction, and certainly not a reaction as intense as that afflicting food stamps. The intervening variable was the imposition, in 1977, of the budget cap mechanism. Policy affects politics, according to the popular adage, just as much as politics affects policy. In this case, the policy budget cap altered the form of political play by inserting a reversion point so painful that most mainstream actors sought to escape it. The outcome was a recurrent dynamic of underestimation, criticism, and eventual emergency adjustment performed as the reversion point deadline loomed.

This should not be a surprise, given the logic inherent to the models developed in chapter 2. Under entitlement rule, the president had the incentive to underestimate food stamp expenditures for the appearance of fiscal restraint. Under budget cap rule, as hypothesized, the institutional incentive for dishonesty shifted to Congress, which systematically underestimated expenditures in order to protect its oversight capacities. The caps were established in 1977 and fixed for four fiscal years. Although the amounts were soon found obsolete, Congress refused to delete dollar specifications, refused to incorporate macroeconomic flexibility, and even refused to accompany necessary threshold revisions in a given year with corresponding revisions for future years. Its goal was to maintain a regular presence in any decision to raise food stamp spending above a minimum level. In the abstract, this was not an unreasonable demand. The practical consequence of such a regular presence, however, was the need to invoke complex legislative procedures under strict calendar deadlines. Similarly, as hypothesized, when no major ideological divisions apply, cap overrides should always supply ample funds to maintain full household benefits. Yet the repeated threat of fiscal crisis was avoided only by repeated emergency legislation. Emergency legislation, in turn, created the opportunity for brinkmanship tricks. It also provided the justification for minor programmatic tinkering and encouraged a perception that something was deeply wrong with the way the food stamp program operated, adding to fundamental discontent.

In a sense, there was a certain disingenuousness to the criticisms of the food stamp program resulting from the cap override process. Legislators had voted for the removal of the purchase requirement at the same time as they had imposed the budget cap. They were aware of the high inflation and unemployment rates in the country and knew the effect these had on welfare outlays. A cynical explanation would be that the cap process allowed congressmen to complain loudly about uncontrollable government spending but then to vote supplemental funds to help a vulnerable constituency, enabling them to claim credit on both sides of the issue. The problem, it was increasingly learned, was that the process was so complex and stressful as to make the game almost not worth playing.

A less cynical explanation of mainstream legislator dissatisfaction is that the cap process narrowly focused congressional attention on spending in excess of the specified threshold, rather than upon the nutritional needs of poor households. Even after admitting that the fixed cap constraint was not defensible, the large amount for cost overruns was still a shock to politicians who had previously promised that necessary restraint had already been achieved. There would always be a certain degree of unjustifiable waste and fraud. Something always could be cut. The frustration, from this perspective, came from the realization that ad hoc tinkering with program rules and regulations, while causing a certain amount of administrative instability, would never be enough to end food stamp budgetary instability. The cap most probably would be exceeded the next fiscal year, again focusing public attention upon the unanticipated excess cost and again forcing remedial action uncomfortable because of both fiscal and calendar constraints.

Program advocates and their liberal allies understood, at least implicitly, the effect of budget cap rules on food stamp politics and policy outcomes. Thus they sought to eliminate all specific dollar limits or to make the limits float based on macroeconomic conditions. The legislative focus would thereby shift to greater tolerance of the food stamp program, it was hoped, because the complex override process would be invoked less frequently and the amount of any spending excess would appear far less dramatic. Failing to soften the caps, advocates nevertheless accepted them as an irritation more than a severe threat. They were the price paid in exchange for the repeal of the purchase requirement. An annual funding emergency, combined with continual minor reforms and political gimmicks, were a small burden tolerable as long as sufficient votes were guaranteed to protect the financial obligation for meeting the nutritional needs of deserving households. President Carter might have been hesitant at times, but his support was there when it mattered. Unified government, with the White House and the Congress dominated by moderate Democrats, kept the overall risk to a minimum.

Conservative opponents of food stamp spending viewed the issue from an opposite perspective. Devoid of program responsibility and outside of most legislative bargaining, they were free to criticize and blame on behalf of allegedly beleaguered taxpayers forced to finance exorbitant and unnecessary program costs. The caps were a valuable tool to highlight the steep rise in food stamp spending over time. Yet the continued growth in outlays, despite the caps, indicated to conservatives that the process during the Carter years reflected more overlook than oversight. Cap overrides would continue until some key political actor stood his ground. Thus, over this period, whereas liberals were bothered by the symbolic message of the system of budget caps but could endure its consequences, conservatives fully endorsed the symbolic message but did not find the consequences powerful enough.

The election of Ronald Reagan threatened to alter this situation. Ideologically, Reagan had condemned the continued expansion of the American welfare state. Politically, having been trapped into the game of supplemental food stamp appropriations for FY 1981, he was determined not to replicate the pattern of emergency cap overrides during his administration. The Carter experience reveals the policy dynamic of the budget cap reversion point under relatively favorable conditions, with unified Democratic party government and generally supportive attitudes; the Reagan experience will show the dynamic under far less favorable conditions, with divided control over the federal government and with intense partisan and institutional disagreement regarding the value of additional food stamp expenditures. The change in political location of the main actors permits exploration of a different set of derived consequences from the formal reversion point models. Nevertheless, the general conclusion will remain unaffected. The net impact of budget caps on food stamp politics and policy was neither dramatic nor beneficial.

Notes—Chapter 5

1. R. Kent Weaver, *Automatic Government: The Politics of Indexation* (Washington, D.C.: Brookings Institution, 1988): 98.

2. *Congressional Record* 123: H 20146.

3. Senate *Report* 95–1058, 76.

4. Jim McIntyre, Memorandum for the President, "FY 1979 Food Stamp Costs—Major Alert," April 4, 1979, WE 10, Box WE-13, White House Central Files, Jimmy Carter Presidential Library.

5. Bob Bergland, letter to James T. McIntyre, Jr., August 9, 1979; James M. Frey, Memorandum for the President, "Enrolled Bill H.R. 4057—Food Stamp Act Amendments of 1979," August 9, 1979. Both in WE 10, Box WE-13, White House Central Files, Carter Presidential Library; U.S. Department of Agriculture, Food and Nutrition Service, "Elimination of the Purchase Requirement in the Food Stamp Program: Effect on Participation and Cost," October 1979, Louis Martin papers, Food Stamp Folder, Box 41, Carter Presidential Library.

6. House *Report* 96–264, 19.

7. *Congressional Record* 125: S 8627.

8. *Congressional Record* 125: H 18068, H 18077, H 18078.

9. *Congressional Record* 125: S 20141.

10. James T. McIntyre, Jr., Memorandum for the President, "Food Stamps," February 12, 1980; Jim Mongan and Florence Prioleau, Memorandum for Stuart Eizenstat, "Food Stamp Funding: Background for Thursday, February 14th Meeting," February 14, 1980. Both in WE 10, Box WE-13, White House Central Files, Carter Presidential Library. Also House *Report* 96–788, 61–3.

11. House *Report* 96–788, 12.

12. House *Report* 96–788, 23.

13. House *Report* 96–788, 16.

14. House *Report* 96–927, 2.

15. Jim Mongan and Florence Prioleau, Memorandum for Stu Eizenstat and Bert Carp, "More FY '80 Money for Food Stamps," May 9, 1980; Jim Mongan and Florence Prioleau, Memorandum for Stu Eizenstat and Bert Carp, "FY 80 Food Stamp Funding," May 12, 1980; and two handwritten notes by Bert Carp, May 9, 1980 and May 13, 1980. All in Food Stamp Folders, Subject File, Domestic Policy Staff—Eizenstat papers, Box 207, Carter Presidential Library.

16. *Congressional Record* 125: H 11446.

17. *Congressional Record* 126: S 31066–7.

18. *Congressional Record* 127: S 10670.

19. *Congressional Record* 127: H 13389.

20. *Congressional Record* 127: S 14045.

SIX

Top Hats: Food Stamp Budget Caps under Divided Partisan Control, 1981–1984

One of the tasks confronting the Reagan administration when it took office in early 1981 was the reauthorization of the entire food stamp program, so that operations could continue and benefits be awarded for FY 1982 and beyond. The new president, unlike his predecessor, announced that he would not countenance liberalized benefits, ballooning costs, or last-minute budget adjustments. Food stamps, to Reagan, represented the quintessential uncontrollable entitlement program, with automatic expenditure growth that burdened taxpayers and insufficient incentives for proper management. With costs that had increased twenty-fold in just a decade, it was an example of good intentions gone amok, resulting in a budgetary time bomb that would soon explode unless defused. "The Food Stamp program," Reagan stated in his February 18, 1981, address to a joint session of Congress, "will be restored to its original purpose, to assist those without resources to purchase sufficient nutritional food." That goal could be achieved yet $1.8 billion saved in FY 1982 "by removing from eligibility those who are not in real need or who are abusing the program."[1]

The president was also committed to the idea of continuing the budget caps as a policy tool helpful in restricting food stamp costs. Any acceptable reauthorization proposal would therefore have to include a new set of caps, specifying an exact dollar amount for maximum spending in each fiscal year. The administration's preference was to make the caps even more stringent than those adopted in 1977, with less allowance for error in annual cost estimates and smaller provision for outlay growth over time. Reagan also expressed an intention to enforce the new cap thresholds upon program operations. Having been trapped into the complex game of cap override immediately upon taking office, he had little inclination to repeat the process.

President Reagan benefited in his task from a conservative shift in Congress. In the 1980 elections, the Republican party gained thirty-four seats in the House and majority control in the Senate. A thermometer of congressional opinion toward the food stamp program showed that the number of members with "nonsupportive" attitudes had increased and now exceeded the number with "supportive" attitudes.[2] Jesse Helms, the new chairman of the Senate Agriculture Committee, was especially antagonistic toward the program, alleging that as much as 40% of all food stamp outlays were waste. Helms was described by one food lobbyist as an ideologue and a bulldog who would not give up even when defeat was assured. "Ten years ago he was considered a kook. Today he is taken seriously and has influence."[3]

The presentation of Reagan era actor positions in a one-dimensional linear model closely approximates the example of ideological expenditure-cap budgeting politics outlined in chapter 2. In that example, a liberal Congress and a conservative president are widely separated by their beliefs, with the president much farther to the right and far closer to Qc. The president (P) is indifferent regarding Qc and x, and thus the space between those two points defines his area of preferable outcomes. Congress has a great aversion to Qc and would accept any outcome to its left. Consequently, there is opportunity for bargaining with the president, with Congress pushing for a compromise outcome approaching x, which is the best it can rationally hope to achieve. The main adjustment to the abstract model, based on actual Reagan era political actors, is caused by the Republican capture of the Senate. Thus the effective position to the left is occupied not by Congress as a whole but by the Democratic-controlled House of Representatives (H). Regarding the Senate, arch-conservative Jesse Helms (JH) assumed the chair of the Agriculture Committee, while the median voter in the chamber was somewhat more moderate (M) (see Figure 6-1).

The existence of a budget cap reversion point influenced the politics and policy of the food stamp reauthorization. During the Carter period, there was an intentional gap between the spending levels entailed by substantive legislation and the spending levels permitted under the budget

Figure 6-1. ***Ideological Budget Game, Fiscal Years 1982–1985***

Republican President—Divided Congress
Budget Cap Rules

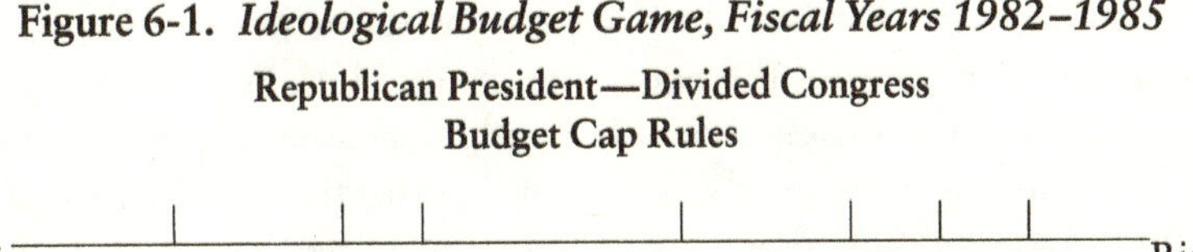

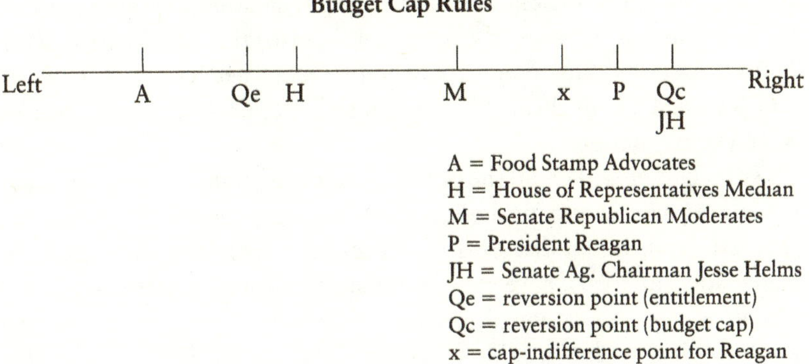

caps. The solution, given a sympathetic political climate, was not to reformulate the policy but instead periodically to override the caps. With program reauthorization scheduled early under the new Reagan administration, it was in the interest of food stamp advocates to test whether a similar accommodation could be achieved. It was, by contrast, in the interest of the president and his conservative allies to respond emphatically, asserting the value of spending restraint and their willingness to enforce such restraint, if required, through the cap mechanism. There was uncertainty whether the administration would actually carry out such a threat. Fear that it might, however, helped to push nutrition advocates to change strategy. Advocates decided to accede to some degree of programmatic cuts, working hard to secure the best compromise possible. They would accept budget caps drawn at that level and pray that expenditures later remained within the bounds.

Success depended on two conditions. First, it was necessary for advocates to form a coalition with conservative Democrats in the House and moderate Republicans in the Senate, thereby delimiting the political power of the president to dictate substantive reforms. Second, it was necessary that the economy cooperate and not drive entailed program costs during the fiscal years of the reauthorization period outside the president's overall spending targets. The advocates were aided by fortunate timing, initially by the onset of macroeconomic recession and then by recovery. Although the president continually pursued greater cuts, he was frustrated by partisan divisions and by an orchestrated campaign focused on the needs of the poor, hungry, and homeless. By 1985 and the next scheduled program reauthorization, institutional stalemate had led to a cautious truce and the Reagan administration had wearied of the battle. Congress thus inserted a bit more room between forecast costs and the budget caps through FY 1990, to better protect against the risk of emergency action.

This chapter will detail the policy dynamic of budget caps under conditions of partisan and ideological division among the key actors, tracing the path from initial discord through difficult compromise to guarded stalemate. The focus, nevertheless, remains the tension between welfare provision and fiscal control, between the needs of poor recipients and the financing made available to satisfy those needs. By the end of this period, it was generally conceded by informed commentators that the caps had not helped to resolve the tension. The imposition of fixed dollar limits on food stamp budget authority had resulted primarily in additional complexity and heightened conflict and had not produced anything approaching rational oversight or more responsible legislative decision-making. The caps would persist into the next reauthorization period more symbolic than effective, with legislators approving specific spending thresholds while seeking to ensure that they would not be exceeded and that the override mechanism would not have to be invoked.

Opening Skirmishes

The entire food stamp program was subject to reauthorization in 1981. Lacking permanent expenditure authority, the program required agreement from both chambers in Congress and from the president in order to permit any future outlay of funds. Given presidential veto power, a Republican majority in the Senate, and an increasingly conservative political tone in the country, President Reagan had considerable bargaining advantage. The consequence for failing to reach agreement regarding reauthorization was no food stamp program at all.

The president's election platform had called for decisive action to curtail entitlement growth and to free up funds better used to help finance a concomitant cut in individual income tax rates. Discussing the Reagan administration's approach to entitlement reform, OMB Director David Stockman said that the fundamental choice was between two basic routes to budget savings—across-the-board reductions versus "targeted selective detailed changes" introduced program by program. The former was simpler to enact and made it easier to show to the public large projected savings. It had been the strategy adopted previously by supply-side conservatives seeking to slice government spending. Minority budget resolutions during the Carter era, for example, had merely demanded a flat percentage diminution in total outlays. Yet, Stockman argued, across-the-board reductions can lack permanence because they do not necessarily affect policy structure, and they can violate equity by failing to "recognize the enormous variety of circumstances" among the benefit population. The Reagan administration therefore opted to emphasize the latter route, which Stockman characterized as "hacking away," recommending a series of detailed policy changes intended to save "$300 million here, $100 million there."[4] For the food stamp program, the sum of these changes equalled $1.99 billion in outlay reductions for FY 1982, representing more than a 15% budget cut.[5] As a second line of defense, aggregate caps would also be reintroduced, set at the level of annual spending anticipated from technical estimates under the revised program rules. Assuming broad macroeconomic revitalization, it was believed unlikely that the cap thresholds ever would be breached.

The problem with the Reagan administration's detailed-changes approach to budget cutting was that each specific reform had to be justified on its own merits, yet the total savings from the collection of reforms had to be sufficient to meet the aggregate target established for acceptable spending. The administration behaved as if program responsibility and fiscal responsibility were fully consistent. Its proposed food stamp reforms were justified for focusing benefits to the truly needy, avoiding duplication, ending unnecessary program costs, and improving service delivery with fewer managerial burdens. These justifications were sometimes transparent. Among the food stamp reforms, those most defensible—such as pro-rating the first month's benefits or limiting gross income to 130% of the poverty rate—saved relatively little money. More than half of the projected amount was to come from reducing food stamp benefits for children receiving subsidized school lunches, harmful to the neediest of households, and from an across-the-board freeze in permissible deductions from gross income, which contradicted the announced goal of recognizing special circumstances.

Presented with the Reagan agenda, program advocates with considerable influence over the Democratic majority in the House had to decide upon a response. The first task was to probe for the seriousness of the administration's intentions, to discover whether it might truly be more concerned with appearances than reality. If so, advocates would reject the most damaging of the Reagan proposals in the House and hope to prevail in conference. A visible symbol of budget control, useful politically to both parties given the ideological tenor in the country, could remain in the somewhat stringent annual spending caps. Reviving the situation that prevailed during the Carter years, the outlay requirements under program rules could become inconsistent with the outlay restrictions under budget rules. Yet, advocates might expect, the prospect of benefit cut-offs to deserving households late into the fiscal year would continue to appear undesirable and thus any threatening caps regularly would be overridden. The process would remain inefficient and uncomfortable, but it would be the least dangerous option to the food stamp program based on the president's announced priorities.

Yet the strategy was contingent upon the administration's agreement to modify or abandon certain proposed cost-cutting program reforms when bargaining with House Democrats, and then upon its reluctance to enforce the budget cap reversion point upon legitimate recipients if projected fiscal year spending threatened to exceed legislated limits. The Reagan administration replied strongly that neither premise should be taken for granted. Quite explicitly, it sought to demonstrate its resolve and thus to indicate that former accommodations would no longer be accepted.

Regarding the cap, the administration claimed that it would not enjoy imposing the reversion point, with its arbitrary and across-the-board approach to cost containment. Yet it did assert, clearly and emphatically, that it would insist upon stringent thresholds unless policy reforms brought food stamp spending within a tolerable range. The administration thus recommended dollar ceilings through FY 1985 that reflected a series of substantive cuts in eligibility and improvements in management, and it warned that the override action accepted for FY 1981 should not be taken as a precedent for future cooperation. As Richard Lyng, deputy secretary of agriculture, told the House Agriculture Committee, "If sufficient funds are not available to provide the established benefit levels to all participating households, then benefits may be reduced to insure we remain within the appropriation."[6]

The Senate Agriculture Committee's Republican majority noted with pleasure the administration's intention "not to return to Congress for additional funding each year, as was customary under previous Administrations," but to operate within proper spending limits. According to the Senate report, "Establishment of reasonable annual appropriation ceilings serve the very useful purpose of ensuring that there will be continual, close congressional scrutiny of the program. If these 'caps' are in danger of being reached, it will indicate the need for further action to hold costs within the authorized amounts." Chairman Helms was even more explicit: "As far as I am concerned, these should be the final figures. If the Administration foresees that the cost of the program will exceed the appropriations, it should implement section 18(b), that calls for reductions in benefits in order to remain within overall spending limits."[7]

Similarly, the Reagan administration sought to indicate that it would not countenance intentional eroding of food stamp substantive reforms, even if the aggregate spending totals were left intact. The first test came over the budget resolution. The House Budget Committee sought to give the president part of what he wanted, sufficient to claim consistency with the prevailing political mood yet cautious enough to avoid blame for cuts to the poor and elderly. Calculated to save $1.0 billion, the Budget Committee's plan for food stamps anticipated no benefit reductions to school lunch recipients and no freeze on allowable deductions. David Stockman reported that the committee's overtures were never considered, "even for a moment . . . we weren't playing horseshoes. Close didn't count."[8] The alliance of unified Republicans with sixty-three "boll weevil" Democrats easily defeated the budget plan on the House floor and replaced it with one far more in accord with the president's wishes.

A second test of the advocates' strategy, giving the administration a full symbolic victory regarding budget totals while refusing detailed substantive commitments, was framed by the House Agriculture Committee. To comply with reconciliation instructions, the committee approved an FY 1982 budget ceiling for food stamp spending that saved the required amount, $1.458 billion, using CBO baseline estimates. However, all specific programmatic reforms to realize these savings were deleted and replaced instead with a promise that the necessary action would be forthcoming later, to be revealed during the actual mark-up of the farm reauthorization bill. By then, it was hoped, cost-cutting considerations would be less salient and the president's legislative momentum would have slowed. Again, the administration completely rejected the overture, which Stockman termed "a pathetic farce" and "a travesty" because it did not in fact change "one comma in the Food Stamp law."[9] Refusing to deal, the administration helped to craft a substitute reconciliation package which prevailed by six votes on the House floor.

The lesson from these opening skirmishes was that the Reagan administration would not be a willing collaborator to partial and symbolic concessions in the direction of welfare restraint. It saw no advantage, whether political or ideological, to continued food stamp budget dishonesty, and thus it used the full legislative powers of the president to insist upon his proposed aggregate amount for spending reduction and upon the substantive reforms needed to achieve those reductions. The cap arrangement provided the Reagan administration with a useful tool in policy bargaining. It maintained a threat of reversion point benefit cuts if for any reason substantive changes were deemed inadequate and anticipated program expenditures exceeded budget targets. The message to food stamp advocates was clear. The strategy of broad spending restraints not met by equivalent policy reforms, even if enacted, would be risky in practical implementation. The political dynamic of food stamp budgeting during the Carter era, with aggregate cap limitations yet periodic legislative overrides, would not be maintained under Reagan.

For food stamp advocates in 1981 to regain the initiative and successfully practice damage control, they would have to move rightward within the boundaries of the president's conservative agenda. The best option available was to devise a broad compromise, acceptable to all Democrats and Republican moderates, supplying them with proposals for policy reform and cost reduction that they preferred over the president's own recommendations. The administration would then be confronted by a unified Congress and the prospect of a divisive fight. There should exist some location for the congressional alternative sufficiently conservative that Reagan would accede. It would not give him everything he wanted but would be constructed to lie within his indifference curve, preferable to no agreement at all. This was the task adopted by congressional leaders, and the consequences can be seen in three different arenas of food stamp politics—the substantive program revisions affecting recipient eligibility and benefit levels, the budget cap placing a ceiling on maximum program expenditures, and the annual appropriation for funds to be expended under the cap.

Within the President's Policy Space

Moving within the boundaries of President Reagan's conservative policy agenda meant that advocates had to accept substantial concessions. They had to propose a series of program reforms that would generate dollar savings approximating the president's targeted amount. They had to fashion the details of those savings in a more palatable form than that offered by the administration. And they then had to win allies from moderate and farm-state legislators, led by Senator Robert Dole, in order to establish an effective bargaining coalition. It was decided to focus energies on preserving a few provisions especially important to the neediest households (for example, no benefit reductions linked to receiving subsidized school lunches), to resist further attacks on the program (for example, mobilizing strongly against Senator Helms's motion to restore the purchase requirement), and to create budget savings through delays rather than through freezes in cost-of-living adjustments. The last of these was particularly inventive. Cost-of-living delays would achieve short-run retrenchment but would limit long-run sacrifices, in a double sense. First, indexation automatically would resume at the full rate some specified time in the future. Second, the food stamp program had a special advantage because it was indexed not to the previous year's totals but rather to objective indicators: poverty income for eligibility and the USDA's Thrifty Food Plan for benefits. Thus the baseline for benefit adjustments, as well as the annual rate for those adjustments, would be fully restored once the delay period expired.[10]

The political compromise was constructed in the Senate Agriculture Committee. In exchange for protecting certain benefits for the elderly and poorest households, the committee sliced deeper into food stamp spending than even the Reagan administration had requested—but with a sizable share coming from indexing delays rather than substantive reforms or permanent freezes. The annual inflation adjustment in the Thrifty Food Plan would occur instead at fifteen-month intervals for the coming three years. There would be no indexing of allowable deductions from gross income during these years. Chairman Helms protested that the savings from the bill would diminish considerably starting in FY 1985. There would be lower food stamp spending during the period covered by explicit Reagan administration target figures, and a dramatic increase in spending afterwards. Yet Helms did not maintain political control over his own committee, over the Senate floor, or over the final conference report on the omnibus reconciliation bill, the vehicle by which the food stamp cuts were enacted in slightly modified form. In a sense, the final outcome can be considered a partial victory for food stamp advocates, for it was probably the best result they could have achieved given the contending forces. Nevertheless, the changes legislated in 1981 were expected to eliminate approximately one million individuals from the food stamp rolls and to reduce benefits for almost all remaining food stamp recipients, with the biggest effect upon the working poor.

With the major program reforms incorporated into the reconciliation act, the principal food stamp item left for the pending farm program reauthorization bill was the budget cap—whether to retain it, for how long, and at what dollar ceilings. The Reagan administration, wary of the recurrence of crisis finance, did not view the caps as a first line of defense in the effort to restrain spending. They were useful, however, as a secondary tool, reinforcing substantive program cuts and ensuring tight implementation. It therefore proposed food stamp reauthorization for four years, fiscal years 1982–1985, with annual expenditure ceilings gradually rising from $10.0 to $10.5 billion. The estimates assumed enactment of all the administration's recommended cuts, plus a 2.5% margin for error. Maximum program outlays would thus be constrained to a level more than 10% lower than prevailed in FY 1981.

The caps in this form were reported by the House Agriculture Committee as part of the farm bill. In a slightly revised version they were reported to the Senate and approved on the floor as part of a separate bill dealing only with food stamp issues. The agriculture committees clearly did not want to abandon so valuable a mechanism for legislative oversight, which guaranteed them intervention into the food stamp program both to voice complaints when costs exploded and to claim credit when providing specially for legitimate welfare needs. "Establishment of reasonable annual appropriations ceilings," said the Senate committee report, "serve the very useful purpose of ensuring that there will be continual, close congressional scrutiny of the program."[11]

Liberal critics claimed that the Reagan forecasts used obsolete utilization data, adopted an excessively rosy economic scenario, and made no allowance for the feedback effect on food stamp costs resulting from cuts made to other welfare programs. Inadequate expenditure ceilings would cause the repetition of, not the escape from, budget crisis. Advocates predicted that the administration, rather than take responsibility for its own faulty calculations, would blame the food stamp program for again operating recklessly and would use the situation to force another round of benefit reductions on the poor. Yet motions to replace fixed dollar caps with flexible caps that varied with macroeconomic conditions failed narrowly in the House committee (where it had passed in

1980) and on the Senate floor. The majority seemed to accept the argument that flexible caps would be a step back toward entitlement budgeting, implying the abandonment of legislated restraint while facilitating some degree of automatic cost increases capable of breaking the federal budget. "We are passing a multi-year bill based on good information," asserted Senator Domenici. "We have excellent advice as to what this is going to cost in the outyears. . . . If our estimates are wrong, put some more money in. But do not turn it closer and closer to an entitlement program, build in indexation, throw away the best estimates, and then wonder why the budget gets out of control."[12]

As the year progressed and the farm bill approached final enactment, budget uncertainty grew. David Stockman informed the president that the recently completed expenditure cuts would not be sufficient to compensate for tax reduction and allow the administration to keep its promise of a balanced budget by 1984. Reagan, on September 24, announced a forthcoming economic package that would include $27 billion of new entitlement and social welfare savings, although he was intentionally vague about the details. At the same time, leading indicators showed signs of a coming recession, which would increase food stamp utilization and raise cost estimates. Just prior to consideration on the House floor, the Reagan administration negotiated a hasty retreat regarding food stamp spending allowances. In exchange for tightening enforcement provisions and further delaying certain cost-of-living adjustments, the caps for the four years, fiscal years 1982–1985, were raised to over $11 billion. Nevertheless, critics noted, because spending predictions were particularly volatile, the thresholds selected "are necessarily arbitrary," and thus "this bill might not finally resolve the question of the cap."[13]

The conference committee was even less optimistic about future estimates. It chose to reauthorize the food stamp program only for FY 1982, with a dollar cap of $11.3 billion, commenting that even this one-year provision "may prove inadequate to allow full funding of benefits."[14] By implication, the entire strategic political game regarding budget caps and food stamp program authorization would have to be played all over again during the coming year and under far more difficult conditions, with the Reagan administration scrounging for further savings while recession increased the number of poor individuals requiring nutritional assistance.

Finally, there was an additional battle in 1981 between Congress and the president concerning the appropriation for FY 1982. The administration, in its quest to keep budgeted expenditures down, predictably underestimated the spending needed to fulfill the year's food stamp obligations. Assuming full substantive reforms and optimistic macroeconomic conditions, it initially requested only $9.8 billion, $1.7 billion less than the previous year, and it was hesitant to expand the request when the assumptions proved less than accurate. In appearance, the administration would look as if it were keeping FY 1982 spending down, placing the onus on Congress if the totals were to be raised.

The administration's opponents had greater leverage over appropriations than over authorization, as long as the amounts were within the legislated ceiling for maximum outlays. The House and Senate appropriated exactly the amount specified in the president's submission, but only for 10½ months, ostensibly to allow for a full cost analysis of the substantive reforms recently enacted. The House Appropriations Committee expressed concern about "unrealistic budget estimates" which lead to "periodic crises." While the administration's revised request made to the Senate in September was slightly higher, this was said to be still knowingly $900 million below the amount "deemed necessary to maintain the program for the full fiscal year at authorized benefit levels."[15]

Congress effectively shifted the initiative back to the president by the technique of partial year appropriations, demanding that Reagan explicitly "request the additional funds which will clearly be required."[16] The consequence was yet another supplemental appropriation for the food stamp program. In his budget message of 1982, the president sought supplemental funding up to the maximum dollar amount permitted under the cap. It was an "urgent request," a technical budget phrase meaning that a delay could jeopardize mandated outlays. The food stamp provision was approved without controversy, although the entire supplemental appropriations bill for FY 1982 was enacted following two presidential vetoes and much procedural wrangling.

The Limits of Acquiescence

By January 1982 the signs of a deep recession were unmistakable. The unemployment rate was 8.8%, on its way to 10.8%. Industrial production was falling toward 1977 levels. The signs of mounting federal deficits were also unmistakable. The administration estimated that expenditures would outpace revenues by more than $100 billion. The CBO figures were even higher and were accompanied by a warning that, despite eventual recovery, the deficit would more than double over the next five years if no changes were made in current policies. To the president and his loyalists, these were merely problems of transition. The economic plan had to be given time to work. The country should not yield to weakness or retreat from the three-sided program of tax reduction, smaller government, and military preparedness. In a show of resolve, the president's response to recession was to further slash domestic expenditures. His 1982 budget submission called for another $58 billion in social spending cuts, including $12 billion from means-tested entitlements.

To most members of Congress, the problem was viewed not as transitory but as more inherent and threatening. Reaganomics had seemingly failed on its promise to ensure both economic growth and fiscal balance. Now further domestic spending cuts were requested, which would be painful to constituents and might be interpreted as political insensitivity toward the economic downturn. Congress was not looking forward to the November elections based on such a record. Liberal Democrats found justification to unleash harsh condemnation. Moderates, particularly among Senate Republicans, would be forced to absorb the burden of constructing a legislative package acceptable to the president and enactable on the floor, knowing that in the prevailing situation they could neither successfully protect individual benefits nor stabilize public finance. As one commentator noted, "Reagan's idea of compromise—given his rather extreme position relative to other politicians on most of these issues—might not look like much of a deal . . . ."[17]

Food stamps were selected for severe cuts in the Reagan administration's 1982 budget proposal. To the president, they represented the quintessential uncontrollable and wasteful entitlement. He was fond of citing the percentage growth in food stamp costs over the 1970s, ignoring the fact that the program was in its infancy at the start of the period and that its outlays were especially sensitive to macroeconomic fluctuations and price inflation. He would repeat an anecdote in which a food stamp recipient bought an orange with a coupon and a bottle of vodka with the change, although USDA officials admitted that such a transaction "would be difficult to make," and they confessed, "We are not specifically aware of the origin of the example that the President cited."[18] Reagan's proposal would cut food stamp spending by an additional $2.3 billion, approximately 19% relative to expected FY 1983 outlays. Allotments would be reduced per dollar of net income, forcing almost all recipients to pay more out of pocket for the same supply of food; the deduction from gross income for work expenses would be terminated, reducing the incentive for gainful employment; special energy assistance would be counted as income in benefit calculations, hurting needy recipients who qualify for more than one form of federal aid; and the states would have to reimburse the federal government for payment errors exceeding a low threshold, penalizing the institutions which directly manage the program. Moreover, responsibility for the entire food stamp program was to be transferred to the states starting in 1984 as part of the president's New Federalism initiative. The administration was apparently concerned more with the level of immediate dollar savings than with distributional equity in the designated means for producing them.

Critics protested that this round of cuts dug much more sharply into the safety net than those of 1981. For example, an elderly couple receiving the basic Social Security and SSI payment would lose 57% of its food stamps. A mother with two children working at the minimum wage and living below the poverty line would nevertheless find her stamps reduced from $66 a month to $9. According to the critics, the easier program changes for austerity purposes had previously been made. Eligibility had been trimmed so that those receiving food stamps already met the president's own definition of the truly needy. The backlog of potential reforms had already been exhausted. "It just doesn't leave much room for more cutting," said former Carter official Robert Greenstein. "We aren't in a situation we were in one year ago when there was more room and we could find more things."[19]

As in the preceding year, the Republican-controlled Senate Agriculture Committee complied obliquely with the president's request, formulating a food stamp package to be included in the omnibus 1982 reconciliation bill that saved slightly more than ordered in the short-run but in a manner that did not substantially affect future years. Expenditures again were reduced primarily by further delays of inflation indexing in the Thrifty Food Plan and in allowable deductions. The Democratic-controlled House Agriculture Committee was less compliant, raising only half of the instructed amount. On the floor, unlike in 1981, the committee majority easily defeated a challenge by conservatives to reinstate more of the president's initial plan. The conference roughly split the difference between the two chambers, adopting modified indexing based on just 99% of the Thrifty Food Plan value.

The agriculture package also contained reauthorization of the food stamp program through FY 1985. Here too President Reagan suffered a relative defeat, as Congress approved program operations for three more years without giving heed to the New Federalism initiative.[20] Regarding the cap, the Senate Agriculture Committee merely accepted the Congressional Budget Office's cost projections, minus anticipated savings from the pending bill, plus a 5% cushion against forecast error. The House committee utilized the same basis but without any margin for error. The conference accepted the House format, adjusted to reflect the final version of all substantive provisions. Budget authority was limited to a maximum of $12.9 billion for FY 1983, $13.1 billion for FY 1984, and $13.9 billion for FY 1985. The Democratic-majority House report mentioned the fallibility of long-range cost estimates in a changing macroeconomy and asked the administration, if outlays threatened to exceed the cap, not to proceed with mandated benefit reductions without first allowing Congress to meet program funding requirements adequately. The Republican-majority Senate report, by contrast, commended the administration for its resolve not to return to Congress for additional amounts each year.

Finally, given renewed program authority and a new set of budget caps, Congress had to enact the actual food stamp appropriation for FY 1983. As before, the administration did not immediately revise its official request consequent to changing economic conditions and the partial defeat of its legislative proposals. It again preferred the appearance of spending reduction to the validity of honest forecasts, and thus it was again criticized in Congress for "the continuing pattern of unrealistic budget estimates for the food stamp program."[21] As before, the House appropriated funds equal to the administration's official request but for less than the full fiscal year. It was not going to volunteer for presidential attack by budget busting and instead strategically sought to shift the onus back to the administration. This time, however, the Senate showed no desire to repeat the complicated process of urgent supplemental action. While indicating its concern with the inadequacy of current USDA predictive models, it approved an appropriation nearly $1.4 billion greater than the administration's request, although still within the cap maximum, and it expressed concern that this still might not be sufficient to meet legitimate needs. The conference delayed a final decision until the president, on December 6, ultimately submitted a revised budget estimate approximating the Senate figure. The House then agreed to retreat from its position and the full-year appropriation was enacted.

The difference in food stamp policy tone and outcome between 1981 and 1982 was caused largely by greater defections from the president's side by conservative Democrats in the House and moderate Republicans in the Senate. The approaching election, the severity of the recession, and the depth of the proposed program cuts all contributed to a diminished willingness of legislators to impose concentrated costs upon a needy constituency. Budget retrenchment promised diffuse social and economic gains intended to arrive some time in the future. That goal now seemed less assured, whereas the means promoted for achieving it were increasingly painful. The president accepted the 1982 reconciliation package as the best deal he could secure given the rapidly changing ideological climate. He could dominate the fiscal agenda and deter any program liberalization, but he could not establish conservative reforms entirely to his liking. This was the pattern of stalemate that characterized food stamp policy and politics over the remaining years of legislated program authority.

To a significant extent, this stalemate was integrally connected to the food stamp budget caps. As enacted, there was virtually no leeway between forecast and allowance. Successful program operation within the caps was dependent entirely on the progress of economic recovery and on the savings projected from programmatic revision. If the recession did not abate as expected, or if the reforms of 1981 and 1982 did not constrain outlays as planned, annual food stamp costs would again begin to exceed their limits, forcing a choice between crisis legislation or mandatory benefit reductions. The president had indicated that he would not tolerantly accept a cap override. The price of his cooperation would most certainly involve the revival of certain substantive changes rejected during the reconciliation battles. Put formally, an equilibrium bargain structured by the indifference point for the president between further program reforms (x) and the cap-induced reversion point (Qc) would predictably shift outcomes further to the right of the congressional median, as compared to an equilibrium bargain constructed under normal legislative conditions. The strategy for program advocates, therefore, was to highlight publicly the problem of enduring hunger in affluent America, reinforcing the alliance with moderates and reducing the credibility of the president's reversion point threat. Primarily, however, they had to hope that unemployment, inflation, and utilization rates proved favorable, automatically keeping costs within the cap thresholds. Given the intensity of food stamp politics, the uncertainty of economic movements, and the history of inaccurate long-run cost estimates, the stalemate of 1982 rested on precarious foundations indeed.

The Conditions of Stalemate

Stalemate over the food stamp program required considerable effort from both right and left. The Democrats had gained seats in the November 1982 elections, improving their standing in Congress, yet the president remained popular and his conservative faith was unwavering. Just to maintain political strength, positions had to be defended and policies proposed. Even if there was little hope of victory, it was nevertheless essential not to cede advantage.

The Reagan administration's budget submission of January 1983 therefore resumed its attack on automatic spending programs that were alleged to be the largest cause of the structural deficit. The food stamp program alone was said to have produced almost $1.1 billion in excess payments. To end waste and corruption, the administration proposed a new method of calculating benefits, mandatory work experience for recipients, and a system by which the states would be held financially liable for overpayment that exceeded 3% of total benefits. It had long been a common political ploy among food stamp opponents to contend that incentives for improved management would guarantee enormous budget savings while not in the least harming deserving individuals. In this case, the data came from a General Accounting Office study for the six months ending March 1981. The error rate for food stamp implementation was high compared to other social welfare payments to individuals. Nevertheless, what the administration failed to note in its public pronouncements was that underpayments to legitimate recipients compensated for one-quarter of the amount reported squandered.

Whereas the conservative position emphasized responsible finance, the liberal position played to sentimentality, condemning persistent hunger and homelessness in a land of plenty. A series of independent studies—for example, by the Center on Budget and Policy Priorities, the U.S. Conference of Mayors, the Food Research and Action Center, and the Citizens Commission on Hunger in New England—discovered a widespread and increasing demand for emergency private food assistance; that a diverse population was seeking such aid; that many among this population were already recipients of public food benefits, including food stamp recipients whose allotments were exhausted before the end of the month; that private food assistance projects were not capable of meeting the growing demand; and that public food assistance programs had in recent years become somewhat less effective in ensuring against nutritional need.

Members of Congress were quick to express concern. Hearings were held around the country to assess the situation. Studies were commissioned to determine what had gone wrong. Speeches were made to denounce recurrent hunger as a national shame, a problem without a legitimate place in a society of vast resources and high moral values. Wishing not to be outmaneuvered, Republicans in Congress declared hunger to be a bipartisan issue. Nevertheless, Democratic opponents seized the opportunity to attack the president's conservative agenda. According to Leon Panetta, "it seems to me, this is the wrong time and the wrong program to seek short-term savings at an unacceptable cost of aggravating hunger in this Nation."[22]

Given political stalemate, Congress resorted to symbolic action. First, the FY 1984 budget resolution established an $8.5 billion reserve fund for domestic programs, including food stamps, to be made available only if budget space was assured and proper authorizing legislation passed. As there was no chance for this to occur, Congress was merely expressing a preference and taking a popular stance. Second, Congress passed a bill ordering the secretary of agriculture to distribute nonessential government food stocks to local food banks, action which the secretary said he was taking already. Third, both the House and Senate adopted nonbinding antihunger resolutions asserting that the federal budget should not be balanced at the expense of increased hunger, that nutrition programs should be protected against further budget cuts, and that the federal government should maintain responsibility to prevent increases in domestic hunger. Fourth, the House established a Select Committee on Hunger, chaired by Congressman Mickey Leland, to study and review programs on international and domestic food assistance. This would help keep the issue salient, hopefully doing for the mid-1980s what George McGovern's Senate Select Committee on Nutrition and Human Needs had done in the late 1960s.

The administration's initial response was to minimize the problem. USDA officials appeared before Congress to detail the range of federal food assistance programs and to insist that they had successfully addressed poverty-related hunger in America. According to Deputy Agriculture Secretary Richard Lyng, these programs were well established and operating as intended. "We feel that current resources devoted to domestic feeding programs are more than adequate."[23] Not all administration statements were so tactful. Presidential counselor Edward Meese allegedly denied that there was any authoritative evidence showing the existence of hunger in America. According to newspaper reports, he claimed that people were going to soup kitchens because the "food is free and it is easier than paying for it."[24]

The administration also sought to neutralize the hunger issue, using investigation as a means of diffusing political pressure. In the fall of 1983, President Reagan established a special Task Force on Food Assistance, to report within ninety days on the extent of America's hunger problem and to make recommendations regarding program improvements. Also scheduled to report around the same time was the President's Private Sector Survey on Cost Containment in the Federal Government, known popularly as the Grace Commission. Predictably, the Grace Commission criticized the food stamp program for glaring inefficiencies. Predictably, the Task Force on Food Assistance, although recognizing that some unspecified number of Americans go hungry, contended that existing programs generally met the demand for basic food assistance, that recent program changes had not significantly reduced the availability of aid, and that private charitable organizations were becoming increasingly effective as part of the nation's safety net.

Both presidential commissions recommended that the states have the option of developing their own food assistance programs, to be instituted in place of food stamps, supported by federal block grants. The Senate Agriculture Committee, led by Jesse Helms, held hearings on the topic but did not attempt to foster legislation. On the other hand, the Task Force on Food Assistance also recommended a number of minor program liberalizations such as easing asset limits, indexing based on 100% of the Thrifty Food Plan, and assuring food stamp access for individuals without a fixed address. These reforms were reported to the House and approved overwhelmingly, 364–39, on August 1, 1984. It was the first significant attempt to expand food stamp benefits since the Reagan era began, but it was clearly an election eve tactic. The Senate made no effort to consider the measure, and the president warned of a veto if it did.

In a sense, the stalemate of the Reagan era during the mid-1980s resembles that of the Ford era during the mid-1970s. The conservative president would have preferred to shift food stamp policy further to the right; a more liberal Congress would have preferred to shift it further to the left. Under the U.S. system of government, with separated institutions sharing power, neither could effect a move without the other. The difference in the logical structure of the stalemate was the form of budget constraint. Under Ford, entitlement rules ensured that all legitimate claims would be met. Under Reagan, budget caps could allow the president to regain the advantage if entailed program costs ever challenged the authorized threshold. The threat depended on the extent of the president's demands and the level of financial crisis he would tolerate in order to advance them. The increased salience of hunger as a political issue helped to reduce the probability that the reversion point option would ever be enforced. Yet the administration's words had in the past been firm, and its cooperation in any cap override would most certainly entail conservative changes in eligibility rules and program operations. Fortunately, the practical test never came. During the four fiscal years covered by this authorization period, 1982–1985, the food stamp budget caps were not breached. However, given the uncertainty of expenditure forecasts and the administration's penchant for systematic underestimation, some risk always remained.

For FY 1983, the Senate had insisted on an honest, full-year appropriation based on expected food stamp costs, and the House and the Reagan administration both eventually conformed. Nevertheless, the appropriation did not prove sufficient. In early 1983 the administration requested another $1.2 billion, almost up to the cap threshold. Congress complied without much controversy, yet the entire supplemental spending bill got bogged down over extraneous issues. On July 7, the USDA informed the states that they should prepare for possible across-the-board benefit reductions. Food advocates protested that the move was illegal because Congress had clearly indicated its intent to adequately fund the food stamp program. However, the administration used the benefit threat as leverage to help break the legislative logjam, albeit on terms favorable to its preferred outcome. The supplemental appropriation was approved in sufficient time and the funding crisis was avoided.

For FY 1984, given presidential underestimation of costs, Congress reverted to the strategy of a part-year appropriation. The House Appropriations Committee, according to its usual practice, accepted the president's official request without amendment, while noting that current estimates showed the need for $766 million more assuming no further legislative changes. It therefore appropriated funds for slightly more than eleven months, to guarantee that the administration would bear the onus for initiating a supplemental request. The Senate, in contrast to FY 1983, concurred. Senator Helms argued that such gimmickry undermined the integrity of the appropriations process; Congress should directly approve the amount it actually intended to spend. The majority leadership responded that the administration had systematically refused to estimate costs accurately; Congress should not voluntarily appear liable for exceeding budget constraints. A supplemental request from the administration was submitted in early 1984 and was later raised, under pressure from the appropriations committees, to $700 million. This was approved without controversy, although again the entire bill was delayed due to its other provisions. This time there was no threat from the administration that the states should prepare for reductions in food stamp benefits.

Appropriations politics for FY 1985 reverted to the pattern of FY 1983. The House noted that the president's food stamp request was $374 million less than needed for the full year, and it again appropriated funds for slightly more than eleven months. The House floor slashed another 1% from this total, as part of an across-the-board reduction in USDA spending. The Senate refused to go along with the part-year appropriation. It added back the 1%, plus another $652 million believed adequate to cover all legitimate costs, despite the fact that this strained budget resolution guidelines. The House receded in conference, permitting the full-year appropriation on the condition that the administration formally requested the higher amount. Yet, again, the amount proved insufficient. Program participation did not decline at the predicted rate during the economic recovery, and thus a supplemental appropriation was proposed and passed in early 1985, adding another $319 million for food stamp spending. While the political games continued, the outcome—adequate program financing as long as it kept within the cap allowance—was not really in doubt.

Conclusion

For each year during the reauthorization period 1982–1985, there was a supplemental appropriation. The Reagan administration underestimated needed expenditures, refusing to adapt its request despite the political stalemate and the probable defeat for its legislative proposals. As hypothesized in chapter 2, confidence that the cap threshold would not be breached increasingly led the president to play as if program entitlement protections still prevailed. Given the ability to posture safely, his annual budget submissions did little more than signal his desire for further food stamp expenditure restraint. Congress twice accepted the administration's totals and shifted the onus back by means of part-year appropriations. Congress twice revised the administration's totals and appropriated funds for the full fiscal year. The nation's economic recovery was longer and more substantial than many experts had anticipated, helping to keep food stamp expenditures within the four-year legislated ceilings. Poverty rates remained higher than at equivalent stages in previous recoveries, meaning that each year's welfare cost forecast was understated. The consequence of these two separate trends was a pattern of annual supplemental appropriations that never quite challenged the cap thresholds. This pattern was not predictable in advance and was not always comfortable in practice. Yet it did facilitate stalemate conditions to continue throughout this period of food stamp spending authority.

The budget caps, although never invoked and never overridden, still influenced food stamp politics and policy during the first Reagan administration. They were essential to the strategic skirmishes in 1981, forcing program advocates to abandon hopes for an intentional mismatch, to give Reagan fewer substantive program reforms in exchange for symbolically strong spending constraints. They were critical to the initial delay of food stamp reauthorization beyond 1982, given mounting economic uncertainty and the desire to avoid unnecessary recourse to the complex process of cap override. They reinforced the stalemate of 1983–84, facilitating the parry-and-riposte of budget supplementals while establishing the boundaries that kept the contest safe. The outcome reflects competing pulls from the two models developed in chapter 2. The president, who saw the caps through the ideological dynamic as a weapon helpful in the battle for cost control, was nevertheless uncertain about the institutional reaction from Congress if benefits actually had to be reduced late in the fiscal year. Congress, which viewed the caps through the institutional dynamic as a weapon helpful for program oversight, was nevertheless wary that the president could use the cap reversion point to establish ideological advantage. Their existence even in the background made the food stamp budget caps a continual threat.

As stalemate persisted through the middle 1980s, it became increasingly routinized. Inertia gradually came to replace attack. The administration was no longer quite so forceful in demanding radical program savings. It slowly tired of a game that promised little budgetary return yet risked criticism for its apparent insensitivity to domestic hunger. Moreover, the salience of rising food stamp expenditures had declined as a political issue once annual appropriations no longer engendered repetitive crisis conditions and emergency relief. The caps, as an indicator of budget restraint, were not easily abandoned. Yet, over time, there was much less desire to make them tight and enforceable. They evolved into a vague limit. For conservatives, the presence of expenditure caps would help to curb liberal efforts at benefit expansion. For liberals, spending leeway under the caps would help deter conservative efforts at benefit contraction. For the moderates in Congress, who held the balance of power, the caps were a reassurance that, if program costs ever again increased dramatically, they would be guaranteed a prominent policy-making role. But it remained their hope that the food stamp budget would continue to escape funding crisis and it was their intention not to manufacture such a crisis by the application of imprudent constraint.

In 1985, Congress reauthorized the food stamp program for another five fiscal years. The reauthorization bill liberalized benefits very slightly and provided somewhat more space between forecast expenditures and the budget cap. Also in 1985, Congress enacted strict limits on permissible federal deficits and invented procedures for automatic expenditure cuts if normal mechanisms failed to respect those limits. The Gramm-Rudman-Hollings provisions changed the reversion point for the federal budget as a whole, analogous to the way that expenditure caps affected the food stamp segment of the budget. Ironically, food stamps and most other welfare programs were exempted from the GRH procedures. In essence, the inherent tension between protecting the vulnerable and establishing budget control was eased specifically for food stamps at the same time as the tension was exacerbated for the entire federal government. The two movements were related. They demonstrate the problem of enforceability, when it is both irresponsible to renege on government commitments to protect social welfare and impossible to ignore their impact upon government financial capacity.

Notes—Chapter 6

1. Ronald Reagan, "Address Before a Joint Session of the Congress on the Program for Economic Recovery," February 18, 1981, *Public Papers of the Presidents of the United States, Ronald Reagan, 1981,* 111.

2. Barbara E. Cohen, "Hunger in America: Legislative Attitudes in Food Assistance Programs" (Ph.D. diss., Brandeis University, 1986): 127–28.

3. David W. Hunt, "Programs Under Siege: Congressional Committee Oversight as a Defensive Strategy Against Budgetary Retrenchment and Termination" (Ph.D. diss., American University, 1986): 153.

4. David Stockman, *The Triumph of Politics* (New York: Harper and Row, 1986): 92.

5. U.S. House of Representatives, Committee on the Budget, Task Force on Entitlements, Uncontrollables, and Indexing, *Impact of the Omnibus Reconciliation Act and the Proposed Fiscal Year 1983 Budget Cuts on Entitlements, Uncontrollables, and Indexing,* 97th Cong., 2nd sess., 1982, 569–70.

6. U.S. House of Representatives, Committee on Agriculture, *General Farm Bill of 1981,* Part II, 97th Cong., 1st sess., 1981, 534.

7. Senate *Report* 97–128, 76, 172.

8. Stockman, *The Triumph of Politics,* 170.

9. Stockman, *The Triumph of Politics,* 195–96, 202.

10. R. Kent Weaver, *Automatic Government: The Politics of Indexation,* (Washington, D.C.: Brookings Institution, 1988): 109.

11. Senate *Report* 97–128, 76.

12. *Congressional Record* 127: S 11987–88.

13. *Congressional Record* 127: H 24783.

14. House *Report* 97–377, 225.

15. House *Report* 97–172, 95; Senate *Report* 97–248, 72.

16. *Congressional Record* 127: H 17610.

17. Joseph White and Aaron Wildavsky, *The Deficit and the Public Interest* (Berkeley: University of California Press, 1989): 206.

18. U.S. House of Representatives, Committee on Agriculture, *Food Stamp Program,* 97th Cong., 2nd sess., 1982, 11.

19. U.S. Senate, Committee on Agriculture, Nutrition, and Forestry, *Oversight on Federal Nutrition Programs,* 97th Cong., 2nd. sess., 1982, 57.

20. Regarding Reagan's half-hearted efforts on behalf of the New Federalism initiative, which included a proposal to devolve food stamps to the states, see Timothy Conlan, *From New Federalism to Devolution* (Washington D.C.: Brookings Institution, 1998): 170–90.

21. House *Report* 97–800, 101.

22. U.S. House of Representatives, Committee on Agriculture, *Review of Fiscal Year 1984 Budget for the Food and Nutrition Service,* 98th Cong., 1st. sess., 1983, 2.

23. U.S. House of Representatives, Select Committee on Hunger, *Alleviating Hunger: Progress and Prospects,* 98th Cong., 2nd sess.,1984, 32.

24. Cohen, "Hunger in America," 87.

SEVEN

Caps Off: The Repeal of Food Stamp Budget Caps in an Era of Fiscal Constraint, 1985–1990

Welfare entitlement grants protection in a double sense. As welfare, it shields needy individuals from some of the inequality inherent to a capitalist labor market. As entitlement, it guarantees funds against rival claimants for budget resources. Expansion of the food stamp program had been the consequence of this double form of protection. The program was only moderately burdensome as a share of total federal dollars, but it became politically salient because of the pace of expenditure growth relative to expectations. The budget caps introduced during the Carter era were intended originally to improve oversight and review if costs did not remain within predicted bounds. During the early Reagan era, they were transformed into a potential weapon useful to those on the right of the legislative mainstream seeking to enforce further policy retrenchment. The latter Reagan years witnessed yet another twist within the basic pattern.

Welfare retrenchment is easiest to accept when the justification is waste and abuse, thereby identifying some portion of recipient benefits as undeserved and thus a safe target for cost reduction. Problems come if retrenchment threatens deeper cuts into the program mission. When the pain imposed upon sympathetic constituencies appears a greater political risk than the gain achieved from expenditure control, budget caps become unenforceable. Automatic spending triggers are redesigned whenever possible, to be more palatable yet less effective as a means of budgetary restraint. Either the caps are made softer and more accommodating, or they are written with exemptions to shelter particular population groups or program types. Regarding food stamps, the cumulative impact of the legislation in 1981 and 1982 was a 13% expenditure cut relative to the projected baseline and a 4% decline in the number of recipients.[1] The campaign by advocates publicizing the extent of hunger and homelessness in America helped make most politicians wary of further action. This chapter will examine the politics of unenforceable caps and hollow restraints within the food stamp program, and also within a set of intersecting controls affecting the federal budget as a whole.

By the middle 1980s, budget concerns had dwarfed all other domestic issues. Contrary to the administration's prognostications, substantial tax rate reduction had produced neither a rapid spurt of economic growth nor compensating expenditure reductions sufficient to balance the federal budget. As deficit totals rose dramatically, all policy became fiscal policy. The process of allocating public funds—how much to spend and for which functions—became increasingly more partisan, polarized, and adversarial. Yet despite such intensity (or possibly because of it), there was an absence of responsible leadership. Revenues were clearly inadequate to match outlay commitments, yet no major actor was willing to shoulder the political liability for retreat, to announce a preference for increased taxation or for lower obligations affecting entrenched interests. "When promises are too large in relationship to available resources," Aaron Wildavsky wrote, "gimmickry . . . grows to epidemic proportions."[2] Frustrated internally and criticized externally for a budget politics of posturing and indecision, Congress finally asserted strict limits on permissible deficits and adopted a formula for mandatory corrections if legislators did not satisfy the aggregate thresholds voluntarily. As with the caps narrowly applied to the food stamp program, these broad Gramm-Rudman-Hollings deficit restraints were not, and could not, reasonably be enforced.

Spending caps during times of pervasive budget crisis are an expression simultaneously of evasion, displacement, and deflection. As evasion, they are an attempt to regain confidence—it can be announced to the public that something positive has been done to solve the budget problem, indicated by present legislation to limit future expenditures. As displacement, they are the product of wishful thinking—tensions faced in the short run might somehow disappear, or at least become less burdensome when confronted in the future. As deflection, they are a statement of good long-run intentions—if the budget crisis happens to continue, an explicit promise exists to deal with it appropriately. Of course, missing from the cap mechanism is any clear and explicit agreement regarding how such future spending limitations actually will be implemented. Aggregate totals cannot be imposed without acceptance of the separate effects which comprise that total. Enforcement of overall expenditure caps entails retreat from certain valuable and valued dollar commitments and thus, absent political adjustment, automatic thresholds will tend to be overridden when the costs of retrenchment appear too severe. An optimist might hope that new institutional rules would induce legislators to face up to the burdens of substantive reform. Yet a cap mechanism established in response to current stalemate, in a practical political world, depends for policy effectiveness upon the suspension of that stalemate. The more likely outcome under conditions of continuing budget crisis should be current symbolism used as a substitute for responsible policymaking.

Regarding welfare, reflected by the particular case of food stamps, the articulated purpose of spending caps was to constrain unintended cost expansion without penalizing the needy poor or exacerbating hunger or malnutrition among American households. The goals were admirable but contradictory. Moreover, neither goal could be abandoned, given simultaneous public concern over the federal budget and household hunger, and given the political deadlock and partisan efforts at blame avoidance. When it is impossible to select one side or the other, it is often best to select them both together. As an expression of policy contradiction, budget caps were expedient in shielding legislators from the need to choose explicitly between available resources and welfare obligations. They could not be criticized for neglecting either expenditure control or the nation's poor. Ironically, the caps could maintain their expressive purpose only on the assumption of persisting equilibrium. If luck prevailed—if economic trends were favorable and recipient demands moderate—the caps could remain in force but never be invoked, saving politicians from the requirement to confront contending policy pressures.

Adapted policy design could help. One possibility would be to set the budget cap reversion point equal to the anticipated reversion point had entitlement rules been allowed to prevail. There would be a visible cap fixed at a level sufficient to appear legitimate yet ample to accommodate all entailed program costs. Under the 1985 food stamp reauthorization, the cap was reinstituted for five further years based on existing program regulations and forecast economic circumstances, plus a small cushion for unexpected circumstances. However, some risk remained. Any ceiling plausibly specified could be exceeded if recipient needs grew or economic conditions worsened; any ceiling established to ensure substantial room beneath it would soon be revealed as counterfeit.

Another possible strategy would be to fix the cap reversion point at a level that might conceivably be breached, but to insulate certain programs or recipients from the repercussions of restraint. Again, there would be a visible cap but protection for identified vulnerable constituencies. However, the more spending that is sheltered, the harder it is to stay within the specified aggregate budget ceiling; the more stringent the budget ceiling, the less spending that safely can be sheltered. The Gramm-Rudman-Hollings provisions of 1985 placed specified limits on the permissible federal budget deficit, but it explicitly exempted food stamps and most other welfare entitlements from the mandatory sequestration process. The obvious risk was that the limits would be exceeded if economic conditions varied from favorable predictions, yet the amounts available from the nonexempt programs might be insufficient to compensate.

Throughout the middle and late 1980s, the tension between constraining spending and protecting welfare continued unresolved and unresolvable. On the one hand, budget caps as the reflection of an enduring policy dilemma could succeed to the extent that they were not effectual. Simultaneous support for expenditure control and public welfare could be maintained only if the caps imposed no significant limits at all. This, however, might prompt analysts to wonder why such a sham cap arrangement was ever necessary, and might lead under conditions of mounting fiscal pressure to a movement to have them tightened. On the other hand, budget caps as an effective means of expenditure restraint could succeed to the extent that they forced legislators to impose the substantive sacrifices that they had consciously evaded at the time the caps were written. Under continuing fiscal pressures, there would be great incentive to loosen any restraint that might potentially be effective. By the end of the decade, the charade was over. Powerful budget caps and generous entitlement protections could not be maintained simultaneously. This was the lesson learned regarding both the expenditure ceilings applied narrowly to the food stamp program and the Gramm-Rudman-Hollings ceilings applied broadly to the entire federal budget. In 1990, both were abolished.

Food Stamp Reauthorization: Liberalization and Leeway

Nutrition advocates expected continued attacks on the food stamp program in 1985. President Reagan had won reelection by an overwhelming margin, which might have been interpreted as a mandate to further pursue his conservative domestic agenda. Concern over the budget deficit made entitlements a likely target. Senate Agriculture Committee chairman Helms was preparing legislation to restore the purchase requirement, reduce benefits, and give program autonomy to the states. In response, advocates planned to publicize the degree of persistent hunger despite the progress of economic recovery. Their vehicle was Mickey Leland's House Select Committee. The instrument was recently published findings by the Physician Task Force organized by the Harvard School of Public Health, showing that hunger was on the rise in America, that it had harmful effects upon physical and psychological well-being, that the percentage of poor individuals receiving food stamp benefits had declined, and that the policy safety net had thus proved inadequate. If previously the food stamp program could have been criticized for growing out of control, it now should be criticized for failing to serve an obvious need.

Somewhat surprisingly, the Reagan administration had very little on its food stamp agenda, even though the entire program was up for legislative reauthorization. Spokesmen for the president called merely for community workfare, stiffer penalties on the states for overpayments, and a fixed federal contribution for state administrative costs replacing the 50% matching grant. Viewing this as tantamount to concession, House Democratic leaders shifted tactics from defense to offense, reviving many of the proposals advanced in 1984. The budget resolution allowed for $400 million in additional spending on nutrition, including food stamps, provided that equivalent cuts were made in other social programs. The House Agriculture Committee reported and the floor accepted reforms that raised asset thresholds, increased special deductions, and adjusted food cost calculations. Debate in committee, commented Leon Panetta, "centered not on the substance of what was proposed, but on its cost."[3] Whereas conservatives protested against benefit increases given budget worries, the Democratic majority responded that these represented minimal restoration to a program that had received more than its share of cuts over recent years. In the Senate, the majority quickly and easily rebuffed Helm's attack, approving instead a series of small administrative corrections. The conference accepted most of the House benefit provisions, at somewhat reduced levels. Although the enacted changes were relatively minor in cost and impact, they represented the first net expansion of food stamp eligibility since budget constraints were imposed in 1977.

Regarding reauthorization and budget caps, the House in 1985 proposed renewing the food stamp program for five further fiscal years, with caps determined by the CBO forecast estimates plus an allowance for error and unanticipated economic changes, increasing from 5% in FY 1986 to 7.5% in FY 1990. "The Committee has no scientific basis for establishing these margins for error but believes they represent a reasonable approach in light of the program's history."[4] The Senate proposed renewing the program for four fiscal years, with a flat 2.5% error allowance. The conference sided largely with the House. The final bill established five-year reauthorization and a gradually increasing margin of error between the predicted cost and that permitted under the budget cap, with the margin ranging from 3% in FY 1986 up to 7% in FY 1990. No such allowance for estimation error had been included in the 1981–82 reauthorization acts.

The new reauthorization also explicitly denied the secretary of agriculture the right to impose across-the-board benefit cuts when outlays were expected to exceed appropriations, unless they also were expected to exceed cap thresholds. This virtually committed the administration, in cases of insufficient funding, to request, and Congress to pass, supplemental appropriations up to the level specified by the cap. Moreover, the committee reports in both House and Senate recognized that Congress consistently had acted to protect food stamp spending capacity and commented favorably about the program's value to needy households.

Among the majority in Congress, there was no desire in 1985 to pull all the teeth from the food stamp spending caps. There was no serious effort to restore entitlement status or to even make the caps float depending on economic indicators. The history of unanticipated program cost expansion and the presence of severe current budget pressures made the reinstitution of fixed dollar caps unavoidable. The goal, however, was to accommodate all entailed nutritional support for the poor while keeping the symbolic promise that expenditures would never again grow out of control. Under conditions of relatively secure economic recovery, the cap was not expected to be constraining and it might even permit small program liberalizations, assuming that the administration would remain acquiescent. Mandated spending up to the budget cap, combined with an arbitrarily defined cushion for estimation error, were intended to reduce the possibility that the food stamp program would ever bump up against enacted spending limitations. This protection would not survive serious market instability, significantly increased utilization, and/or significantly higher food prices. Yet mainstream legislators certainly believed that adequate leeway had been provided and thus the contradiction between expenditure control and welfare provision would no longer actually have to be confronted.

Gramm-Rudman-Hollings: Budget Caps Minus Entitlements

If the politics of food stamp budgeting in 1985 was relatively calm, the politics of aggregate federal budgeting was partisan and acrimonious. Compromise over the budget resolution was constructed in the Senate with considerable difficulty. This was challenged, from one side, by the president who insisted upon greater military spending and greater cuts in social programs. It was challenged, from the other side, by the House majority, which insisted on higher tax revenues and full cost-of-living adjustments in Social Security. A budget resolution finally was adopted, but the corresponding reconciliation bill failed to clear Congress by the year's end. Given sharp ideological divisions and looming federal deficits, the same battle would be fought again each successive fiscal year, and under conditions that increasingly made the choices more painful and coalitions more difficult to secure.

Over the post-World War II period, the federal government consistently had run deficits. These were always less than 3% of GDP, aside from wartime and recession. The high, during the recession of 1975–76, had been 4.4%. This pattern was broken during the Reagan years. The deficit was equal to 6.3% of GDP during the recession year 1983, and it was still greater than 5% long after recovery commenced. Even more significant, the amount that persistent deficits added to the federal debt prior to the Reagan era systematically had been smaller than the increment in the national product. Thus the ratio of gross federal debt to GDP declined, from 96.7% in 1950 to 33.5% in 1981. This trend was reversed beginning with Reagan. By FY 1986, gross debt had climbed above 50% relative to GDP, with no slackening in sight.

The political response to government deficits in the United States is not always commensurable to its objective economic consequences. The actual effect of such a dramatic increase in federal indebtedness was a matter of technical debate during the Reagan years. Its emotional significance was much more evident. Congressional leaders worried that the combination—institutional budget deadlock amid substantial budget deficits—implied that the government had failed at the task of self-management, that elected officials were incapable of balancing factions and reconciling differences sufficiently to construct coherent policy, that the American political system itself had succumbed to the forces of fractionalization and segmentation, and that it no longer was capable of representing the national interest. Cast in terms of competence and legitimacy, the deficit problem was thought to require a drastic solution.

The Gramm-Rudman-Hollings (GRH) provisions, approved as part of a bill to raise the allowable debt ceiling, inserted a new, deficit-constraining reversion point into the game of federal budgeting. GRH set a limit on the estimated annual federal deficit and lowered that limit over time, from $172 billion in FY 1986 down to zero in FY 1991. The mandated maximum deficit each year was to be embodied in the congressional budget resolution and enforced by the corresponding reconciliation and appropriation acts. If these failed to achieve the specified target, GRH required an automatic "sequester" for across-the-board spending cuts, divided evenly between defense and nondefense accounts and to affect all but explicitly exempt programs, sufficient to produce the necessary savings.

The underlying problem can be understood as a formal paradox. There was no easy political accommodation among intransigent actors, each of whom sought substantial deficit reduction but differed dramatically regarding the means to achieve it, concerning the appropriate mixture of military spending, domestic spending, and tax revenue. The ordinary method of constructing agreement usually entails logrolling. Yet any probable political logroll involving the means would produce less deficit reduction than each of the actors would choose independent of the need to compromise. Thus the budget deficit level that might be achievable from political bargaining among the key institutional actors would be generally unacceptable. By contrast, the deficit level generally acceptable to the main institutional actors would be unachievable because of their divisions regarding means.

The solution involved two moves simultaneously. First, Gramm-Rudman-Hollings established a strict reversion point imposing the consensus level of deficit reduction. No political compromise over the pieces could be enacted unless it brought the anticipated deficit down to this level. Such a compromise would be extremely difficult to negotiate, evidenced by the fact that it was not produced despite clearly announced intentions prior to the enactment of GRH constraints. Second, the GRH provisions increased the cost of failure to reach voluntary compromise that achieved the required amount of deficit reduction. The new reversion point not only specified a dollar deficit threshold but also imposed a mandatory mechanism for enforcing that threshold if politicians could not find the will to do so. It was hoped that the threat of an automatic, arbitrary, and across-the-board sequester would induce actors to reach an agreement closer to their separate interests, at the same deficit level. As such, it would have an effect upon both policy preferences and bargaining strategies. As one senator observed, "The genius of GRH . . . is that it profoundly changes the consequences of inaction."[5]

The question is, why would political actors by an enormous majority insert a new deficit reversion point forcibly into the budget game at a level that normal deliberations would refuse to produce? To the "proceduralists" in Congress, the issue was the apparent breakdown of legislative comity and order. Their hope was that the prospect of sequester would be so horrendous that actors would drop intransigent demands, reduce the intensity of partisan controversy, and work together to achieve budget consensus. To the "outcomists" in Congress, the issue was the absolute size of the budget deficit, and thus any measure that brought the net deficit as quickly as feasible down toward zero was preferable to the expected settlement from normal budgeting. A politically negotiated outcome satisfactory to various entrenched interests would be wonderful if it also achieved fixed deficit requirements. Otherwise the reversion point would apply, which to them was not so terrible a prospect given the alternative. Finally, to the "ideologists," both left and right, the motivation was to guarantee that the other side visibly shared the onus of retrenchment. Resigned to deficit reduction, this apparently was more important than avoiding costs oneself. Liberal Democrats believed that the president would be forced to accept a bargain that included tax increases in order to save military expenditures from a sequester. The president and his conservative Republican allies believed that the liberals in Congress would be forced to accept a bargain that included welfare spending cuts so they would not have to impose deep, across-the-board, and therefore illogical reductions on nonexempt domestic programs. Supported by an unusual and bipartisan coalition, the omnibus bill incorporating GRH provisions was passed in both the House and the Senate by a nearly 2–1 margin and was signed by the president on December 13, 1985. According to Senator Warren Rudman, it was "a bad idea whose time had come."[6]

The consequences of GRH are almost predictable from our discussion of the budget caps in the food stamp program. There are two main lessons: that creative procedures rarely substitute for policy solutions, providing no escape from inherent dilemmas; and that aggregate restraints cannot be imposed without accepting the consequences to the parts, which becomes especially complicated when welfare entitlements are placed at risk.

Regarding the former, the insertion of GRH procedures left untouched the underlying conflicts that had reduced Congress to gridlock. Proponents intended that the fear of sequester would force actors to bargain in good faith and in a more timely manner. Yet the power of GRH came only when sequester loomed as a viable threat. Actors therefore had even greater incentive to delay and play brinkmanship, refusing to show any signs of weakness while hoping that their ideological opponents would be the first to concede. The result was further intransigence of institutional position and further refusals to take the first steps toward negotiation. Budget resolutions and appropriations bills stalled. Budget politics were afflicted by continual crises and emergency solutions. Consensus was most easily found in support of optimistic economic forecasts, budget tricks, and vague promises that made the deficit constraint somewhat less tight. GRH, observed White and Wildavsky, "did not force the major actors to come together; they merely found it easier to agree on palliatives and gimmicks that might prevent sequester."[7] Such gimmicks helped the deficit ceilings to survive for two fiscal years. In the third, when large-scale expenditure cuts seemed unavoidable, the ceilings were rewritten for the sake of political peace.

FY 1986 was in progress when GRH was enacted. Although the predicted deficit was $42 billion above the specified $172 billion ceiling, the law limited any first-year sequester only to $11.7 billion, meaning that the target would be missed. For FY 1987, the GRH deficit ceiling was

$144 billion. None of the requisite appropriations bills and no reconciliation progressed through Congress until after the start of the fiscal year. Salvation eventually came by means of "blue smoke and mirrors"—a favorable economic forecast, a one-time windfall from the revenue-neutral tax reform of 1986, estimated receipts from asset sales, accelerated tax collections, and scheduled expenditures postponed until the start of the coming year. Yet creative accounting did not affect core spending priorities and could not help against the baseline for FY 1988, when the scheduled deficit ceiling was lowered to $108 billion. Again no appropriations bills progressed, with neither political party accepting the burden of retrenchment. Fortunately, a Supreme Court decision forced legislative reformulation of the sequestration procedures, providing a welcome opportunity to alter the deficit thresholds. According to revised GRH rules, the ceiling for FY 1988 would be $144 billion, identical to the year before. The ceiling for FY 1989 was reduced slightly, to $136 billion, but a $10 billion cushion in practice meant that no critical choices were required from politicians until after the 1988 presidential elections. Gradual annual deficit reductions would then resume and a balanced budget was promised by FY 1993, two years later than originally planned.

Even with the relaxed ceilings, FY 1988 appropriations saw continued conflict and a renewed threat of sequester. Gridlock was broken only after the start of the fiscal year, under the impetus from "Black Monday," when the Dow Jones average fell ninety-five points. Congress and the president then negotiated a two-year truce, somewhat raising defense outlays and revenues while protecting most domestic spending. The agreement held through FY 1989, but only by using friendly economic forecasts. The actual deficit for FY 1989 was $154 billion, well above the $136 billion threshold, but no player had the incentive to protest and resume the budget wars. The tension between programmatic priorities and deficit limits was transferred to the incoming president. George Bush would soon learn, as had his predecessor, that institutional mechanisms rarely provide an escape from inherent policy dilemmas. In FY 1990, there was a relatively small sequester when budget negotiations broke down. This was only a prelude to FY 1991 when a major budget crisis reoccurred. The response, yet again, was to rewrite the reversion point rules and ease the deficit thresholds.

The other relevant lesson regarding GRH, also predictable from our discussion of food stamps, concerns the specific tension between welfare provision and aggregate spending control. In the attempt to avoid burdening poor and vulnerable households, most welfare programs were explicitly exempted from the automatic sequester if voluntary agreement did not achieve the legislated deficit targets. Technically, there were three different kinds of program exemptions: those completely removed from sequestration (including Social Security, Medicaid, and food stamps); those subject to sequestration for part of their annual inflation adjustment (Medicare); and those subject to sequestration up to the full amount of their inflation adjustment (civil service and military retirements), leaving the remainder of spending exempt.[8] As a consequence, only 46% of the total federal budget was vulnerable to sequester.

Nevertheless, entitlement costs were fully counted in the deficit totals that triggered the GRH procedures. Relatively uncontrollable expenditures comprised a major portion of total federal outlays. Their growth had contributed appreciably to the perceived deficit crisis. Their fluctuations, contingent upon economic conditions, could help make the expected federal dollar shortfall much greater than permitted under GRH rules. Yet the entitlement outlays that helped to constitute the problem were consciously removed from the mandated solution. Welfare protection and budget control were simultaneously declared incompatible but integrally related. (The same logic applied to taxation. Fluctuations in tax revenues affected the government's ability to achieve the deficit standard, but taxes under GRH were not necessarily raised when the standard remained unmet.)

The exemption of entitlement programs from the solution was challenge enough. Advocates for the poor and elderly had no cause to expose these benefits to compromise. Insulated from mandatory cuts, entitlements could always do better from the reversion point than from political bargaining. Ostensibly, the entire budget was subject to adjustment and reconciliation prior to the deadline for across-the-board spending reduction. In practice, however, entitlement advocates would rationally respond to program risk with delay and obstruction, knowing that the closer the sequester deadline, the stronger their strategic position. A disproportionate burden from restraint therefore fell upon nonexempt domestic items, accounts that had suffered most under the Reagan budgets of the early 1980s and by default were the prime targets again. A popular joke in Washington was that, "if you were planning on flying anywhere, you had better do it soon. But if you wanted to smuggle something, wait a while; GRH cuts would cripple the Customs Service."[9] The exemption scheme could have functioned had the amounts at stake been small and bargaining relations cooperative. With large deficits and partisan intransigence, the consequence was only to increase pressure where the strain was already evident and to reduce chances for reasonable policy agreement.

The inclusion of entitlements into the deficit problem complicated matters even further. Pressure under GRH for spending reduction would result not just from the conscious decisions of legislators but also from exogenous movements in the economy. Policymakers could make significant strides toward achieving deficit totals yet finish in a worse situation than when they began. During the viable years of GRH, official economic prognosticators tended to forecast a rosy scenario, in which both unemployment and inflation would remain low. This translated into favorable budget estimates and lower deficit predictions than actually happened. The real threat arose once the long, gradual macroeconomic upswing came to an end. This occurred during the early 1990s. Prompted by recession combined with the Gulf War, the federal deficit climbed to a record high despite a decade of prior expenditure cuts. The GRH ceiling could not be met, in large part because tax revenues were automatically lower relative to a nonrecession baseline and entitlement outlays were automatically higher. Yet the GRH sequestration process could not force tax revenues up to that baseline, nor could it force entitlement outlays down. The result was a severe budget crisis. Not surprisingly, the political system deadlocked. The entire apparatus of Gramm-Rudman-Hollings ultimately was abandoned and another, much milder framework was installed in its place.

Gimmicks aside, there were only two routes of escape—either remove entitlements from the calculation of the deficit problem or include entitlements in the sequester deficit solution. The former would give specified welfare programs clear priority over deficit reduction. According to this plan, the GRH deficit target would be adjusted depending on economic conditions, facilitating countercyclical fiscal stabilization and cushioning the shock to many households when unemployment rates rose. The response from conservative Republicans was that flexible ceilings would not ensure rapid progress toward a balanced budget, but instead protected high government spending within the cloak of a deficit reduction bill. Many conservatives therefore embraced the latter option, denying all GRH exemptions, which would give aggregate deficit totals clear priority over welfare policy programs. "These programs are typically low-income, means-tested programs which are good and worthy programs," said one Republican representative. "But they should no more be exempt from sequester than any other program of the Federal Government. We ought, insofar as possible, to subject everyone to the process."[10] The Democratic response was that the social safety net must be guaranteed and lobbyists, especially on behalf of the elderly, worked hard to reinforce that perception. A regard for equity, plus concern over possible electoral repercussions, made the conservative escape impractical. The demand for effective deficit reduction made the liberal escape insufficient. Yet the budget crisis of 1990 determined that the GRH arrangement was no longer feasible in its prevailing form.

The specified cap for FY 1991 was $64 billion. In January 1990, early in the planning cycle, the Bush administration estimated that the figure could be met assuming a moderate amount of new expenditure reduction. By the start of the fiscal year, the deficit forecast was nearly $300 billion, requiring cuts equal to approximately half of all federal discretionary spending. The size of the cut "was so unthinkable, so potentially damaging to the national economy and national security" that it became a "foregone conclusion that GRH would be repealed, reformed, or quietly put off until another year."[11] Budget decision-making in 1990 was characterized by extreme levels of institutional conflict, ideological intransigence, partisan maneuver, and leadership failure. It was noteworthy for months of special summit negotiations that eventually collapsed, for President Bush's reversal regarding his "read my lips" pledge for no new taxes, for stalemate so fundamental that the fiscal year began only by means of continuing resolutions, for a bipartisan agreement ultimately negotiated between the administration and congressional elites that was rejected in the House by a large bipartisan majority, for a dramatic federal government shutdown over the Columbus Day weekend, and for a final budget package constructed primarily by the Democrats in Congress with the president's acquiescence. Although that package included both spending cuts and tax increases, it was still far from sufficient to meet the legislated GRH deficit ceiling.

As part of the 1990 agreement—in a section formally entitled the Budget Enforcement Act (BEA) and incorporated as Title XIII of the reconciliation bill—the existing deficit ceiling for FY 1991 was abandoned. In place of all subsequent thresholds, a new plan was established calling for $50 billion in deficit reduction for each of the five coming fiscal years. However, the plan also included a version of the liberal escape, with intentional flexibility that adjusted the annual target in order to reflect prevailing economic and technical assumptions, changes in budget concepts and definitions, and any pressing emergencies (such as the savings and loan bailout and the costs of the Gulf War). In addition, the BEA also adopted a weak version of the conservative escape imposing certain mandatory corrections upon entitlement growth. The act divided the federal budget into five distinct areas, separated by "fire walls." Discretionary expenditures in the areas of defense, international affairs, and domestic programs were each given their own dollar targets and sequester process. Normal spending above the target figure would have to be met by compensating reductions to be found within the same expenditure category. For federal revenues and for mandatory expenditures (including welfare entitlements), the BEA process allowed the dollar targets to be adjusted annually for inflation, recession, utilization, levels of household need, and virtually all other relatively uncontrollable factors outside of congressional choice or regulatory rule-making. In essence, entitlement spending could grow over time as long as it was not caused by changes in underlying policy. Yet any increase in cost attributable to programmatic reform would have to be met by Pay-As-You-Go (PAYGO) compensating reductions from elsewhere in the entitlement budget category.

The crisis of 1990 therefore resulted in a shift from strict deficit limits based on part of the budget to weaker spending limits affecting all items in the budget. Aggregate targets were made flexible but in exchange there was no assurance of deficit reduction. Entitlements were incorporated into the new process but in exchange there was no mechanism to compel retrenchment. The alternative, fixed dollar targets and welfare exemptions, had proved politically unenforceable and programmatically unwise. Gramm-Rudman-Hollings as a mechanism designed simultaneously to better control the federal budget yet protect distributional equity was inescapably drawn into crisis, causing it to be abandoned.

Food Stamps without Controversy: Farewell to the Caps

Returning the focus back to the food stamp program, the fiscal-year period of reauthorization, 1986–1990, was comparatively calm. The program had been insulated from the budget crises and drastic spending cuts of GRH. The Reagan administration had long since launched its attack on food stamp excesses and liberal advocates had long established their defenses. Aggregate cost concerns, symbolized by the budget cap,

Figure 7-1. ***Ideological Budget Game, Fiscal Years 1985–1990***

Republican President—Democratic Congress
Budget Cap Rules

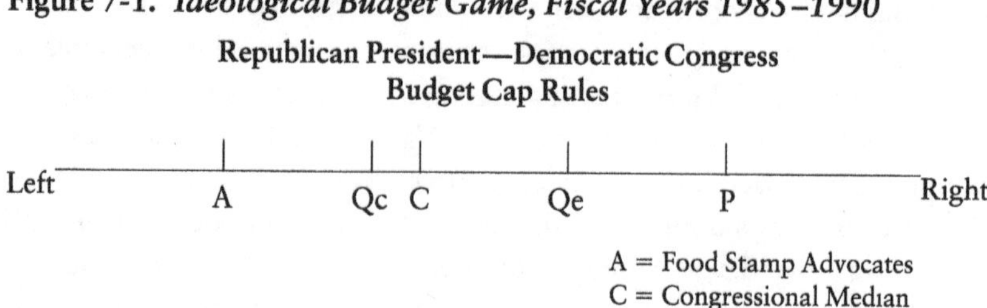

A = Food Stamp Advocates
C = Congressional Median
P = President Reagan
Qe = reversion point (entitlement)
Qc = reversion point (budget cap)

restrained demands for higher benefits. Household nutrition concerns, symbolized by the leeway granted under the cap, forestalled pressure for greater savings. Policy was meant to stay within these boundaries because virtually all actors agreed that the budget caps, as an effective tool of spending restraint, were in practice unavoidable but unenforceable. The tension between secure welfare benefits and constrained expenditure growth was thus not resolved but was held in abeyance. Mainstream legislators tended to accept the principles on each side of the tension, and they preferred not to be compelled to decide between them. With little to gain and much to lose politically, food stamp budget decision making became far less conflictual and more routine. After so many years of bitter controversy, there was finally some respite and relief.

Without disturbing the overall peace, however, minor games of strategic advantage continued. The nature of these games can be deduced from the revised cap dynamic, represented in Figure 7–1. From the ideological right, the loose cap and program spending considerably below that threshold gave food stamp budgeting more of an entitlement-like appearance. The legislated cap (Qc) was located to the left of expected program costs under existing law (Qe), making it irrelevant as a constraint. The Reagan administration therefore was free to focus entirely on Qe. It could safely and systematically play dishonestly, underestimating costs for appearances of expenditure restraint. Moreover, it could resume its criticism of program waste and fraud, which unnecessarily raised entailed expenditures, and thus it proposed managerial reforms to move Qe somewhat rightward. From the ideological left, the loose cap and program spending below that threshold supplied an opportunity to seek slight program expansion. Given that Qc was above Qe, there was budget room to expand entailed costs leftward. A tight cap would have made this impossible, for higher benefits would bring higher costs and thus a much greater chance that the reversion point would threaten core commitments. Now, however, liberals could propose reversing some of the painful program restrictions enacted earlier in the decade, since funding limits were no longer a complete barrier. Both ideological positions were reasonable and predictable given the revised budget cap arrangement. Their fates during the second Reagan administration depended upon the divided partisan control over government institutions.

For each fiscal year during this reauthorization period, President Reagan's food stamp budget submission underestimated expected spending. The request always assumed new legislation that would limit the total amount of federal government assistance to the states for their administrative costs and would impose severe penalties on states with high error rates. The proposal, with its accompanying attack on wasteful spending, came entirely from the White House and received minimum support from USDA officials. There was no chance that Congress would accept the idea and little belief that such a change would generate the savings predicted. Thus USDA spokesmen simply went through the motions defending it before the relevant committees, content that the exercise would keep the topic of management efficiency and administrative costs in public view and would help motivate the states to improve performance. Nevertheless, it meant that the president's budget for food stamps continued to be dead on arrival, systematically insufficient for entailed program needs.

In response, Congress decided to play honestly. Given the reduced popular salience of food stamp politics, there was little to gain from persistent skirmishes that used part-year funding to force the administration to revise its request. Without having to worry about visibly bearing the political onus, the appropriations committees in both House and Senate chose to fully fund the program based on current law. The committees were content simply to detail the faulty Reagan assumptions in their annual reports. They also became increasingly more critical regarding the accuracy of the administration's economic forecasts, upon which program utilization and food price estimates were based. With continued economic prosperity, there was no need for a supplemental appropriation for fiscal years 1986 and 1987. In FY 1988, based on updated cost projections, the Senate committee raised funding nearly $1 billion above the administration's initial request, sufficient to prevent a supplemental bill. In FY 1989, economic optimism ran a bit too high and a small supplemental appropriation was approved without controversy. Importantly, the dollar distance between food stamp outlays and the legislated expenditure cap widened over these years, meaning that the ceiling on maximum expenditures presented no essential threat to normal food stamp program operations.

On the other side, the existence of budget room under the cap encouraged food stamp advocates to seek modest program expansions. The initial pretext was to better serve the homeless. Attention to the topic was prompted by the hearings of Congressman Mickey Leland's select committee and by a report of the U.S. Conference of Mayors claiming that existing regulations made it difficult for the homeless to qualify for food stamps. Although the administration argued that current provisions were more than ample, this was a heartstrings issue difficult to oppose without appearing insensitive. In 1986 Congress attached to the antidrug bill a separate title intended to improve food stamp eligibility for the homeless and to permit the use of stamps in shelters and soup kitchens. In 1987 Congress attached to a general bill on homelessness provisions to encourage food stamp outreach and expedite the processing of applications. It also raised by $9 per month the special deduction from gross income for high shelter costs, which had been frozen from 1981 to 1983 and now lagged behind inflation, on the justification that it would help those on the brink of homelessness avoid the choice between affording housing and affording food.

A further opportunity to reverse the program contractions of the early Reagan era came with the major welfare reform bill of 1988. The original proposal from the House Ways and Means Committee called only for a study regarding improved coordination between AFDC and food stamps. The House Agriculture Committee instead attached a substantive food stamp title to the welfare bill. The new title was explicit about coordination, calling for simultaneous applications for food stamps and cash welfare, federal matching grants for food stamp information efforts, and automatic food stamp eligibility for cash welfare recipients. In addition, echoing the job training theme of the overall bill, the food stamp title proposed higher gross income deductions for work and child care expenses and new performance criteria for state employment training programs. Advocates expressed frustration about their inability to pursue a comprehensive nutrition agenda to ensure adequate benefits. As Leon Panetta complained, "we cannot deliver on real benefit reforms that are needed until we get our fiscal house in order." His goal, strategically, was to begin by "an incremental process, and that is not all bad."[12] The proposed food stamp title, however, was ignored by the Senate and deleted by the conference, in part because it raised the total cost of the welfare package.

Food advocates then decided to risk a separate bill. It meant exposing the reforms to a direct vote, with no disguising the budget price. The Senate Agriculture Committee even added provisions to the House title that gradually raised the basic food stamp benefit, ostensibly to compensate for indexing delays, and that revised state implementation penalties to recognize errors from underpayment as well as from overpayment. The operative political axiom is that when food stamp policy is portrayed as a matter of preventing hunger among the needy, it commands widespread popular support; when portrayed as a matter of ballooning costs and suspect recipients, it is an easy target for condemnation. The fact that 1988 was an election year contributed to the former. The leeway under the budget cap reduced fears of the latter. The small food stamp reform bill thus won bipartisan endorsement in committee and surprisingly easy passage on the floor. The administration, although opposed, was not especially vigorous regarding the matter, and the president cooperated by signing the bill into law in time for credit-taking before the November election.

The change in tone and substance of food stamp politics, from the first days to the final days of the Reagan administration, was quite dramatic. An era that began with a cap-induced funding emergency ended with a cap-accommodated slight liberalization; that began with presidential aggressiveness to make an example of this particular program ended with apparent presidential indifference; that began with political pressure to cut waste and dramatically lower costs ended with minor budget games but no great spectacle and with bipartisan reassurances that low-income people would always receive the nutrition assistance guaranteed to them. The contradiction between expenditure control and welfare entitlement remained suspended but not resolved. In this form, the issue would be left to the incoming Republican president.

The Bush administration had no ready agenda regarding food stamps and it openly adopted a more conciliatory posture than its predecessor. Bush was more concerned with the aggregate budget than with the specifics of its composition. The change in attitude was evident almost immediately. For the small FY 1989 supplemental appropriations bill, the new president merely asked Congress for "such sums as may be necessary" to ensure adequate funding for the remainder of the fiscal year.[13] He took a similar stance with the revisions to the FY 1990 budget. The Reagan administration's request, as usual, had assumed savings that never would be enacted. The House, as usual, appropriated the full amount based on current law using Reagan's own economic forecasts, although it severely criticized the administration for inaccurate assumptions. The Senate, as usual, utilized its own, revised forecasts, which raised the appropriation significantly. By the time of the conference, cost projections showed the need for an even higher allowance. The final appropriation was $15.7 billion, more than $1.6 billion over the amount initially requested. Throughout the course of these adjustments, the administration maintained a posture of permissiveness. Keeping away from the details, President Bush simply expressed support for full funding of benefits to qualified recipients, as long as the sum did not exceed the expenditure ceilings specified under existing law.

Even this posed a problem. The downward trend in household participation that began in the mid-1980s had ended. Inflationary adjustments to the Thrifty Food Plan were higher than originally anticipated and recession was on the horizon. As part of a FY 1990 dire supplemental appropriation, the House approved $510 million more for the food stamp program. The Senate approved $705 million. The conference approved $1.2 billion, based on the latest cost estimates from the USDA, although it made the amount "available only to the extent an official budget request, for a specific dollar amount, is transmitted to the Congress."[14] There was good reason for caution. These additional funds placed food stamp appropriations above the budget cap for FY 1990, which remained at $15.97 billion. Suddenly, without anyone expecting it, the tension between program costs and guaranteed benefits threatened to explode again onto the legislative agenda. The Bush administration would be pressed to decide whether to act like Reagan, who used the threat of the reversion point to bargain for reforms consistent with conservative policy preferences, or like Carter, who considered the prospect of mandatory across-the-board benefit cuts so distant from his policy position that he would endorse a cap override to protect adequate funding. It would be a test for Bush's proclamation of a "kinder and gentler" yet still fiscally conservative government. Similarly, if the cap threshold were exceeded, Congress would be forced to decide how far its newly found liberalism extended. It was easy to defend food stamp benefits when budgets were accommodating; now, with program costs escalating, it would be much more difficult to overturn a visible expenditure constraint and permit higher welfare outlays, especially if the president proved less than cooperative.

Policymakers decided to watch and wait. During passage of the FY 1990 supplemental appropriations bill, agriculture committee members in both House and Senate referred to food stamps as a mandatory spending program. Yet no legislation was advanced to override the caps. All the relevant actors seemed to accept the value of adequate funding, but none seemed anxious to initiate remedial steps. Importantly, no actor threatened reversion point brinkmanship. The administration asserted appropriations authority only up to the cap threshold. Although USDA officials became a bit nervous as the fiscal year drew toward a close, participation and cost estimates in fact proved slightly exaggerated. FY 1990 food stamp outlays remained just below the authorized ceiling. This was only partial consolation. Recession once again proved that budget limits pinch hardest in times of the greatest social need. The food stamp caps deterred flexibility in times of economic instability. Rather than facilitating public sector compensation for declining private sector incomes, they instead promised lower nutrition benefits to those poor households already suffering from market conditions. The recession irrefutably showed that, in the long run, the choice between budget control and welfare protection could not successfully be neglected or escaped. Moreover, a further explosion of food stamp costs was predicted for the coming fiscal year. The entire food stamp program was also up for reauthorization, and the subject of budget caps would then be reconsidered.

The 1990 reauthorization was included as part of the general farm bill. The food stamp section was named in honor of Congressman Mickey Leland, who died in a plane crash while on a relief mission in Ethiopia. The Bush administration had little to recommend, wishing neither to challenge Congress with spending retrenchment nor to abandon existing restraint with program liberalization. In the House, bipartisan support for incremental benefit expansion continued. The committee bill proposed raising allotments to 105% of the Thrifty Food Plan to compensate for indexing lags, increasing the shelter cost deduction to help guard against homelessness and disregarding the first $50 of child support payments to encourage support from absent fathers. On the House floor, some ideological conservatives attacked the bill for boosting food stamp costs in a period when deficits were exceeding GRH limits and entitlements appeared out of control. The leadership from both parties responded that hunger was a high moral issue and that slightly higher food stamp costs were acceptable within House budget projections. The motion to delete all program liberalizations failed, 83–336.

Financial concerns were not so compliant by the time the bill was considered in the Senate. Institutional stalemate had resumed, the annual budget resolution had not passed, and the pending budget summit with the president made prospects for new spending uncertain. The Agriculture Committee leadership had ready a bipartisan proposal similar to the one enacted by the House, but it could not be presented to the floor without license under the budget resolution. The farm bill, as reported by committee, therefore contained no food stamp section. It would be offered as a friendly amendment to the extent that budget allowance was provided. In the end, this amendment could contain nothing more than minor and technical provisions advertised as a no-cost option. The conference was similarly obliged. Without budget capacity, it could approve no significant changes in eligibility, deductions, or benefit levels. The main new provisions concerned only penalties for illegal trafficking, a system of electronic transfers for food purchases, the use of estimated deduction costs for the elderly and homeless, and a $10 minimum for annual inflationary adjustments. The conference report expressed "disappointment that important changes and improvements to the Federal food assistance programs" had to be deleted "because of the budget crisis facing the Nation." Nevertheless, the report insisted that the "original goals remain," and it hoped that "the important and necessary improvements can be made in the future."[15]

The food stamp program was reauthorized for another five years, from FY 1991 through FY 1995. The bill also eliminated all dollar caps limiting the maximum annual amount for food stamp expenditures. The formal recommendation came from the Bush administration and was consistent with its request, seen during the supplemental appropriations for FY 1989 and FY 1990, that funds be guaranteed sufficient to meet all legitimate program needs. Budget caps, said USDA assistant secretary Catherine Bertini, "threaten to interrupt the flow of benefits to recipients and place unnecessary burdens on Federal and State program managers." Open-ended authorization would eliminate "unnecessary procedural steps" and would "streamline the appropriations process in the event that unanticipated changes in law, participation, or food prices cause program costs to rise."[16] Apparently, the dangers to recipients and the complexity of adjustment were more significant to the Bush administration than any increased leverage gained from cap-induced strategic advantage. Unlike Reagan, President Bush expressed a preference for strong welfare protection over expanded opportunities for program oversight or for interventions to advance a more conservative program agenda.

Congress allowed the cap to be abolished quickly, easily, and without controversy. The food stamp title simply authorized to be appropriated "such sums as are necessary . . . to carry out the provisions of the Act."[17] The provision was slightly ambiguous regarding the restoration of full entitlement status. Expenditures remained subject to annual appropriations, but those appropriations were no longer subject to legislated ceilings. Whereas previously the secretary of agriculture had to report whether outlay trends during the year might compel reductions in the value of allotments issued to eligible households, now the secretary must report whether a supplemental appropriation would be needed to support entailed program operations. Whereas previously the secretary of agriculture had to direct the states to limit benefits if outlays were projected to exceed authorized spending limits, now the secretary must direct the states to limit benefits if outlays exceeded the actual appropriation. However, since the appropriations committees were instructed to provide all necessary funds and they had never failed to comply with supplemental money in order to ensure that every qualified household received its complete food stamp allotment, there was little actual threat of funding denial implicit in the bill. Entitlement status, in spirit if not quite in law, had returned. The complicated budget game of fixed food stamp expenditure caps, which began with the Mathis amendment of 1977, had come to an end.

A simple explanation for the termination of the food stamp caps is that they were no longer either necessary or expedient. It had been ten years since food stamp expenditures had last bumped against the cap threshold. Since then, the political salience of food stamps had diminished and Congress had continually demonstrated its commitment to fully fund the program. Despite recurrent battles over appropriations estimates during the Reagan years, sufficient adjustments had always been achieved, whether from revised initial totals or from supplemental action. Prior to that, despite recurrent cap crises during the Carter years, the appropriate expenditure authority had always been provided. The food stamp budget ceilings now could be seen as cumbersome in operation and irrelevant in effect. As such, they might be repealed without protest.

This explanation is mistaken on two counts. Objectively, it assumes that the problem of food stamp cost control had been solved. Yet there had been unanticipated supplemental appropriations for the past two fiscal years, one of which seriously threatened the cap threshold. Projections for future spending were similarly uncertain. With the country in recession, participation and program outlays were increasing dramatically. Moreover, relatively uncontrollable welfare expenditures in general were making it ever more difficult to meet aggregate Gramm-Rudman-Hollings deficit constraints. In a sense, the objective situation in 1990 was akin to that in the middle of the 1970s. The forecast again was economic instability, partisan conflict across government institutions, and rising anxiety over entitlement obligations and the level of government spending. It was under such conditions that cost concerns had before moved to the center of the food stamp agenda. It was neither obvious nor necessary that these cost concerns had now become less relevant to food stamp budgeting, or that they were managed with greater ability.

Subjectively, the argument that the caps in 1990 had visibly outlived their usefulness assumes that the tension inherent to entitlement budgeting between individual benefits and aggregate fiscal control had been resolved convincingly in favor of the former. This is also mistaken. Since the middle 1980s, the liberal campaign focusing on hunger and homelessness had aroused considerable sympathy. Recent reforms had in part reversed program contractions imposed during the early Reagan era. At the same time, however, aggregate budget fears had grown and increasingly dominated the legislative agenda. It was under such conditions that elected officials had before resorted to creative procedural experimentation in the attempt to escape a difficult policy dilemma. There is no reason to believe, in abandoning the food stamp spending caps, that politicians had now fully understood the implications of welfare entitlement and were willing to live with the fiscal consequences of their policy commitments.

What had occurred, in contrast to 1977 when the Mathis amendment was enacted, was that the practical consequences of the spending caps had become fully evident. The politics of food stamp caps had progressed through three different periods. Each represented a different variant of the fundamental tension between expenditure control and welfare provision. In none of them did the caps contribute to a satisfactory solution.

Initially, during the late 1970s, the articulated problem was entirely internal to the food stamp program, emphasizing extraordinary cost expansion and worries over excessive waste, fraud, and abuse. The justification for the caps, from this perspective, was to improve oversight, raise management efficiency, and encourage conscious choice when outlay demand surpassed expectations. The promise was that program obligations could be lowered without risk to deserving recipients. The complication was that spending growth was not primarily caused by internal management failure but by fluctuations in the external economy. Food stamp constraints would have negligible effects upon macroeconomic stabilization. Yet macroeconomic instability threatened the ability of the food stamp program to protect household nutrition. As a consequence, the caps consistently were overridden, although not without procedural complexity and political gimmickry.

In the second period, during the early 1980s, the focus of budget cap politics expanded somewhat, as part of a conservative policy agenda that denounced swollen government and personal dependency. Allegedly, food stamps were representative of excessive welfare liberalization. The caps became a useful right-wing instrument for bargaining over retrenchment, because the across-the-board cuts from the reversion point were far less preferable to liberals than a series of reforms that reduced eligibility and tightened administration. The promise, yet again, was that the truly needy would not suffer. The complication was that dramatic cost savings, demanded by the Reagan domestic strategy, would not result from marginal reforms. Congress balked at the prospect of greater program reductions, complying primarily by delaying certain indexed benefits. Larger savings required a dedicated reversion point game player willing to impose a legislative logjam and substantive deprivation. Such a player might hold the agenda for a while, but the tendency of mainstream politicians to support orderly procedures and to defend constituent welfare would soon be revived. An aggressive conservative would then either become isolated, as did Jesse Helms, or would retreat into indifference, as did President Reagan.

In the third period, during the later 1980s, the focus of food stamp cap politics was almost entirely external to program operations. The overriding problem was the level of the federal deficit. Financial crisis intensified the tension between welfare benefits and budget contraction.

Yet politicians, quite naturally, sought to escape especially hard tradeoffs. Furthermore, the impact of food stamp spending control would be minor relative to aggregate budget needs. Caps therefore became more a symbol than an effective weapon. The promise was that they would preserve the appearance of restraint while accommodating reasonable program benefits and all anticipated costs. The complication was that wishful thinking could not deter economic realities. Recession brought FY 1990 outlays dangerously close to the cap threshold and threatened nutrition assistance to otherwise deserving households. Symbolic caps could easily turn into substantive caps, forcing upon actors explicit choices in a turbulent partisan setting where neither cost overruns nor benefit cuts appeared an attractive option.

The elimination of the food stamp expenditure caps did not occur because the objective problem of entitled spending pressing against budget limits had disappeared or because the subjective tension between welfare benefits and overall fiscal priorities had been solved. Rather, there was no comfortable solution to the inherent dilemmas of entitlement budgeting through the application of program-level caps. The cap process was designed at a time of growing political concern over total costs with a concurrent disinclination to retreat from existing benefit guarantees. The caps originally were intended to provide an incentive to encourage program managers to contain unnecessary expenses and improve administrative efficiency, and they assumed rational legislative decision making if the resulting savings did not keep costs from exceeding a plausible threshold. Unfortunately, the caps did not—and could not—specify exactly why such rationality would prevail or how it would enable politicians to decide, if required outlays ever challenged the threshold, between the competing values of nutrition assistance and budget constraint. Over the brief history of the food stamp caps, the inherent policy tension increased as the focus of the budget problem expanded from program excess to welfare excess to deficit excess. Concomitantly, the ability of food stamp restraint to offer relief, while protecting nutrition benefits for households declared to be truly needy, systematically declined.

Moreover, to be effective, the food stamp cap thresholds depended on a delicate balance between economic projections and program needs. That balance would be upset whenever food prices rose and/or utilization rates increased much faster than anticipated. Each period in budget cap history experienced at least one such episode of market instability.

Congress could always set the caps consistent with current forecasts and override them if necessary. However, cap overrides at best engendered procedural complexity, crisis appropriations, and an irresistible temptation to tinker. At worst, they awarded tactical advantage to those politicians willing to threaten household nutritional benefits as a means to compel concessions. On the other hand, Congress could instead set the caps with margins to insulate benefits from economic instability. The desired balance again would be upset, as the caps would then become merely perfunctory, giving the appearance of restraint without impact on expenditure control. Moreover, even perfunctory caps can become tight when economic conditions deteriorate rapidly.

By 1990, Congress had witnessed all of these various alternatives. Legislators had tired of continuing political battles and were frustrated in their efforts to reconcile microlevel policy changes with aggregate expenditure thresholds. They could find no advantage in imposing on a program delivering valuable nutritional assistance to the poor a series of specific yet arbitrary outlay constraints that would be inherently either merciless or irrelevant. Logically, they responded by repealing the cap mechanism that foisted fruitless options upon them. Nevertheless, the underlying conditions that made the food stamp budget caps initially attractive remained politically relevant. The need for adequate welfare state protection was still counterpoised against fears of deficit spending and uncontrollable entitlements. In such situations, policy experiments that once appeared quite dead have a way of returning to the active political agenda.

Conclusion

Budget costs become politically salient when viewed in the aggregate. Yet the individual policy pieces that comprise the sum are valued by deserving and/or powerful constituents. Expenditure constraints placed upon the aggregate therefore are unenforceable, unless the burdens they impose on the pieces are also acceptable. Yet expenditure constraints are placed upon the aggregate largely because retrenchment decisions regarding the pieces cannot be made. The locus of conflict is displaced but the level of conflict often intensifies. The conclusion is that procedural innovations cannot substitute for tough policy decision making.

Gramm-Rudman-Hollings was the culmination of a new centralization in congressional budgeting, intended to replace a haphazard process that allegedly was incapable of controlling costs, determining priorities, or protecting the future. As the GRH experience showed, however, effective centralization depends on the ability to make aggregate choices imposing order upon the individual components. When such choices are politically unfeasible, or when the resulting order is unwelcome, or when the components cannot thrive within this structure, the new centralized decision-making procedures fail. Paradoxically, if the relevant political actors can cooperatively decide upon the budgetary framework, then formal constraints are largely irrelevant. If they cannot cooperatively decide, then formal constraints will usually heighten inherent tensions. Constraints thus can succeed only when political actors are generally agreed what has to be done and need only a slight incentive pushing them towards completing the bargain. This was certainly not the situation faced during the late 1980s, a period remarkable for budget emergencies and partisan stalemate. There was little reason for legislators to absorb the popular reprisals from retrenchment, since the impact on the federal deficit was small and calls for further restraint were relentless despite a decade of agonizing effort.

The situation is exacerbated when welfare considerations enter the equation. There is always pressure to safeguard programs offering material protections to the most vulnerable in society. During the late 1980s, the democratic demand to assert greater budget control was matched by the democratic demand to ensure adequate public support for the needy. The combination proved intractable. Expenditure caps could not be enforced if the perceived consequence was a significant retreat from antipoverty and antihunger commitments. GRH therefore exempted most welfare spending from mandatory sequestration. The caps applied specifically to the food stamp program were intentionally loose so as to protect beneficiaries from reversion point threats. Presumably too powerful to be effective, procedural restraints were made symbolic and then eliminated.

The greater the social frustrations regarding public spending and deficit projections, the more politicians fear for their capacity to govern. The greater the fears regarding governance, the higher the temptation to use caps as an institutional means of control. The greater the policy control required from caps, the less they are capable of delivering restraint—especially when social welfare commitments are at stake. The less the caps can deliver, the more prone they are to crisis. The greater the tendency toward crisis, the more the cap mechanisms contribute to social frustrations and concerns regarding governability. One possibility for escape is to restructure the caps, praying desperately that they will prove more effective in their next iteration. The other solution is to trivialize or repeal the caps, but this means that politicians forsake the appearance of budget control. After 1990, the new Budget Enforcement Act did not necessarily force federal expenditure or deficit totals down. The PAYGO provisions did not constrain the growth of welfare outlays already entailed under existing law. The food stamp program itself was returned to entitlement status. Yet pressures for stricter spending restraints remained, and the demand for caps would reappear by the middle of the coming decade.

Notes—Chapter 7

1. CBO estimates, cited in Aaron Wildavsky, *The New Politics of the Budgetary Process* (Glenview, IL: Scott, Foresman, 1988): 340.

2. Wildavsky, *The New Politics of the Budgetary Process*, 212.

3. House *Report* 99–271, 793.

4. House *Report* 99–271, 165.

5. Joseph White and Aaron Wildavsky, *The Deficit and the Public Interest* (Berkeley: University of California Press, 1989): 442.

6. Howard E. Shuman, *Politics and the Budget*, 3rd ed. (Englewood Cliffs, NJ: Prentice Hall, 1992): 184.

7. White and Wildavsky, *The Deficit and the Public Interest*, 516.

8. R. Kent Weaver, *Automatic Government: The Politics of Indexation* (Washington, D.C.: Brookings Institution, 1988): 62–63.

9. White and Wildavsky, *The Deficit and the Public Interest*, 509.

10. *Congressional Record* 131: H 9599.

11. Daniel P. Franklin, *Making Ends Meet: Congressional Budgeting in the Age of Deficits* (Washington, D.C.: Congressional Quarterly Press, 1993): 63–65.

12. U.S. House of Representatives, Committee on Agriculture, *Welfare Reform Proposals*, 100th Cong., 1st sess., 1987, 3.

13. House *Report* 101–78, 6.

14. House *Report* 101–43, 71.

15. House *Report* 101–916, 1086.

16. U.S. Senate, Committee on Agriculture, *Preparation for the 1990 Farm Bill*, Part XIV, 101st Cong., 2nd sess., 1990, 155.

17. House *Report* 101–916, 1105.

EIGHT

Old Hat: The Return of Entitlement Politics and the Revival of Budget Cap Proposals, 1991–1994

By the early 1990s, America had experienced the fiscalization of the entire federal policy agenda. Virtually every debate had become a budget debate; virtually every program faced potential retrenchment; virtually every new proposal was scrutinized for its immediate public sector costs more than for its long-run social benefits. The budget deficit loomed as a primary symbol for the dissatisfaction average Americans felt regarding government. Fiscalization produced two interrelated political tendencies. The first was a fundamental conservatism in policy outlook. Emphasis shifted from what needed to be done to what safely could be afforded. A budgetary focus favors the critic claiming that internal operations need to be purged of wasteful inefficiency. Advantage goes to the politician demanding contraction in the size and scope of government. The terms of debate help to bias the outcome. Entitlements, as mandatory expenditures responsive to social conditions more than to government intentions, become especially vulnerable to attack.

The second inherent tendency was a policy perspective that emphasized aggregates over specifics. Budget opposition is derived from the totals—the sum of federal tax revenues does not equal the sum of federal expenditures, resulting in persistent deficits. By contrast, budget support lies in the details—each individual program has its own rationale, coherence, and constituency. Fiscalization produced a profound distrust of whether these two competing pressures successfully could be reconciled, especially given the fragmentation of interests and institutions characteristic of the U.S. political system. By implication, it engendered anti-political as well as antigovernment sentiments. Increasingly, there was concern that the chaotic pressures from American democracy would overwhelm orderly decision making, and thus reforms were proposed to strengthen the instruments of central control.

In this context, expenditure caps slowly reappeared on the U.S. legislative agenda. Political memories are short and policy solutions are few. The PAYGO system introduced in 1990 largely codified the budgetary status quo. Conscious policy changes that increased costs or decreased revenues had to be matched by compensating adjustments, but automatic cost increases or revenue decreases generally were permitted. As such, PAYGO would prove a barrier both for those who sought substantive innovation and for those who sought stricter fiscal constraint. The remaining years of the Bush administration saw continued deadlock but a reduction in the intensity of the fight. Clinton's election was encouraging to those wishing for change, yet the trend toward fiscalization proved irresistible. The president's economic revitalization program thus quickly evolved into a deficit-reduction program. Across the ideological spectrum, politicians began to flirt with the idea of renewed budget caps, which would visibly restrict government spending in the aggregate and dominate the forces of political fragmentation. The Republican legislative victory of 1994 ensured that new cap proposals would be considered seriously in Congress.

The food stamp program in effect had been restored in 1990 to entitlement status. Spending during this period was no longer restrained by legislated limits on budget authority. As a corollary, food stamp politics returned to the entitlement dynamic seen previously during the 1970s. Considered from the perspective of empirical testing, the events from the period 1991 to 1994 offer further confirmation for the hypotheses derived from the models discussed in chapter 2. As before, with entitlement rules under conditions of divided party government, there was a tendency for the president to underestimate costs and for ideological partisans to employ exaggerated rhetoric and symbolic offers. The baseline was guaranteed and reform unlikely, establishing priority to the reversion point and freeing actors from the consequences of strategic play. As before, with entitlement rules under conditions of unified Democratic government, there was moderate food stamp liberalization, bridled by the amount of available federal funds. As part of the bargaining over entailed costs, welfare liberals conceded the imposition of somewhat greater aggregate budget controls, which in turn encouraged deficit hawks to demand even more stringent barriers. Unlike in the 1970s, however, food stamps during this period were not on center stage. Instead, they were only a small component in a much broader debate over the growth of mandatory spending programs. Yet the issues in this broader debate were similar in tone and logic to those which previously had focused on food stamps alone. Moreover, the new policies proposed for entitlement limitation would have a major impact upon the food stamp effort.

Food Stamps under PAYGO: President Bush Plays as Ford

The PAYGO provisions of the 1990 Budget Enforcement Act replaced deficit control with expenditure control. The act formally distinguished two categories of federal spending—discretionary spending under the supervision of the annual appropriations process, and direct spending mandated by the terms of substantive legislation. For the former, strict dollar limits were imposed with exceptions for emergency situations. Anticipated excess within each distinct subject area would have to be met by compensating voluntary reductions or by involuntary sequester. For the latter, no fixed ceilings were imposed, but rather spending was accommodated up to the level determined by prevailing law. Totals therefore would be flexible given shifting inflation, unemployment, utilization, and recipient need. Congress certainly was not prohibited from altering the terms of prevailing law, but any resulting increase in anticipated outlays would have to be matched by programmatic cuts elsewhere in the direct spending category or by a sequester. The consequence was a strong prejudice on behalf of existing allocations. Under PAYGO, current priorities were maintained, no program changes were necessitated, and few changes were feasible politically.

Food stamps were listed within the direct spending category of the Budget Enforcement Act. Legislation had removed all caps from the program although expenditures still required Appropriations Committee approval. It was almost a complete return to entitlement status. During the mid-1970s, the appropriations committees had been ordered to fund the food stamp program adequately to meet all legitimate demand. It was unclear whether such an explicit order now existed. Nevertheless, as Allen Schick observed, food stamp spending had "never been regulated by the appropriations process," and the Budget Enforcement Act certainly placed the program with other entitlements in a category defined by the absence of discretionary choice in the annual budget review.[1] In practice, if not absolutely in law, the food stamp budget over the fiscal-year-period of program authorization, 1991–1995, was governed by the entitlement reversion point. Not surprisingly, food stamp politics and policy during the remaining years of the Bush era paralleled the experience of the Ford era. Again there was a Republican president confronting a Democratic Congress; again there was gradually rising concern over entailed costs; again program reforms were blocked by the division of institutional power. As under Ford, the president tended to underestimate anticipated costs. Congress responded relatively honestly, although strategically it insisted that the president cooperate in making the estimate adjustments needed to ensure full funding of benefits. As under Ford, congressional Democrats had an agenda of program liberalizations that would raise costs above the reversion point, yet the impossibility of action produced a game of position taking and political intransigence. The only new element was the requirement of PAYGO that any legislated increase in spending for one mandatory program be met with compensating reductions in others. This added an internal restraint upon liberal reform, reinforcing the external restraint from divided government.

Entitlement budgeting implies the dominance of the reversion point, as we have seen, in two different senses. First, regarding annual appropriations, neither the president's official request nor the amount initially allocated by Congress are necessarily to be taken seriously; adequate program funding ultimately must be provided. Second, regarding spending revisions, entitlement status encourages extreme rhetoric and irrelevant proposals; the failure to reach legislative compromise merely leaves the status quo intact. The Bush administration was quick to grasp the political advantages of the former, assuming a strong economic recovery in order to underestimate needed outlays. This gave the appearance of fiscal restraint and helped push deficit projections down while placing the onus for adjustment upon Congress. Thus, for FY 1991, Bush requested $100 million less for food stamps than had been appropriated for FY 1990. This was despite the fact that participation had recently climbed above twenty million persons—nearly 10% of the population—for the first time since the mid-1980s and despite fears of continuing recession that would keep utilization and costs high. The appropriations committees in both House and Senate strongly criticized the administration for "inaccurate assumptions which grossly understate the cost of the program."[2] Responding honestly based on existing estimates, they added over $2.2 billion to the amount, making the total appropriation $19 billion, although $823 million would be made available only after a formal request by the White House.

Even this proved to be insufficient. As the recession continued, full funding of benefits required a major supplemental appropriation, which was attached to a "dire emergency" bill intended to pay the civilian costs of the Gulf War.[3] The administration's proposal was duplicitous. It called for indefinite authority to spend if necessary to sustain benefits through the end of the fiscal year, but it formally requested only $200 million while noting that as much as $1.5 billion might be required. Thus the administration could claim that it supported relief against economic hardship and that it had kept supplemental costs down. Congressional committees again chastised the USDA for its inability to provide accurate estimates, and they added the full $1.5 billion to the appropriation. Yet they also played a small political trick in response, making the amount above $200 million available upon the receipt of an official request from the administration. The result was that, by the end of the fiscal year, food stamp appropriations for FY 1991 were increased by nearly one-quarter over the president's original submission, complicated by some minor but predicable institutional gamesmanship.

For FY 1992, the Bush administration asked for $23.2 billion in the food stamp spending, with $2.5 billion of that amount to be a cushion available only if absolutely needed and explicitly requested. The House Appropriations Committee awarded $1 billion less, claiming that it had tired of consistently erroneous cost projections and indicating that the president would have to initiate a supplemental proposal in order to secure full funding. The Senate instead played honestly and added $500 million to the administration's submission, noting that current estimates already forecast spending well into the cushion amount. The conference reduced the Senate total by $300 million and insisted that the president had to issue an explicit request to obtain the last $1.5 billion of the total. With economic recovery proceeding, albeit hesitantly, the $23.4 billion appropriation proved sufficient, although there was some late concern in the aftermath of Hurricane Andrew.

For FY 1993, the Bush administration tried a variant on the tactic of underestimation. It projected $22.7 billion in necessary spending, less than the previous year, and added a $5.3 billion cushion to protect against economic uncertainty. The former figure was obviously too low but it gave the appearance of restraint. The latter figure was obviously too high but it protected the administration against charges of callousness. Both were helpful in an election year. Both, however, left Congress without a credible figure upon which to base its deliberations. The House Appropriations Committee, citing testimony from USDA officials, cut the total request by more than $2 billion. The Senate committee, not wishing to bear the onus, simply approved the full $29 billion. The conference approximately split the difference. Program utilization declined gradually with economic recovery, and the amount finally appropriated for FY 1993, over $28.1 billion, was far more than necessary. All of these minor budget games hardly mattered, as food stamp spending was now generally considered mandatory up to the level of need. In fact, the games could proceed freely precisely because food stamp spending was considered mandatory, making such minor political play completely safe.

The second implied consequence of entitlement status concerns the efforts of advocates and critics seeking to move the reversion point, Qe, closer to their preferred outcome. Under divided partisan government, there are no restraints upon aggressive demands, rhetorical excess, and symbolic gestures because there are no potential budgetary costs resulting from coalition failure or nonagreement. From the right, President Bush—like Ford before him—viewed Qe to be artificially too high and he renewed the attack on food stamp fraud and waste, arguing that $100 million was abused annually through illegal trafficking. Bush was not inherently suspicious of the food stamp program, as Ford seemed to be, but rather focused primarily upon saving federal funds under tight budgetary conditions.

It was the liberal Democrats in Congress, arguing from the left that Qe was defined too low, who most seized the opportunity for aggressive ideological play. A number of reforms had been deleted from the 1990 food stamp reauthorization because of budget constraints. Both the House and Senate agriculture committees in 1991 approved liberalization packages that raised the basic allotment to 105% of the Thrifty Food Plan, removed maximum limits from the excess shelter cost deduction, exempted the first $50 of child support payments, and indexed permissible automobile asset values to the inflation rate. The announced aims of the so-called Mickey Leland Hunger Relief Act included responding "to the hunger emergency afflicting American families and children," attacking "the causes of hunger among all Americans," ensuring "an adequate diet for low-income people who are homeless or at risk of homelessness," promoting "self-sufficiency among food stamp recipients," and assisting "families afflicted by adverse economic conditions."[4] The House version even proposed returning food stamps to complete entitlement status, removing the provision that ordered the states to reduce household benefits if appropriations were insufficient.

The Bush administration expressed opposition to the bill. The secretary of agriculture objected to the cost, which threatened to exceed $5 billion over a five-year period. The expansion of food stamp benefits was termed "not warranted and ill-timed." Instead of reducing entitlement spending from baseline levels, the reform would "assure substantial, automatic increases" and would "lock in spending priorities for years to come."[5] Despite the impassioned justification by partisan liberals and their announced high priority for food stamp reform, no legislation was advanced in Congress during 1991. The dominant hurdle was not the veto threat from the Bush administration. A veto might even aid in the political effort to portray the president as aloof and indifferent. Rather, the deterrent was the PAYGO requirement, which necessitated compensating revenue enhancement or entitlement reduction if food stamp costs were to grow as a consequence of conscious policy choice. The committee leadership in both House and Senate promised not to bring the bill to the floor until a funding offset was secured. The House Ways and Means Committee chairman Dan Rostenkowski, whose domain included taxation and most federal welfare programs, promised to be helpful. However, absent a financing mechanism capable of commanding sufficiently broad support, the Leland bill could not proceed.

A solution eventually was found via the Family Preservation Act sponsored by the House Ways and Means Subcommittee on Human Resources. The act intended to create a new entitlement for state foster care and adoption efforts. Most of the Leland food stamp provisions were attached to the bill, the main exception being the increase in the basic allotment relative to the Thrifty Food Plan. The entire package would be financed by a 10% surtax on individuals with taxable incomes above $1 million. Reported to the House in July 1992, the measure was transparently a partisan maneuver to co-opt the rhetoric of family values and embarrass the president in an election year. According to Leon Panetta, "everyone has their own interpretation of what family values are. But surely the most fundamental value that has to be present in every family is the protection of our children, providing for their security, providing for their safety and ensuring that they are fed."[6] The Family Preservation Act was a convenient vehicle for food stamp reform to ride. The needs of America's children was an issue commanding automatic sympathy. The proposed "millionaires' tax" highlighted the differences between rich and poor. Any legislator standing against aid to poor children in order to shelter the income of the wealthy might certainly feel vulnerable to attack. Republicans in the House condemned the measure for its antiquated "tax-and-spend" philosophy, raising taxes to fund a new entitlement. More important, they emphasized the overtly political character of the bill and warned that it had not "a ghost of a chance of being signed into law" by the president.[7] The House passed the Family Preservation Act in a vote divided along party lines. In the Senate, the foster care and tax provisions, without the food stamp title, were attached to a separate bill establishing enterprise zones for inner cities. In this format, the package was approved by Congress. The absence of food stamp reform did not matter. The bill was vetoed by President Bush on the day preceding the 1992 elections.

Food Stamps under PAYGO: President Clinton Plays as Carter

In a parallel fashion, Bill Clinton during his first two years in office played the game of entitlement budgeting in a manner analogous to that initially played by Jimmy Carter. Both were Democratic presidents supported by unified partisan control of government institutions. Both were southern moderates without Washington experience. Both were deeply ambivalent when forced to choose between the conflicting goals, higher spending for social fairness or lower spending for deficit reduction. Both accepted some liberalization in the rules governing the food stamp program, but to achieve this expansion in entitlement benefits both were compelled to accept procedural limits on the extent of entitlement rights. Finally, both soon lost control over the budget debate, unleashing forces from the right that excoriated welfare spending and held it liable for much of the nation's financial and social problems. The main difference between them, given the perspective of this book, is that by the time Clinton took office the problem of budgeting entitlements had become a dominating issue in U.S. domestic politics, in which food stamps were a contributing but relatively minor part.

Clinton ran for president on a platform of economic populism, promising a middle-class tax cut, a stimulus package for short-term growth, and greater long-term public investment in human and physical resources. He had not given much thought to budget issues, although he did pledge to cut the federal deficit in half within four years. Upon taking office, Clinton was confronted with a reestimate from the outgoing Bush administration sharply raising the predicted fiscal shortfall. This prompted an intense debate among the Clinton advisers regarding how much to maintain the original program and how much to modify it.[8] The inherited deficit was deeper than anticipated, yet the president's electoral constituency and his call for policy change demanded new initiatives. The final package announced in February 1993 was carefully balanced to accommodate certain administration spending priorities while also promising lower deficits, including a combination of program cuts and tax increases to reassure financial markets and help keep interest rates down.

Clinton's first year was characterized by intensifying budget battles. The first item placed before Congress was the FY 1993 supplemental appropriation incorporating $16.3 billion in short-run economic stimulus. It was approved by the House but encountered a resolute Republican filibuster in the Senate. This was both a test of the president's political influence and an opportunity to sharpen the rhetoric for the coming phase of partisan conflict. The Democratic leadership somewhat misjudged majority sentiment, suffering when Clinton's proposal was portrayed more as spending for higher deficits than as spending for needed job creation. Ultimately Congress passed only $4 billion in extended unemployment insurance coverage. The second item was the FY 1994 budget resolution. Approved by a party vote, it was generally consistent with the president's aims, although it contained somewhat more deficit reduction and left considerably less room for new infrastructure investment. Next was the reconciliation bill, which carried the main substantive details of the Clinton program. Confronted by intense ideological pressures, the administration had enormous difficulty in securing a minimum winning coalition. In the process of negotiation, its social and economic plan primarily became a fiscal plan. Quantitative budget numbers predominated and qualitative policy concerns faded. With his political reputation on the line, the president employed the ample resources of his office in the effort to produce an agreement and obtain sufficient votes for its passage. The eventual reconciliation bill was enacted by the smallest of possible margins, by one vote in the House and by a tie in the Senate with Vice President Gore deciding. Finally, late in 1993, House moderates and conservatives sought another round of spending cuts. Although opposed by the White House, a floor amendment to attach major deficit reduction to a minor administrative restructuring bill failed by only six votes in the House. The entire measure was then bottled up in Senate committee.

Food stamp liberalization was included as part of the reconciliation bill. The House Agriculture Committee seized the opportunity to again revive the so-called Leland provisions, which it deemed "a long-overdue set of changes that expands the Food Stamp Program's ability to meet the food needs of low-income Americans."[9] The proposed changes included increasing the basic allotment to 104% of the Thrifty Food Plan, raising deductions for excess shelter and childcare costs, excluding from income the first $50 of child-support payments, indexing against inflation the maximum value of vehicles when calculating the asset limit for eligibility, simplifying the definition of a household, and revising certain administrative practices. The estimated cost of the House bill was $7.3 billion over five years, yet according to the CBO the amount was allowable under PAYGO rules within the context of the entire budget resolution. The administration gave support to the food stamp liberalization, and Democrats in committee defeated Republican efforts to lower the cost or defer action until a full welfare reform proposal was submitted.

No equivalent food stamp title was included in the Senate version of the reconciliation bill. Substantively, the Senate bill needed greater expenditure savings in exchange for reducing anticipated tax receipts. Procedurally, the Senate was bound by the "Byrd rule," which prohibited extraneous matter in a reconciliation bill and thus made any provision that did not involve deficit reduction liable to a possible point of order. The consequence was a political show-down in conference. Conservatives resisted all additional spending provisions. Liberals, especially those representing urban and minority constituencies, considered certain higher-cost items (e.g., food stamp liberalization, funds for inner city enterprise zones, and an increase in the Earned Income Tax Credit) integral to their party's platform and prerequisites for support. The eventual compromise retained the Leland food stamp provisions except for the benefit adjustment relative to the Thrifty Food Plan. As a result, there would be no general increase in allotments, but certain kinds of recipients would receive more favorable treatment. Welfare liberals thus obtained a large part of the nutrition package that otherwise would be blocked under PAYGO budget rules; the compromise helped ensure their support for the conference version of the reconciliation bill. Fiscal conservatives were satisfied that the new food stamp provisions would now cost one-third the previous estimate; the compromise helped ensure that no point of order was raised on the Senate floor. Freed of any cap and accommodated under reconciliation, Congress could then approve much of the long-delayed Leland food stamp proposal.

President Clinton's approach to welfare entitlement in 1993 was moderate. Regarding contributory programs, he sought small cuts in health care and raised the amount of Social Security payments taxable for upper income individuals. Regarding means-tested programs such as food stamps, he helped promote small increases in benefits especially for working households with children. Yet he was generally content to allow mandatory spending to rise as individual eligibility and economic conditions dictated. More substantial changes would have to wait for his welfare and health policy initiatives, although the prospects for either were fading rapidly. This was not satisfactory to the fiscal hawks within his party insistent upon greater deficit control. In order to appease them and to secure their votes for the reconciliation bill, Clinton granted three different kinds of concessions. Each was minor in its policy impact but significant in its symbolism.

The first concession ensured Clinton's support for the continuing visibility of entitlement spending as part of the budget and deficit debate. In order to win the pivotal vote of Congresswoman Marjorie Margolies-Mazvinsky, the president promised to host a conference on entitlements in her suburban Philadelphia district. In order to win the pivotal vote of Senator Bob Kerrey, he promised to establish a bipartisan commission on entitlement reform. The Philadelphia conference, held in December 1993, attracted extensive news coverage and broad participation. Clinton delivered a long and pedantic lecture full of detail regarding the character and cost of various entitlement programs. His main conclusion was that "the culprit is health care costs,"[10] but he did not explain how comprehensive coverage and lower costs would be reconciled. It was an exercise apparently designed to sidestep controversy and avoid commitment.

The entitlement commission began with a bang but ended in a whimper. The president's executive order establishing the commission gave it broad leeway to examine entitlements and their long-term effect upon the budget in order to "help chart a future for Congress and for the country." The thirty-two commission members included prominent legislators and civic leaders. The two commission chairs, Senators Kerrey and Danforth, hired an expert staff and carefully organized the schedule for hearings. Their goal was to develop an interim report outlining the problem and identifying a "laundry list" of possible reform options, with the expectation that the commission eventually would "reach consensus" on a specific course of action.[11] The final report issued in December 1995 agreed only on the value of continuing citizen education and the need to take a long-term viewpoint on budget issues.[12] That report contained five conflicting sets of policy recommendations, each with its ideological proponents, none of which succeeded in commanding majority support or popular enthusiasm. There were a number of reasons for the commission's failure. Discussion was so focused upon long-run trends that it virtually ignored the short-run deficit problem, reducing the incentive to accept painful political prescriptions. The chairmen developed their own, controversial policy recommendation in private and submitted it to the other commissioners just a week before the vote, allowing them little time for explanation, argument, or adjustment. The existence of revenue-raising tax reform on the commission's agenda angered partisan conservatives. The primacy of Social Security reductions upset partisan liberals. By concentrating almost entirely on lower costs, the commission's agenda did not always distinguish among the entitlement programs, did not consider possible reasons why mandatory spending might be justified, and did not address how entitled benefits aided needy individuals in the population. Finally, the commission was eclipsed by the election campaign of 1994 and the prominence given to the Republican leadership's proposed "Contract with America." Any project that challenged the prevailing political winds "after the election . . . was sailing against a hurricane."[13]

The second concession granted by the Clinton administration concerned the strict enforcement of PAYGO procedures. The administration originally had not been prepared for the consequences of these procedures and thus was surprised when discretionary spending limits precluded many of the investment initiatives planned for the economic revitalization program. Soon, however, the administration became a willing captive to these limits. Strict enforcement placed the White House in opposition to many executive branch agencies. PAYGO institutionalized no-saying, since any additional programmatic cost required compensating cuts elsewhere—in other programs supported by other political constituencies. Each small change in policy therefore demanded an all-out political assault by its advocates, deterring virtually all policy innovation. For example, food stamp officials were blocked from proposing legislative reforms to better conform management practices and eligibility rules with those of AFDC, which would have improved state-level efficiency and possibly saved money over time. Strict enforcement also interfered with routine administrative decision making. Food stamp officials were prevented from expanding outreach efforts to enroll already eligible households when it was decided that not only the cost of the outreach program but also the cost from all resulting household enrollments would be scored as an explicit policy change for budget accounting purposes. Program officials were allowed to request $13 million to help implement an Electronic Benefits Transfer system to replace food stamp coupons only when Congress consciously overturned an OMB decision scoring the spending as discretionary rather than mandatory. The effects of such constraints were hardly momentous, but the tone was indicative of the growing distrust of entitlement programs prevalent throughout American politics.

The third Clinton administration concession to deficit control concerned the reintroduction of a mechanical restraint on entitlement spending, albeit in a very weak version intended more for appearance than for effectiveness. During the 1993 budget debate, some fiscally conservative House Democrats flirted with the idea of further social welfare benefit reductions to substitute for the president's proposed energy tax increase. This idea was unacceptable to the administration, yet something had to be done to secure their political support. In a deal constructed shortly prior to the House vote on the reconciliation bill, both sides agreed to a plan ordering the president to propose some means of paying for all entitlement spending above a specified target, or else explain explicitly why the target should be revised. This new entitlement review process was incorporated into the House version of the bill but not the Senate version, where it was blocked by the Byrd rule preventing extraneous matters. In conference, House members receded from their provision because it would make "the entire conference report subject to a point of order in the Senate and thereby endanger final enactment of the reconciliation bill." Moreover, the conference noted, President Clinton had promised "to establish by Executive Order a mechanism for monitoring entitlement outlays and making recommendations to address overages."[14] The Executive Order was issued on August 4, 1993, the day before the vote on the final reconciliation version, and the House immediately revised its rules of procedure to conform. The new process was a critical element in the narrow Clinton administration victory.

Under PAYGO as established in 1990, entitlement expenditures could increase without limit provided that the cause was an entailed consequence of existing policy rather than a deliberate change in policy. The entitlement review process imposed further constraints. The OMB was instructed to forecast, within thirty days of the passage of the reconciliation act, entitlement costs for fiscal years 1994–1997. This would establish annual entitlement targets, which could be adjusted for fluctuations in caseload but not for inflation rates higher than anticipated at the time of the initial forecast. Congress had to be notified and presented with a full analysis of the variance if entitlement spending was expected to exceed the fiscal year target by more than half of one percent. The president was ordered to recommend offsetting the excess over allowance with either specified spending cuts or tax increases, or else had to recommend that all or some of the amount be permitted and supply a clear justification. The House Budget Resolution had to incorporate budget savings at least equal to the amount recommended by the president. If such savings produced less than a total offset for the excess over targeted entitlement spending, this would have to be approved by a separate vote. Without such action, according to House rules, neither the budget resolution nor the thirteen regular appropriations bills could be considered.

As a limit on entitlement spending, the new controls certainly were not strong, nor were they intended to be. There was no mandatory enforcement of the entitlement targets. The president need not request savings to offset any spending excess. The House need not accept the president's recommendation. The Senate had chosen not to alter its rules and participate in the process. The restraints were focused only at the macrolevel and gave no hint how cuts might be applied to individual programs. There was no procedure for negotiation and no sequester provision threatening across-the-board reductions if negotiations failed. Moreover, there was no great political desire to implement the controls on entitlement spending, even if there was agreement to have them written into the reconciliation bill. Considerable cost increases could be accommodated without them ever being invoked. The main trigger was inflation rates substantially above forecast, and inflation had proved relatively moderate in recent years. Thus there was absolutely no fear for entitlement spending during fiscal years 1994 and 1995. Economic recovery, along with low inflation and low interest rates, caused the federal deficit to fall to $200 billion, the equivalent of approximately 3% of GDP. Regarding the food stamp program, the FY 1994 appropriation for $28.1 billion was $2.5 billion less than the administration initially requested, because utilization had declined and costs were far under projections. For FY 1995, the $28.7 billion appropriation was identical to the administration's request and was approved without controversy.

Nevertheless, entitlement spending during this period faced a gradually tightening noose. The review process was introduced without much foresight, as a mechanism accepted primarily to win votes for the reconciliation bill. It reflected the short-run outlook that dominates much of American politics and policymaking. Given weak enforcement and the brief lifetime of previous budgetary constraints, the Clinton administration and the Democratic majority in Congress clearly thought it was a minimal risk to take in exchange for a major legislative gain. Yet consequences are not entirely predictable. Symbolism has a way of affecting substance. For example, the food stamp caps of 1977 initially assumed a considerable leeway that disappeared rapidly at the unexpected onset of high inflation. In the highly partisan environment of the middle 1990s, it was not obvious how any equivalent situation would be managed.

Furthermore, the entitlement review process magnified the danger in a different way. It was a Democratic president, when establishing the new process by Executive Order, who spoke of "our chronic failure" to manage government finances, who called the recurrent deficit problem a major cause of increasing citizen cynicism, who announced that his plan would "go the extra mile" to ensure results different from those in the past, and who openly and proudly declared, "No longer can we permit entitlement spending to soar out of control without some concrete action being taken to restrain it."[15] Policy is sometimes demanded equal to the rhetoric. The president's own reasoning could be used to legitimate entitlement limits far more substantial than those now introduced for purposes of political expediency. Clinton's antideficit program depended upon continued economic growth, administrative efficiencies, and major health care reform. It was vulnerable to criticism from those insisting that control over finances could always be stricter, that deficits could be reduced faster, and that entitlement costs could further be restrained. If these were a major cause of government failure and public discontent, then the existing weak budgetary strictures were evidently insufficient. The number of steps the president would take toward fiscal conservatism were small given his background, beliefs, and partisan constituency. Yet for every step he took in that direction, his Republican opponents would demand that he go farther. Thus welfare entitlements and the size of the deficit were issues used successfully against the Democrats during the 1994 congressional elections. As the tenor of the political debate became increasingly more conservative, proposals to revive strict expenditure caps were advanced, differing somewhat by their definition of the reversion point and the enforcement mechanism for noncompliance. The Republican victories of November 1994 carried the potential to unleash them.

Spending Caps Return to the Political Agenda

Gramm-Rudman-Hollings had imposed strict limits on the total federal deficit but exempted entitlements from the mandatory sequestration process. PAYGO included entitlements in the sequestration process but did not impose strict limits on their growth. Increasingly, given the fiscalization of federal policymaking, this arrangement was challenged by those claiming that the only effective route to deficit control was through effective entitlement control. Not surprisingly, expenditure caps returned to active political consideration. They were proposed in different forms by Democrats and Republicans, presidents and congressmen, politicians and scholars. This section will briefly document the revived presence of entitlement caps in budget policy debates during the early 1990s and the mounting pressure to have some sort of cap formula instituted for federal welfare spending, including food stamps.

Consistent with its oversight role, the House Budget Committee in late 1991 conducted an extensive review of the nation's economy, the federal deficit, and the impact of the 1990 budget agreement. A report on long-term prospects authored by chairman Leon Panetta concluded "that resolving the deficit issue and making the necessary investments in growth, productivity and fairness should be the highest priority of the

Executive and the Congress over the coming ten years." The Democratic chairman of a Democratic-majority committee insisted that the effort "must begin immediately," and should include "sufficient entitlement cuts . . . to achieve annual savings of $55 billion to $105 billion below current law (that is, below the baseline) by FY 2001."[16] The report examined both substantive changes to entitlement policy and general enforcement procedures to compel spending reductions. Regarding the latter, "The Committee recommends the design of a cap, enforced through the budget process, on the growth of entitlement programs, in order to reduce their underlying growth rate to a sustainable figure." Panetta recognized the potential contradiction between entitlement caps and low-income assistance. He admitted the tension between aggregate spending controls and the multiplicity of policymaking jurisdictions in Congress. Yet he treated these as mere "technical issues" to be resolved in order to make the cap workable. "The concept of an entitlement cost cap is strongly endorsed by the Committee; and it deserves to be examined, carefully defined, and ultimately enacted."[17]

President Bush cited the House Budget Committee report in his January 1992 budget message. It provided justification for his own proposal, a fixed cap on the growth of mandatory spending. The PAYGO provisions, the budget message asserted, are "valuable and workable" but "there is a vast area of spending they do not reach: the entire structure of automatic expenditure." Mandatory programs constituted more than half the federal budget; continued rapid growth was expected over the coming five years. Restraining the growth of these programs therefore was one of the keys to effective deficit control. The president proposed to cap mandatory federal expenditures in the aggregate and to permit annual increments equal to the change in population plus the change in the Consumer Price Index plus an additional 2.5% (1.6% after the enactment of health reform). Any breach in the cap threshold would trigger a sequester imposing broad cost reductions, with only Social Security spending exempt. "This one procedural reform," the budget message insisted, "would go a long way toward remedying the most serious weakness in the discipline system of the current Budget Enforcement Act."[18] An "entitlement cost cap" was featured prominently in President Bush's campaign for reelection, although it was never incorporated into the administration's own budget estimates and the president carefully avoided providing substantive detail indicating where any savings relative to the current baseline might fall.[19]

A slightly modified version of the Bush proposal was advanced by the Republican leadership in both the House and Senate. It was offered as an amendment to the 1992 Senate Budget Resolution by Peter Domenici, cosponsored by fiscally conservative Democrats Sam Nunn and Charles Robb. According to the Domenici amendment, annual entitlement growth (exempting Social Security) would be limited to the inflation rate plus the change in the eligible population for each specific program, plus an additional growth allowance to facilitate transition declining from 2% in 1994 to zero by 1997. The debate on the Senate floor reflected the tensions inherent to entitlement budgeting and control. Cap proponents defended the whole against the parts. Procedurally, there was need to impose greater congressional supervision over that section of the budget flying on automatic pilot. (Yet the very purpose of entitlement status, advocates replied, is to grant specified programs special defenses against appropriations uncertainty and political discretion.) Substantively, there was need to impose control over the most rapidly growing portion of the budget, in order to mitigate the impact of entitlement spending on the deficit and limit its domination over other policy priorities. (Yet the very purpose of entitlement status, said the advocates, is to protect specified benefits, especially those serving needy and vulnerable households, against competing priorities and aggregate restraint.) "Frankly," claimed Domenici, "there are going to be all kinds of speeches . . . about this terrible plan and how it is going to hurt people." But he asked each beneficiary group, "before they get worked up about this, they listen to what is being proposed and they evaluate whether they want to be part of saving the United States economy or do they want it to go bankrupt?" He felt certain that they would answer, "Be fair in your reforms, in the changes here and there; we will sacrifice a bit; we will get a little less than we have grown used to spending," for otherwise we will endanger the economic health of the country and the prosperity promised to our children.[20]

Welfare cap opponents, by contrast, challenged the need for greater restraint, contending that it was a partisan move to help finance extensive tax cuts for the wealthy. More important, they defended their duty to the part against the claims of the whole. Mechanical budget procedures based on an arbitrary spending threshold would result in unwise and inequitable policies. Only a few entitlement programs had consistently experienced inflationary cost increases greater than the overall CPI. A more reasonable approach would narrowly address these programs, especially Medicare and Medicaid, and would carefully detail all proposed reforms. (Yet a cap mechanism gains plausibility exactly because such targeted program reforms are not politically practical.) A more compassionate approach would not threaten a reduction in benefits to the neediest of households, for reasons irrelevant to their standard of need. (Yet a cap mechanism gains effectiveness as a bargaining tool exactly because of the looming danger of such an undesirable outcome.) Opponents of the Domenici amendment argued that the cap proposal was a vulgar exercise in misdirection, for it appeared to impose budget control while hiding legislative responsibility for the policy changes or human suffering that might result.

The resolution to the Senate debate in 1992 came by means of political stratagem. The Democratic leadership in the Senate moved an amendment to exempt veterans programs from the proposed spending cap. Fiscal conservatives anticipated that formal entitlement control would be a symbol that mainstream legislators would be hesitant to reject. Welfare advocates regained the political advantage by first forcing legislators, in an election year, to choose whether to include veterans in the cap process. If they voted against the amendment, they would anger a powerful constituency. If they voted for it, they would undermine aggregate entitlement control and open the door for further exemptions. The Senate chose the latter option, exempting veterans benefits by a 66–28 margin. Domenici then withdrew his amendment from floor consideration. The basic issue, however, would emerge again and again.

In 1993, the Republican alternative to the Clinton budget promoted spending reductions in place of the administration's suggested revenue increase. The minority substitute to the Senate budget resolution included strict limitations on the growth of Medicare and Medicaid outlays. The Democratic leadership replied that this was an ill-timed move, as it would pre-empt the comprehensive health care reform scheduled to be considered later in the session. The Clinton administration was known to be considering a cap on health care costs, although ultimately it was not included in the reform package submitted to Congress.[21] In order to give the administration time to develop its own proposal, the leadership instead offered a sense-of-the-Senate resolution noting that the main cause of entitlement growth came from soaring Medicare and Medicaid costs and recommending that any forthcoming health reform should include substantial savings. The motion was approved overwhelmingly.

The Senate also considered a floor amendment from Sam Nunn to cap the growth of each individual entitlement program, allowing merely for changes in eligibility, plus inflation, plus a temporary allowance for the transition period. Whereas the 1992 cap effort grouped all entitlements together, threatening reductions in some due to the extraordinary expansion in others, the 1993 amendment adopted a more diverse approach, thereby penalizing just the offenders (particularly in health care, but also potentially in student loan and nutritional assistance programs). If outlays for any given mandatory program breached the cap, Congress would have sixty days to enact substantive changes bringing its spending back into line or else would face an automatic budget sequester for the amount in excess over allowance. Cap critics complained that it was capricious and unjust to deprive needy households of their benefits. Cap proponents replied that it was the only way to contain entitlement programs growing out of control. In part to protect the pending health care reform and in part to escape a politically difficult roll call vote, the Senate tabled the Nunn amendment, 51–47.

In 1994, the locus of debate shifted to the House. The House budget resolution of March included a sense-of-the-Congress provision calling for enforceable limits on the growth of entitlement spending. The Democratic leadership adopted a minimalist interpretation of the provision, moving in July merely to codify and clarify the terms of the president's executive order of the previous year. Disappointed by this action, Congressman Charles Steinholm, a fiscally conservative Democrat, proposed tight caps on the growth of total entitlement spending in order to force tough choices upon Congress. Steinholm's amendment proposed a mandatory sequester that included all entitlement programs, including Social Security. This was unacceptable to most legislators in an election year, and thus the amendment failed, 37–392. The Republican leadership equally complained that the majority bill was insufficient, that it was "another one of those warm and fuzzy, feel good but phony budget process fixes that does not fix a thing."[22] Their proposal was to insert an annual entitlement limit into each year's budget resolution along with instructions to the authorizing committees to produce the policy changes necessary to satisfy that limit. It would make budgeting for mandatory programs much more like budgeting for discretionary programs. Yet this proposal was unacceptable both to welfare liberals objecting that the net result would excessively constrain benefits for needy households and to avowed fiscal conservatives objecting that the net result would insufficiently constrain the total amount of entitlement spending. The Republican alternative thus failed, 194–233.[23]

As the year progressed, budget pressure on the administration grew. In October 1994, the leadership in Congress contrived to prevent the so-called A-to-Z deficit cutting plan from coming to the floor for a vote, and it negotiated a series of side agreements to guarantee that the discharge petition did not receive sufficient signatures. One of those arrangements allowed for Congressman Orton to present a sense-of-the-Congress resolution stating that current trends in entitlement spending were not sustainable and that Congress must act to resolve the long-term imbalance between entitlement promises and available funds. Orton's goal was to ensure that the issue of mandatory program budget control remained visible on the policy agenda, but critics replied that it was an ineffectual gesture and a waste of legislative time. The rule to allow floor consideration of Orton's motion failed, 83–339. In the end, therefore, no significant entitlement legislation was approved by either the House or Senate during the 103rd Congress. Yet the debate had become increasingly raucous, the rhetoric increasingly assertive, and the likelihood of action increasingly probable. Deficit reduction had emerged as a surprisingly popular cry. In a world in which raising taxes meant political suicide, in which discretionary spending already had been severely trimmed, and in which the notion of a public obligation to protect adequate welfare was increasingly under attack, it was logical to expect that the demand for effective entitlement restraint would reemerge with a vengeance.

Simultaneously with movements inside Congress, the idea of fixed dollar caps on the growth of entitlement outlays was receiving more favorable treatment in the academic community. Much of the impetus came from scholars of the pluralist school seeking to promote greater interest group competition as a means of reconciling preferences and improving the policy balance among organized factions. In the words of Aaron Wildavsky, the political scientist most responsible for the integration of pluralist theory and budgeting practice, "Since no single group can impose its preferences upon others within the American political system, special coalitions are formed to support or oppose specific policies. In this system of fragmented power, support is sought at numerous centers of influences. . . . Nowhere does a single authority have power to determine what is going to be in the budget."[24]

Unfortunately, Wildavsky argued, over the last twenty-five years the competitive budget game of interest group bargaining had largely been supplanted by a cooperative budget game of interest group subsidization. The norms of moderation, incrementalism, and balance eroded considerably. In their place came budgeting by addition, in which all claimants with access could obtain and secure benefits, resulting in higher domestic spending and rising deficits. Entitlement rules contributed importantly to this new budget order, escaping annual review while establishing privilege to those programs fortunate enough to win designation. Citizens were becoming increasingly dissatisfied by a budget politics devoid of norms and controls. In Wildavsky's view, interests were winning more but enjoying it less. Yet voluntary retrenchment was illogical. The situation, in game theoretical terms, is an n-person prisoners' dilemma. If other claimants retreated from their demands, aggregate budget pressures would ease and so it would be safe for any single group to pursue self-interested favors. If other claimants did not retreat from their demands, then aggregate pressures would persist regardless of the behavior of any single group and so the group would be foolish to abandon the pursuit of self-interested gain. The implication is, whether or not other factions accept benefit sacrifices, a rational interest group will continue to demand benefits; thus all rational groups will continue to demand benefits; therefore negative budget externalities will persist despite general condemnation. Wildavsky's conclusion was that Americans needed rules to bind themselves against the temptation toward mutually disastrous action, to be achieved by placing limits upon budgeting by addition and forcing stronger competition among interests for the available federal resources. His recommendation was a constitutional amendment linking the change in total outlays to the change in the nation's GDP.[25] However, he was practical enough to know that the dispersed and decentralized forces of American politics could likely overwhelm any budget regime that first seeks to define the aggregate total and then allocates separate amounts by means of subtraction.[26]

Following a parallel logic, for example, health reform spokesman Theodore Marmor proposed a "global budget" to help contain Medicare outlays. Expenditure caps, argued Marmor, compel providers to negotiate agreements regarding the rationing of services. They would help replace the present system that merely pays all reasonable and customary charges, not by the dictates of a central authority but instead by giving organized interests a stake in restraining each other's costs. "Limiting Medicare's budget will eliminate its perennial tendency to foil budget planners with unpredictable rates of growth, it will keep its expenditures in line with inflation, and it will force the tough decisions and hard bargaining necessary for cost control."[27] Similarly, to select just one further example, Allen Schick in his superb textbook on the federal budget process writes that a cap on entitlement spending is the leading candidate to fill the hole in the PAYGO system of budget control. The cap "can be made to work" with careful design, such that it specifies in law the trigger conditions and the formula by which savings would be achieved and allows Congress the option to eschew entitlement cutbacks if this accords with its political and budgetary priorities.[28]

Finally, as the 1994 elections approached, the need for entitlement caps was proclaimed by two important extra-parliamentary bodies. The first was the ill-fated Bipartisan Commission on Entitlement and Tax Reform. The proposed reform package coauthored by its chairmen, Senators Kerrey and Danforth, included a 10% cut in entitlement spending, apart from Social Security and health care, by the year 2000, and a cap on further program growth limited to inflation and population change. The justification was to "share the costs of planning for the future" and to "ensure that our tax dollars are spent judiciously." Among the other plans debated by the commission, an entitlement cap was accepted as a means of budgetary savings in the alternative package advanced by more conservative commissioners, while it was rejected as too sweeping and inequitable by the liberals.[29]

The second was the "Contract With America" issued by the House Republican Conference and used as a platform in the 1994 campaign. The contract's draft "Personal Responsibility Act" called for a strict cap on total spending by AFDC, SSI, and housing assistance programs. Growth would be linked to inflation plus changes in the national poverty population, and reconciliation instructions would require that the authorizing committees of Congress make the substantive changes in policy necessary to comply with the spending caps imposed. The food stamp program was not included here. Instead, it would be grouped with a number of other nutrition programs and replaced by a consolidated block grant to the states, with funding set at 95% of the aggregate amount for the separate programs and allocated to the states relative to their proportion of economically disadvantaged individuals. Growth in nutrition block grant spending would be limited to the percentage change in the U.S. population and the percentage change in the food component of the Consumer Price Index, calculated for the preceding fiscal year. Explicitly, entitlement status for welfare households would be terminated as a necessary corollary of these cap arrangements.[30] The "Contract with America" was merely a campaign document, but Republican legislative victory in November 1994 made it inevitable that some form of entitlement cap proposal—including the revival of caps applied narrowly to the food stamp program—would appear prominently on the agenda for the 104th Congress.

Conclusion

The inherent logic of entitlement budgeting dominated food stamp politics and policy during the last years of the Bush and the first years of the Clinton administrations. The pattern of strategic behavior had been seen before. Food stamp play under Bush was analogous to that under Ford—partisan stalemate meant policy equilibrium at the entitlement reversion point, freely permitting cost underestimation and rhetorical excess. Food stamp play under Clinton was analogous to that under Carter—unified Democratic governance meant moderate policy liberalization but increased concern over uncontrollable cost pressures. Entitlement budgeting during these years, moreover, prompted the return of spending restraint proposals to the legislative agenda. Accepted in a very weak form by moderates seeking to assuage deficit fears, they helped give validation to certain more extreme claims that the aggregate national budget was endangered by the special protections granted to the welfare segment. Cap proposals in different versions thereafter appeared as a mainstay of dissenting spending resolutions, especially from fiscal conservatives.

To their proponents, entitlement spending caps had become an indicator of one's political commitment to significant deficit reduction. They would assist legislators to constrain the upward drift in government outlays and regain conscious choice over more aspects of the budget. The hope seemed to be, despite a skepticism drawn from the past, that the introduction of the proper institutional mechanism would somehow help establish the correct policy balance. Yet there was no easy consensus regarding how a successor to Gramm-Rudman-Hollings would be constructed and enforced; how to treat old age retirement and health care, the largest entitlement categories; or how to ensure welfare cost containment when the poor are most vulnerable to the fluctuations of macroeconomic fortune. Differences in political partisanship and policy beliefs deterred action during the initial two Clinton years, while pressures continued to build.

The familiarity of the observed political behavior during this period, 1991–94, should be taken as evidence that the form of budgetary rule strongly influences the character of budgetary behavior. Individuals react to the formal structures of politics in relatively predictable and stable ways. The return of food stamps to effective entitlement status entailed a change in reversion point, affecting as hypothesized the strategic positions adopted and policy proposals advanced by interested actors. Beneath the apparent flux of everyday political contests lie certain logical patterns available for social science analysis and prediction. The main difference in food stamp entitlement politics between the late 1970s and the early 1990s was the increased fiscalization of the U.S. legislative agenda. The extent of budgetary conflict had expanded enormously and thus the issue of entitlement control included but went far beyond the food stamp program by itself. Importantly, however, the dilemmas of policy choice, reflected in the recurrent entitlement cap debate, remained invariant. Despite increased scope and intensity, politicians continued to confront the tensions between recipient guarantees and spending restraint, substantive adjustments and procedural mandates, welfare equity and democratic discretion.

Notes—Chapter 8

1. Allen Schick, *The Federal Budget: Politics, Policy, Process* (Washington, D.C.: Brookings Institution, 1995): 123–26.

2. House *Report* 101–598, 111.

3. On the politics of "Dire Emergency" supplemental appropriations in 1991, see Daniel P. Franklin, *Making Ends Meet: Congressional Budgeting in the Age of Deficits* (Washington, D.C.: Congressional Quarterly Press, 1993): 129–30, 139–51.

4. House *Report* 102–396, 1; Senate *Report* 102–252, 1.

5. House *Report* 102–396, 24–26.

6. *Congressional Record* 138: H 7548.

7. *Congressional Record* 138: H 7557, H 7560.

8. Regarding the continuing tension between program expansion and fiscal restraint, see Bob Woodward, *The Agenda: Inside the Clinton White House* (New York: Simon & Schuster, 1994); and also Elizabeth Drew, *On Edge: The Clinton Presidency* (New York: Simon & Schuster, 1994).

9. House *Report* 103–11, 16.

10. William J. Clinton, "Remarks at a Conference on Entitlements in Bryn Mawr, Pennsylvania," December 13, 1993, *Public Papers of the Presidents of the United States, William J. Clinton, 1993*, 2163.

11. William J. Clinton, "Remarks on Establishing the Bipartisan Commission on Entitlement Reforms and an Exchange with Reporters," November 5, 1993, *Public Papers of the Presidents of the United States, William J. Clinton, 1993*, 1904–05; J. Robert Kerrey and John C. Danforth, Letter to Commission Members, June 8, 1994, Papers of the Bipartisan Commission on Entitlement and Tax Reform.

12. Bipartisan Commission on Entitlement and Tax Reform, *Final Report to the President* (Washington, D.C.: U.S. Government Printing Office, 1995).

13. Congressman Thomas Downey, quoted in Eric Pianin, "Entitlement Panel Fails to Set Plan," *Washington Post*, December 15, 1994, sec. A: 18.

14. House *Report* 103–111, 966.

15. William J. Clinton, "Remarks on Signing Executive Orders on Budget Control and the Deficit Reduction Fund and an Exchange with Reporters," August 4, 1993, *Public Papers of the Presidents of the United States, William J. Clinton, 1993*, 1333.

16. U.S. House of Representatives, Committee on the Budget, "Restoring America's Future: Preparing the Nation for the 21st Century," a report by Leon E. Panetta, Serial CP-5 (1991): 2, 17.

17. U.S. House of Representatives, Committee on the Budget, "Restoring America's Future: Preparing the Nation for the 21st Century," a report by Leon E. Panetta, Serial CP-5 (1991): 20–21.

18. Office of Management and Budget, Executive Office of the President, *Budget of the United States Government, Fiscal Year 1993*, Part I (1992): 15–17.

19. Congress of the United States, Congressional Budget Office, "An Analysis of the President's Budgetary Proposals for Fiscal Year 1993," March 1992, 10; Viveca Novak, "Entitlements Waltz," *National Journal*, (October 17, 1992): 2364–68.

20. *Congressional Record* 138: S 5415–18.

21. Adam Clymer, "White House Drops Concept Of a Cap on Health Spending," *New York Times*, October 29, 1993, sec. A: 1, 9.

22. *Congressional Record* 140: H 5973.

23. These votes provide an excellent illustration of the power of the congressional leadership to structure the sequence of legislative decision-making. Mainstream Democrats preferred the codification option; mainstream Republicans preferred the budget resolution option; deficit hawks preferred the entitlement cap option. None of the three were certain of a majority. The Democratic leadership preserved procedural fairness, subjecting each option to a floor vote, but arranged the order of voting so as to ensure victory for its preferred position. The budget resolution proposal was considered first,

which was defeated by a coalition of Democrats and deficit hawks, each of whom had a preferred, live, option on the agenda. The entitlement cap proposal was considered second, which was defeated by a coalition of mainstream Democrats and Republicans, both of whom feared the political reaction from a fixed cap that included Social Security. This left codification as the sole option remaining on the agenda, which was supported relative to the status quo by many legislators who had demanded more aggressive action because it was the only entitlement control move then available.

24. Aaron Wildavsky and Naomi Caiden, *The New Politics of the Budgetary Process,* 3rd ed. (New York: Addison Wesley, 1997): 266.

25. Aaron Wildavsky, *How to Limit Government Spending* (Berkeley: University of California Press, 1990).

26. Joseph White and Aaron Wildavsky, *The Deficit and the Public Interest* (Berkeley: University of California Press, 1989); Wildavsky and Caiden, *The New Politics of the Budgetary Process,* 163–68, 258–59.

27. Theodore Marmor, "The Medicare Solution," *The Washington Monthly,* September 1995, 37.

28. Schick, *The Federal Budget,* 202–03.

29. Bipartisan Commission on Entitlement and Tax Reform, 27, 36–37, 116–17, 152, 246–47.

30. House Republican Conference, "Contract With America," *Legislative Digest,* September 27, 1994.

NINE

Block Heads: Food Stamp Budget Control and the Politics of Welfare Reform, 1995–1996

According to the "Contract with America" issued by the House Republican Conference in September 1994, the party's blueprint for welfare reform would include a cap on the "spending growth of AFDC, SSI and numerous public housing programs, and the mandatory work program established under the bill." The cap would equal "the amount spent the preceding year for these programs with an adjustment for inflation plus growth in poverty population." Food stamps were not to be included within the cap, but instead would be consolidated with a number of other nutrition programs into a block grant to the states, "funded in the first year at 95 percent of the aggregate amount of the individual programs."[1]

According to the House version of the Personal Responsibility Act, passed by the new Republican majority in March 1995, AFDC, child and foster care, school meals, and special nutrition aid for pregnant women and young children would all be transformed into block grants to the states funded approximately at current levels. Yet the block grant option intentionally was rejected for the food stamp program, which would be retained as a federal entitlement but with its expenditures capped. Unless overridden by explicit legislation, program obligations could not exceed the amount of the current CBO estimate, adjusted only for the provisions of the welfare reform act.[2]

The Senate and final versions of the 1995 welfare bill maintained this curious reversal from the original "Contract," in which AFDC would be transformed into a block grant while food stamps would become a capped entitlement. Regarding budget status, the main change made to the food stamp program in conference was the specification of strict dollar ceilings for given fiscal years, parallel to the situation that prevailed from FY 1977 to FY 1990. Expenditures were authorized for seven years, with a fixed maximum of $25.4 billion in FY 1996, declining to $24.6 billion in FY 1997, and then rising slowly to $29.8 billion by FY 2002. The secretary of agriculture was instructed to monitor projected outlays and to report regularly to the House and Senate agriculture committees. "If the Secretary finds that program funding requirements for a year will exceed allowed obligations, the Secretary must direct States to reduce allotments to the extent necessary to stay within the obligation limits for the year."[3]

President Clinton vetoed this version of the welfare bill on January 9, 1996, claiming that it "was designed to meet an arbitrary budget target rather than to achieve serious reform."[4] The farm bill enacted in March 1996 authorized food stamp appropriations through FY 1997 without any mention of an expenditure cap. The revised Personal Responsibility Act passed in midsummer and signed by the president simply extended this authority through FY 2002. Similarly, the balanced budget agreement of 1997 negotiated between Congress and the president contained no cap provision affecting food stamp expenditures, not even a specified ceiling on the growth of mandatory outlays. Therefore, although threatened throughout the 104th Congress by more stringent forms of budget rule, the food stamp program ultimately retained its standing as a welfare entitlement. In essence, it is a story of what did not happen.

This chapter will consider food stamp politics and policy during the recent era of welfare reform. The argument proceeds in three stages. First, attending to the increasing fiscalization of welfare provision in America, it analyzes block grants as a complex budget arrangement, involving a fixed appropriation from the federal government to the states, a formula distributing this allocation among the states, and a set of autonomous spending decisions by the states that might or might not prove adequate to meet recipient need. Each of these was controversial. Second, the chapter considers the fate of food stamp expenditure controls during the legislative battles of 1995–96, examining the reasons why the program escaped devolution to the states and then tracing the retreat in Congress from block grants to caps to restored entitlement. Third, the chapter distinguishes two alternative routes to welfare savings—a top-down approach based on aggregate controls that is relatively unspecific regarding their effect on individual provisions, and a bottom-up approach based on a number of small, separate, and substantive cuts in eligibility and benefits that may not necessarily meet aggregate targets. In the end, food stamps under welfare reform reflected the latter route. Nevertheless, the evidence will show that formalized expenditure limits remained an active item on the policy agenda, and that the eventual legislative decision not to utilize them was based primarily on short-run political expediency. Despite past experience and the intense debates of the early 1990s, there was virtually no intentional consideration of the tension between nutritional sufficiency and budget control, no careful deliberation, and no emerging policy consensus.

Much recent attention has been devoted to the case of means-tested cash support, as AFDC was transformed in 1996 into the Temporary Assistance to Needy Families (TANF) block grant to the states. The purpose of this chapter is to show that there was a strong fiscal dimension to the demand for welfare devolution and that there were fiscal patterns other than devolution embodied in the Personal Responsibility Act. The principal outcome from this brief but frantic period of policy reform—for those programs like food stamps that escaped assignment to the states and for the federal budget overall—was a series of bottom-up cuts affecting individual provisions but no effective top-down limitations upon entitlement status. The combination is potentially unstable to the extent that it signals simultaneously restrained and unconstrained welfare spending. Thus it might well prove transitory given the onset of new fiscal pressures.

Block Grants as a Form of Budget Rule

John Engler, the Republican governor of Michigan, appeared before the Ways and Means Committee in mid-January 1995 and placed on the table before him a high stack of documents representing the rules and regulations for AFDC, food stamps, and Medicaid. The complexity of these programs, the inconsistencies across them, and the propensity for micromanagement from Washington, he said, comprised a barrier that limited flexibility and deterred efforts to lower the poverty rate. Speaking on behalf of Republican governors, Engler called for block grants to the states to replace these separate programs, in order to foster innovation and permit more efficient operations. "Washington has had 60 years to tackle the welfare problem. It is time to give the States a chance. Certainly we can do better than the current Federal system that is represented by these rules and regulations."[5]

Part of Engler's justification was that a system of welfare block grants would save the government money. "How much money can we save with nationwide reform? Plenty."[6] Yet Engler was hesitant to estimate the value of increased state flexibility in terms of a percentage to be cut from current program costs. Instead, he indicated that the governors were willing to accept a fixed allocation from the federal government, possibly a five-year freeze using FY 1995 as the baseline. "I think the best solution," Engler told the House Agriculture Committee a few weeks later, "is to say, 'Here, States. Here's the money for the Food Stamp Program.' And then we'll write the rules to make sure that they work."[7] Not all commentators were so sanguine. The attractiveness of the block grant plan, argued some critics, lay in the promise of reduced federal responsibilities, both financial and substantive. It is a politician's dream to spend less money yet avoid blame for the consequences. "Block grants," said Senator John Breaux of Louisiana, "are like taking all the problems that we have with the welfare program and putting them in a box, then wrapping it all up, tying a bow around it, and then mailing that box of problems to the States, saying: Here, it is yours. It is a block grant. It is a block grant of problems with less money to help solve those problems. That, I think, is not a solution."[8]

In a sense, a block grant can be seen as a form of budget rule that constrains the amount available for program spending, comprised of three different elements. First, there is the federal outlay to the states. If this dollar amount is specified by the authorizing legislation for some given number of years, then the block grant operates as a strict allocation that cannot be altered without explicit congressional action. If the amount is not specified or if the authorizing legislation establishes only a maximum ceiling, then the block grant is subject to the annual appropriations process and must compete against other possible uses of government funds. Either way, a welfare block grant entails the abandonment of entitlement status, for the level of federal spending is no longer adjusted automatically given changing recipient demand and macroeconomic conditions.

Second, there is the distribution of federal block grant expenditures among the states. For example, a distribution that copies the existing apportionment gives advantage to those states with abnormally generous program enforcement or abnormally high rates of current utilization. Yet a distribution that is tied to underlying population need (for example, the percentage of households living under the poverty threshold) provides a windfall to states that have made little effort to enroll and/or serve their poverty households. The choice of formula for state allocation thus invites political conflict, as the potential winners and losers will struggle over their slices of the fiscal pie.

Third, there are the funding decisions adopted by the separate states. The states desire to receive their block grants free from all restraints and conditions. This would ensure maximum flexibility and reward states for lowering their welfare burdens. The federal government would prefer regulations to ensure that the money it contributes actually is spent to assist recipient households. This would prevent states from arbitrarily reducing payments and using the funds for other purposes. Similarly, the states desire the liberty to pocket all administrative cost reductions as an incentive to more efficient operations. The federal government would prefer to share in any potential savings. At issue is the degree of permissible state autonomy within the new budgetary arrangement. Such autonomy, however, becomes risky during recession or natural disasters, when there are extraordinary and unanticipated claims for program benefits. One option is to establish an emergency federal fund or to require the states to establish their own, yet this violates the principle of local responsibility. The alternative is to leave the states alone to find supplemental dollars from higher taxes or competing programs if they wish to avoid denying welfare benefits despite rising need.

By implication, the tension between guaranteed assistance and budget discretion remains inescapable, although it is given a slightly novel articulation within the block grant format. The difficulties of adequate welfare provision absent entitlement protection are magnified under block grants, given the presence of multiple levels of government and the interactions between them. Yet the opportunities for spending constraint are also magnified through a combination of a limited federal outlay, a set formula for apportionment, and the separate state appropriations responsive to local conditions. Each of these three elements, we shall see, were visible in the debate over the Personal Responsibility Act, potentially regarding the proposed food stamp block grant but with important consequences regarding the TANF block grant enacted to replace AFDC.

The first element concerns the total amount of federal spending. When introducing the Personal Responsibility Act before the Senate, Robert

Dole listed three fundamental justifications—state autonomy, a strong work requirement, and substantial cost reduction. "No program with an unlimited budget will ever be made to work effectively and efficiently. Therefore, we must put a cap on welfare spending."[9] A strict limit upon federal obligations equally was a strong motivation for the advocates of the food stamp block grant. Those seeking to attach such a provision to the bill spoke of the "dramatic and rapid increase" in food stamp costs over time, faster than the growth in population and caused in part by insufficient oversight and faulty program management. They cited an opinion poll showing that 60% of Americans believed the budget deficit should be reduced by cutting food stamps.[10] The potential reduction in federal food stamp outlays threatened to be quite sizable. For example, a USDA analysis showed that a block grant as originally proposed in the "Contract with America" would diminish government nutrition outlays in FY 1996 by more than $5.1 billion, the equivalent of 12.7%. As the block grant would be adjusted only for changes in U.S. population and the inflation rate during the previous year, the gap predicted for spending under existing versus decentralized nutrition programs would widen over time. Moreover, the actual gap might be even larger as economic forecasts often err. The USDA simulated the five-year pattern of spending on the assumption that the proposed block grant rule had been implemented in FY 1989 and compared the result to real program costs. For FY 1994, the deficiency would have been more than $12.5 billion, producing more than a one-third cut in nutrition outlays. This would have had a clear and adverse impact upon dietary intake and public health, especially among children of low-income families.[11]

Block grant defenders denied that lower federal spending would affect program benefits, citing the administrative efficiencies expected from greater state autonomy. Yet the claim was contradicted by evidence from a series of USDA demonstration projects conducted during the 1980s that attempted to standardize and simplify food stamp benefit calculations for families already found eligible for AFDC. In all cases, the efficiency savings were modest. "This should not be that surprising," asserted Robert Greenstein, executive director of the Center on Budget and Policy Priorities. "In every state, the same agency already administers both the AFDC and food stamp programs, and the two programs use the same application forms."[12] Greenstein also argued that block grant reductions in federal nutrition spending would probably be much larger than anticipated because of its discretionary status within the budget process. The USDA calculations were based on the ceiling for possible expenditures. "The amount actually appropriated would likely be below the ceiling, as is true for most discretionary programs."[13] Food assistance would have to struggle annually against other spending priorities. Programs with weak political constituencies tend to fare poorly, especially during times of budget austerity with increasingly intense competition for a shrinking pool of available funds. President Clinton made a similar point before the National Conference of State Legislatures, using the example of the Community Development Block Grant while he was governor of Arkansas. The dollar amount "was held constant for a decade. So in real terms, it got smaller and smaller and smaller."[14] To conservative delight and liberal dismay, the impact of a potential block grant on federal nutrition spending would most likely be substantial.

The estimated fiscal impact on the food stamp program was purely hypothetical, as Congress ultimately did not choose to transform it into a block grant to the states. The parallel controversy concerning AFDC, however, was quite real. Early in the debate, the Department of Health and Human Services reported simulation results for a five-year welfare block grant fixed at 103% of spending for FY 1987. By FY 1993, federal outlays would have been 26% lower than actually occurred, with 47 of 50 states receiving less funds.[15] The final version of the Personal Responsibility Act was incorporated within a reconciliation bill, in part to symbolize that the effort to slow the growth of welfare spending was an aspect of an overall strategy to reduce the federal deficit.[16] Nevertheless, the states were allowed to select a favorable baseline for the TANF block grant and they were guaranteed the full $16.4 billion appropriation through FY 2001 to protect against discretionary budgeting in Congress. In fact, according to CBO projections, the TANF block grant would initially award more money to the states than they would have received under the prior law, which served as an incentive for enactment. Over time, however, economic and population changes would produce a shortfall, which by FY 2002 was expected to exceed $1 billion.[17] Critics loudly complained that any fixed grant scheme would prove inadequate, with rising dollar deficiencies compared to current law that would not be matched by reduced caseloads or greater efficiencies.

The second aspect of block grants as a form of budget rule concerns the formula for fund allocation among the states. Each formula produces a different pattern of relative winners and losers, thereby engendering controversy. Regarding the potential food stamp block grant, the USDA estimated the payment distribution for a system based on the number of eligible households per state and found wide cross-state disparities. Compared to FY 1996 actual spending, fourteen states would sacrifice as much as 20% of their food stamp funds. Texas would lose more than $1.1 billion, whereas California would gain $650 million.[18] The states that would suffer most were the ones with greater utilization rates, for they would have comparatively high current food stamp costs relative to the eligible population. In response, advocates for the food stamp block grant in Congress proposed a five-year plan based instead on the level of actual FY 1994 food stamp payments per state. The problem here, as President Clinton pointed out, is that states' demography and job opportunity structures change at different rates, and thus it will be very difficult to devise a fixed yet equitable "formula that keeps you from getting hurt . . . over a 5-year period." He expressed doubt, as assistance needs evolved over time, that any block grant system could keep pace with the demands faced by many individual states, locking them "into a real bind."[19] Under entitlement, food stamps had acted somewhat as a stabilizer, automatically adjusting payments to help economically disadvantaged states facing increased nutritional demand. A long-term block grant formula grounded upon a single base year prevents that flexibility. Unless supplemented by a state's own resources, program rules would no longer guarantee funding adequate to ensure that all qualified individuals—regardless of location within the U.S.—could escape going hungry.

Again, a distributional issue that merely threatened to affect food stamps was in fact a matter of serious contention with regard to the actual block grant that replaced AFDC. The House bill would apportion the TANF grant among the states based upon their previous share of federal family assistance spending. In addition, a small fund was made available to compensate states that had experienced population growth. The Senate Finance Committee deleted this supplemental fund, and thus it proposed to allocate grant money to each state equal exactly to the amount paid for AFDC and related programs in FY 1994. This incited a protest from southern and southwestern senators claiming that any formula defined by the old welfare regime merely replicated the status quo and discriminated against states that had historically low benefit levels or were experiencing rapid population growth. The response, especially from northeastern and midwestern senators, was that no state should be forced to cut its welfare effort because of a dramatic reduction from the funding level it currently receives. The month-and-a-half delay between the committee report and Senate floor consideration was in part caused by an intraparty Republican dispute over the funding formula. The eventual compromise was to maintain retrospective funding, giving states the option of the 1995 amount, the 1994 amount, or an average of 1992–94 amounts. In addition, there would be a supplemental fund of $878 million (later reduced to $800 million by the conference committee) reserved for states with below national average benefit levels and above national average population growth rates; states with considerable variance from either threshold would also qualify. Nevertheless, this was not sufficient to satisfy all the critics. Amendments were attempted on the Senate floor to revise the supplemental fund based on the growth rate for poor families within a state and to revise the entire allocation formula based simply on the number of poor children. The effort was made again in 1996, when the welfare bill was revived and later enacted.

Finally, the effectiveness of a block grant system depends on the activities of the individual states. The degree of federal control over state appropriations constitutes the third aspect of such grants as a budgetary arrangement. Regarding food stamps, a federal block grant would entail the establishment of fifty different state programs, each with its own set of eligibility rules and benefit levels, thus abandoning any national commitment to ensure a minimally nutritional diet for all Americans. Given complete autonomy, a state need not maintain its current level of financial commitment. "The Governors may decide," said Senator Richard Lugar, "in fact, to use the money for something else. If you happen to be a citizen of one of those States, you are out of luck."[20] Lugar also feared a competitive "race to the bottom," because states that could keep their surplus federal dollars would have an incentive to set benefits low relative to their neighbors, so as not to serve as a magnet for needy populations.

A different concern about state-level financing was based on unintentional rather than intentional deficiencies, especially from unanticipated changes in economic conditions. During times of recession or natural disaster, program demand increases but state revenues decline. As Delaware governor Thomas Carper warned, "The day will come when state economies are in a slump, and when that day comes families who never dreamed they would be dependent on food stamps will need them, and states won't have the resources to provide them."[21] This was the subject of a colloquy between Senators Kent Conrad and Rick Santorum, the former a Democratic critic and the latter a Republican supporter of food stamp block grants. Conrad used the example of Florida, which had stable food stamp utilization for a number of years before suffering in the early 1990s the combined effects of deep recession and Hurricane Andrew. "No block grant could have responded to the increase in families that needed food stamps in Florida during this time. No State would have been able to predict or prepare for this dramatic growth in demand for food assistance." Santorum replied that prudent state planners should have the wisdom to prepare for emergencies, saving a share of allocated dollars in a rainy day fund. Conrad doubted whether sufficient funds would ever be saved. Santorum responded that a state could always speed up the pace of appropriations or use its own resources. Conrad claimed that it was wrong to put children at risk because of possible planning mistakes. Santorum agreed that some risk always exists, but that governors are not fools and that the decision should be theirs to make. "If their eyes were not open, they certainly are open now as a result of our discussion." Conrad answered, "the notion that Governors are put on notice because we in the Senate have a debate at 3 o'clock in the afternoon on Friday is probably not a very reliable thing for any of us to depend upon."[22]

Again, an issue that was hypothetical with regard to the food stamp program was instead quite significant as AFDC was replaced by a block grant system. Regarding intentional deficiencies, the initial bill gave the states virtually complete independence to use federal TANF funds as they found reasonable. Moreover, nothing in the act was "intended to limit in any way the manner in which a State may spend its own funds on aid for needy families."[23] Critics claimed that this was irresponsible because it merely turned federal funds over to the states, and they demanded language requiring that the states maintain the level of their prior welfare effort. In the search for support from moderates in Congress, the provision was altered over several iterations. The final bill insisted that the states continue to spend at least 75% of the amount they previously had allotted for AFDC, 80% if they had failed to place a required number of welfare recipients into the workforce. Significantly, the Senate explicitly rejected an amendment to mandate that the states actually guarantee fully funded benefits to all households that they had defined as legitimately qualifying for aid, which would have reestablished entitlement, although at the state level. Regarding unintentional deficiencies, the initial bill contained little protection against economic downturn except for a rainy day loan fund of $1 billion ($1.7 billion in the Senate version) that the states could draw upon in emergencies but would have to repay with interest over three years. The final act added an incentive to the states to establish their own rainy day reserves and established a $2 billion contingency fund available to states experiencing high and rising unemployment rates or welfare caseloads. Such provisions helped to make the Personal Responsibility Act more palatable to legislators concerned about the limits of state financial capacity.

A block grant system entails more than the devolution of welfare rulemaking and administration from the federal government to the states. It is also a budget arrangement useful for constraining expenditures, a fact that was apparent to proponents and opponents alike. As a budget arrangement, a block grant implies the rejection of entitlement protections. There no longer exists a promise that funds will be provided sufficient for all enrolled individuals to receive the benefits for which they are eligible under prevailing law. Fiscal deficiencies could occur at three different levels: the national level because federal appropriations need not be maintained equal to the initial commitment; the distributional level because the apportionment formula need not reflect changing conditions among the states; and the state level because spending by each of the fifty separate welfare programs need not be adequate to meet recipient demand, especially in times of economic recession or natural disaster. Block grant proponents celebrated the opportunity to take welfare off of automatic pilot, thereby increasing political control over the extent of public charity. They downplayed the attendant risk, believing that greater state innovation would reduce caseloads and program costs. Eliminating entitlement would provide an extra incentive for individuals to end welfare dependency and for states to pursue efficiency. Block grant opponents were far less optimistic. One striking aspect of the Personal Responsibility Act is the fact that AFDC ultimately was transformed into the TANF block grant, whereas food stamps were left unchanged as a federal entitlement. It is a surprising asymmetry, hardly predictable from the Republican "Contract with America."

Food Stamps and Welfare Reform

To conservative welfare reform advocates, there was no logical reason to treat cash and food assistance differently. The Republican governors regularly demanded that both programs be transformed into block grants to the states. More than fifty Republican members of Congress, mostly freshmen, signed a letter urging that policy remain loyal to the original "Contract." It was contradictory to redesign AFDC in a fundamental fashion but merely tinker with food stamps. Devolution of welfare to the states allegedly would improve flexibility and innovation, control costs, decrease fraud, and cut bureaucratic red tape. If true in general, it should also be true for food stamps. The new Republican majority had promised bold and consistent action, and it should seek nothing less than comprehensive welfare reform. The governors, announced one legislator, deserve independence to help solve the welfare problems they understand best. "To only give them two-thirds of the tools they need is like playing golf without a putter. You can't finish."[24]

Yet Congress, despite Republican leadership, did not comply. The House Ways and Means Committee had quickly decided that it would favor the Republican governors over the "Contract with America," and thus it adopted a block grant system in place of AFDC. The House Agriculture Committee, however, rejected both the governors' appeal and the original "Contract," preferring a lesser reform. Chairman Pat Roberts expressed "real reservations" regarding block grants at the very first committee hearing of 1995. Instead, he declared, his prime mission was to clean up fraud and make the food stamp program more cost-efficient.[25] Supported by Bill Emerson, chairman of the subcommittee on nutrition, Roberts warmly praised the idea of "one-step shopping" for individuals receiving benefits under multiple welfare programs. To promote integration and compatibility, the House bill proposed that states have the option to establish one uniform set of eligibility and benefit rules for those families applying simultaneously for TANF and food stamps. The goal was simplification in implementation and management. Nevertheless, it was a far step from eliminating food stamps as a federal entitlement. The House Agriculture Committee voted 5–37 against transforming food stamps into a block grant. A block grant amendment offered on the House floor failed 114–316, with Republicans divided almost evenly and Democrats opposed almost unanimously. The Senate Agriculture Committee similarly refused the block grant option, and a substitute motion on the Senate floor failed 36–64, with one-third of Republicans joining the Democrats by voting against it.

Given the challenge from the ideological right, the Republican agriculture committee leadership had to explain its preference, retaining food stamps as an entitlement program while rejecting devolution to the states. The main justification offered by Roberts in the House and by his equivalent Richard Lugar in the Senate was that food stamps were a necessary safety net for those who rely on public assistance. According to Lugar, "there must be a safety net, basically, for eating, for nutrition—a safety net against starvation in this country."[26] This was especially valuable given the transition to a new welfare system in the states. The freedom to experiment, it was argued, would be enhanced by the existence of a secure nutrition entitlement remaining at the federal level. Food stamps, with a uniform national benefit structure linked to net income, had always served an equalizing function given the wide disparities in AFDC payments by state. It could now provide a backstop against possible TANF program deficiencies. In addition, the agriculture leadership expressed worry that a block grant establishing separate state food assistance programs would not sufficiently protect against fraud and abuse, and that it could not ensure appropriate job training for able recipients. Chairman Roberts even asserted that there was nothing in the Republican "Contract" that actually called for "block grants of cash" to be given over to the states.[27]

The Republican governors protested and were placated by somewhat greater policy discretion. After a 2½-hour meeting and conference call, the House Agriculture Committee agreed to permit any state with a functioning Electronic Benefits Transfer system (using debit cards in place of food coupons) to receive its food stamp funds as a block grant. This was largely symbolic in the short run as, despite thirteen years of urging from Congress, only Maryland currently could qualify and most states were years away from operating such a system. In addition, the House committee agreed that welfare beneficiaries holding a job in private industry, paying at least $350 per month, could get their food aid in cash rather than stamps. Governor Engler conceded that these changes were in the right direction, although they were hardly satisfying to the states seeking more dollars and less federal control. Equally, however, the changes were frightening to food stamp proponents concerned about maintaining nation-wide protections against hunger. "This could be the beginning of the end of the food stamp program," warned Robert Fersh of the Food Research and Action Center.[28]

The leadership's explanation was somewhat superficial and not necessarily convincing. If the states could be trusted to manage the TANF block grant, then why not food stamps? If welfare recipients deserved an adequate safety net, then why only in nutrition assistance and not cash? The inconsistency in treatment stripped some of the luster from the self-proclaimed Republican revolution and strained the unity among Republican ranks in Congress. Behind the articulated justification, however, are four other reasons why food stamps were retained as a federal entitlement despite a partisan declaration on behalf of devolution.

The first reason concerned the structural differences between food and cash assistance programs. For example, it is far more complicated to administer a welfare arrangement that prints, distributes, and redeems special coupons, as opposed to one that merely awards cash to eligible households. A number of states, with governors less attached to the new Republican agenda, were hesitant about the responsibility of managing an independent food stamp operation. In addition, food stamps had always functioned as a single, national-level program, although it used state welfare offices for implementation. By contrast, AFDC historically had been established as a joint partnership, with each state writing its own eligibility and benefit rules within broad federal guidelines and providing a share of the necessary funds. Cash assistance to needy families was already partly under state control. It was therefore easier to imagine a block grant substitute and easier to implement the change. Finally, food stamps, as an in-kind program narrowly targeted for nutrition support, was more secure emotionally in the hearts of the American public than AFDC, which simply provided more discretionary dollars to households with substandard earnings. The belief that no one should go hungry in a land of abundance could be counterpoised against the popular demand to radically and swiftly fix the so-called welfare mess. The lesson is that political decisions made in the past have a distinct impact on the present, as the inherited structure of policy affects the perceived need for and plausibility of reform options.

The second underlying reason involved the institutionalization of decision making. The agriculture committees in the House and Senate were at first hardly enthusiastic about food stamps. Practical necessity, however, gradually gave way to acceptance. The next generation of committee members was more willing to integrate a new set of issues—nutrition, environment, trade—within the broad domain of legitimate concerns. Moreover, an increasing percentage of Agriculture Department dollars flowed toward these areas, as opposed to more traditional commodity support programs. There was also political reward from greater attention to these new issues, for they had appeal in all congressional districts, giving the committee importance beyond the narrow constituency of farmers.[29] By contrast, AFDC was placed within the jurisdiction of Ways and Means in the House and Finance in the Senate, which are taxation committees primarily and which also have responsibility for Social Security and Medicare. The taxation committees found little political gain, but lots of bother and blame, from their policymaking obligation regarding family cash assistance. Therefore, Agriculture would be far less willing to diminish its policy responsibility by means of a block grant to the states than Ways and Means. Chairman Roberts had developed a reputation of fighting for his committee's interests and autonomy, which sometimes led to personal conflicts with other Republican leaders. As he declared, "I must caution those who say, just send us the money with no oversight, no strings attached, and let us run the programs. This committee is not prepared to abrogate our responsibility."[30] Ironically, the decentralization of Congress into standing committees helped prevent the decentralization of the food stamp program to the states.

The third reason was the presence of organized interests. Nutrition groups predictably protested that a block grant for food stamps would signal a retreat from the nation's commitment to feed its hungry. Yet many agriculture interest groups also registered opposition, forming an unusual but powerful alliance that had no parallel in the case of AFDC. According to a USDA study, a nutrition block grant would significantly reduce agricultural purchases and farm incomes. Based on the initial draft of the Personal Responsibility Act, the USDA estimated a large fall in retail food sales, between $4.25 and $10.5 billion, affecting earnings in both food production and marketing industries while costing more than 100,000 jobs. The report detailed the projected losses in a series of food sectors and predicted, from an economy-wide econometric model, long-run and lasting changes "in the composition of output and in the distribution of employment," with effects that "would be felt most heavily in rural America."[31] Farm interests over time had become reliant upon the additional income received as a consequence of food stamp payments. A number of agricultural lobbies, including both producers and grocers, communicated their fears to Congress. By severing the direct link to a national nutritional standard, there was no guarantee that a block grant would maintain current payment levels. By allowing the states independence to design their own programs, there was no guarantee that stamps would be issued that targeted benefits solely for food purchases. Thus, for example, Wayne Lord of the National Peanut Association wrote to Senator Lugar "to urge you in the strongest possible terms to oppose proposals, such as those included in the Personal Responsibility Act (PRA), to replace current federal food assistance programs with block-grant funding."[32] Not surprisingly, it was farm state legislators who were most willing to defy the Republican "Contract" in order to protect the federal food stamp program.

The fourth reason for the differential treatment of food stamps and AFDC concerned the pending farm bill. Most agricultural support programs required reauthorization in order to permit spending for FY 1996 and beyond. Typically, commodity subsidies and food stamps were joined together to facilitate rural-urban logrolling. The 1995 farm bill promised to be especially controversial, as Chairman Roberts and the House Republican leadership were advancing a major reform based on free-market principles. Replacing many government protections and regulations, farmers would be guaranteed fixed payments that would decline over time regardless of economic conditions or planting decisions. The announced goal was to gradually wean American agriculture from federal dependence. Roberts's "Freedom to Farm" proposal encountered strong opposition, especially from dairy and cotton commodity interests. In the quest for votes, food stamps were a means of attracting legislators with districts minimally affected by the battle of agricultural perspectives. Roberts and his allies were not about to sacrifice this valuable bargaining chip to the welfare bill while the farm bill was pending. The House Agriculture Committee report announced this fact in the same paragraph that declared that the food stamp program would retain its entitlement status, stating that further program amendments might be considered and "this section may be revisited . . . if deemed necessary" during the consideration of the farm bill later in the year.[33]

In sum, food stamps were protected from the ideological movement toward welfare block grants by old-fashioned political pressures. On the basis of institutions, symbols, interests, and strategy, food stamps were far better positioned than AFDC to ward off the challenge from the states. Those legislators wishing for a more sweeping reform, including Senator Robert Dole, who espoused block grants in his campaign for president, ultimately had to concede that they just did not have the votes.[34] Despite the promise of the "Contract with America," the practical politics of food stamps dominated over policy consistency and conservative principles.

Caps On and Off

The argument of this chapter has been that block grants can be seen as a complex form of budget control, but that food stamps were not transformed into a block grant mainly for pragmatic reasons. The Republican leadership certainly never abandoned the goal of restraining costs. According to the House Agriculture Committee, "it is time to limit the automatic increases built into the food stamp program."[35] Similarly, Agriculture chairman Roberts told Congress that it must take "the food stamp program off of automatic pilot" and discontinue "the pattern of ever escalating, runaway costs."[36] The committee target was to reduce food stamp spending by $16.5 billion over five years. The political coalition that had protected program integrity against devolution would not save it from budget-cutting reforms, especially when the alternative was deeper incisions into commodity subsidies.[37] The savings in the House bill came from a combination of substantive and arithmetical changes. Substantively, consistent with the announced conservative agenda, benefits were denied to most legal aliens and were restricted to ninety days for non-working but able-bodied individuals aged eighteen to fifty with no dependents. Arithmetically, the inflation adjustment to the Thrifty Food Plan was limited to 2% per year, and the standard deduction from gross income, the excess shelter cost deduction, and the excludable asset value for automobiles were all frozen at 1995 levels.

Finally, to ensure that spending remained within expected levels, a cap was reimposed on total food stamp appropriations. Annual obligations could not exceed the current CBO estimate, adjusted for the impact of the Personal Responsibility Act. The committee report favorably cited the example of the Mathis amendment of 1977 and called for a return to its emphasis on strict spending restraint. If entailed outlays in any given year were forecast to breach the cap, the secretary of agriculture would be required to reduce allotments across-the-board unless Congress took explicit action either to override the ceiling or to modify program rules. Certain nutrition advocates, such as Robert Greenstein from the Center on Budget and Policy Priorities, had indicated their willingness to accept restored food stamp spending caps. If politicians wanted to limit the total amount of program spending, it was a better option than block grants, especially given the past history—Congress effectively had escaped cap strictures whenever they actually endangered recipient benefits. Unlike the past, however, it would now be more difficult to override cap thresholds under emergency conditions because, under the provisions of the Budget Enforcement Act, every deliberate increase in mandatory spending had to be matched by a compensating rise in taxes or by cuts in other mandatory programs.

The Republican House of Representatives food stamp provisions provoked immediate condemnation from congressional liberals. Toward the end of a long and heated Agriculture Committee mark-up session, one frustrated Democratic critic proposed renaming the bill the "Food Stamp and Commodity Reduction to Make Americans Hungry Act." The minority report complained that the proposed changes were inspired primarily by cost reduction. The report praised the bill for rejecting the block grant option but found it hypocritical because the reasons used to defend food stamps as a federal program were contradicted by the specific provisions adopted. Food stamps could not truly be considered a safety net if certain needy individuals would be deprived of benefits when they failed to quickly find a job. It could not be called a protection against malnutrition if allotment indexing was limited to 2%, especially because the USDA had predicted a 3.5% annual increase in the cost of food. It could not be defended as flexible given changing economic circumstances if yearly dollar expenditures were capped and there was no automatic correction for the growth in recipient demand that occurs during unforeseen recession. "We must conclude that the majority's bill is a cost savings bill, nothing more. . . . Merely cutting the Food Stamp Program at some arbitrary level is not reform and no one should mistake it as such."[38]

The Clinton administration was disturbed by the House bill yet pleased that it could be attacked as a narrowly Republican venture. In the Senate, however, administration spokesmen adopted a more cooperative tone. The new agriculture secretary, Dan Glickman, announced that the president would veto any welfare bill that turned food stamps into a block grant or jeopardized the nutritional safety net. He offered a set of relatively tame reform recommendations but also indicated "we will work with you" to find additional savings that minimized harm to "the basic feeding and nutrition mission" of the program.[39] Following Glickman's suggestions, the Senate Agriculture Committee draft bill generally adopted lower thresholds but permitted automatic adjustments for changing conditions. For example, it fixed allotments at 100% (rather than 103%) of the Thrifty Food Plan but fully accommodated annual increases based on the changing cost of food. It reduced the standard deduction from gross income (from $138 to $124 per month) but resumed indexing beginning in FY 2003. It deleted strict budget caps but authorized spending only through FY 2002. On the other hand, pressure from the Republican right had to be appeased. Each state would be given discretion to take its food stamp money as a block grant, provided that 80% would be spent on food assistance and no more than 6% would be used for administrative costs.

The object for the Republican leadership in Congress was somehow to balance fiscal savings and program integrity in a manner capable of attracting bipartisan support and, it was hoped, acquiescence from President Clinton—despite the ideological threat from conservatives to the right demanding full devolution (while hoping for a veto in order to pursue further partisan attacks against the president), and despite the ideological threat from liberals to the left protesting all benefit reductions that might increase hunger (while hoping for political deadlock in order to further wage public battle against the Republican Contract). Bipartisan balance, maintained precariously on the Senate floor, was even more forbidding in conference where the House and Senate versions had to be reconciled. For example, the conference deleted the Senate provision allowing states the choice to select a block grant with its food stamp funds, yet it expanded the House provision permitting the block grant option not only for states with Electronic Benefits Transfer systems but also for those with especially low error rates or those willing to pay from their own funds the cost of excess errors. With regard to an annual spending cap, the conference followed the House and reimposed the cap, although the ceilings were somewhat relaxed. Appropriations would be authorized for seven years, with the legislated maximum rising gradually from $25.4 billion in FY 1996 to $29.8 billion in FY 2002. Whereas in 1990 the Bush administration viewed such caps as an unnecessary complication to reasonable entitlement budgeting, in 1995, under a different political and fiscal configuration, the new Republican majority advanced them as a useful instrument for expenditure control. Ironically, only five years after their elimination, specified limits upon food stamp outlays were on the verge of policy re-enactment.

Yet budget caps for the food stamp program were never in fact reinstated. First, the Personal Responsibility Act was incorporated as part of the 1995 omnibus reconciliation bill. As such, it became embroiled in a furious partisan budget battle that resulted in the shutdown of nonessential government services from November 14 to 19 and again from December 16 to January 6. Inclusion within the broader measure protected the welfare titles against a filibuster and allowed its savings to be scored as part of the Republican seven-year balanced budget plan. Inclusion also meant that the section re-establishing the food stamp budget caps had to be deleted, as the Byrd rule in the Senate prohibited extraneous matters in a reconciliation bill. The issue became moot, however, as President Clinton vetoed the huge reconciliation bill, claiming that it "would cut deeply into Medicare, Medicaid, student loans, and nutrition programs; hurt the environment; raise taxes on millions of working men and women and their families by slashing the Earned Income Tax Credit (EITC); and provide a huge tax cut whose benefits would flow disproportionately to those who are already the most well-off."[40] Second, the Personal Responsibility Act was then sent to the president as a free-standing bill, approved by Congress in mid-December 1995 with a few minor changes intended to attract additional support. This version contained the food stamp spending cap provision. Republicans hoped that President Clinton would be trapped by his own past rhetoric into accepting it. Instead, the president issued another veto. While announcing his willingness to bargain in good faith, he declared this particular bill unacceptable as the deep spending cuts fell "hardest on children" and the structural changes had "little connection to the central goal" of moving people from welfare to work.[41] Last, there was still another iteration of the Personal Responsibility Act that cleared Congress in mid-1996 and eventually was signed into law by the president. Yet this version did not contain any mention of cap limitations upon food stamp spending. At the end of the long ordeal, the program remained as it was at the outset—a federal entitlement in which the government was obligated to provide funds for all eligible households adequate to satisfy the full level of their legitimate benefit claims.

In early 1996, the welfare bill became part of the election year politics of appearance and position-taking. President Clinton, in his State of the Union address, called upon Congress to send him a bipartisan reform measure that he could sign. Robert Dole and the Republicans, fearing that any such compromise bill would not be sufficiently strict, preferred simply to criticize Clinton for blocking popular legislation. While the

Personal Responsibility Act languished, the farm bill received immediate attention. Its titles had been included in the 1995 reconciliation package vetoed by the president. If not revived, the food stamp program would soon exhaust its authority to spend and most other agriculture provisions would revert back to the wording adopted in 1949. The House approved a new version based on "Freedom to Farm" principles and the Senate Agriculture Committee did likewise. Yet the controversial character of the bill combined with the need to move quickly made the measure vulnerable to a filibuster on the Senate floor. Chairman Lugar thus also advanced an alternative version, written specifically to appease Patrick Leahy, the most influential Democrat on the committee, which added sections concerning conservation and rural development initiatives and reauthorizing the food stamp program for seven more years without any cap restrictions. According to Leahy, "a farm bill is no longer . . . just about growing crops or amber waves of grain. A farm bill is about feeding the American people. It is about the elimination of hunger in one of the wealthiest nations in the world."[42] Moderate Democrats were now given an option other than total opposition.

While Lugar's more conservative bill did not gain enough support for cloture to shut off debate, the Lugar-Leahy compromise fell just one vote shy. Assuming that it would probably garner sufficient support once all the senators had returned from spring break, it was granted floor consideration and approved with minor amendments. Yet hurdles remained in conference. Many Republicans were loath to permit food stamp extension without accompanying reform, thereby abandoning the leverage needed to enact substantial savings. Counter-pressure came from the Clinton administration. Agriculture secretary Glickman, in an eleven-page letter to lawmakers, expressed the USDA's reservations regarding the "Freedom to Farm" system of guaranteed yet declining crop subsidies, but listed a number of provisions—including reauthorized nutrition programs—that could help avert a presidential veto.[43] The need for hasty resolution influenced the final outcome. The conference accepted most of the Lugar-Leahy amendments. Regarding food stamps, the program was reauthorized for two years, through FY 1997, rather than seven, in order to facilitate reconsideration if welfare reform returned to the active agenda. To better satisfy both Leahy and Glickman, however, no ceiling was placed on permissible outlays. It was always possible that budget caps could have been reintroduced during some later examination of food stamp provisions. Yet this was unlikely in the short run according to the norms of legislative behavior. The concession had already been made as part of the bargaining over the farm bill. Under ordinary conditions it is thought to be deceitful to renege on a deal already concluded, and as such the proposal for caps on food stamp spending was withdrawn—at least temporarily—from policy deliberations.

Therefore, when interest in welfare reform revived in early summer, a large number of issues were treated as already settled. Given Clinton's rising popularity and the approach of elections, a number of congressmen felt the need to claim credit for a major legislative accomplishment, even if it meant sharing praise with the president. The critical retreat occurred when the Republican leadership dropped its demand that Medicaid also be transformed into a block grant. The resulting draft bill was somewhat more moderate than the one prepared in 1995. Regarding food stamps, the most important difference was full program reauthorization without expenditure ceilings through FY 2002. In addition, the Senate floor voted 53–45 to drop the option for states to elect a food stamp block grant if they had implemented electronic benefits or showed low error rates, and the conference complied in order to appease the secretary of agriculture and the White House. The final bill thus contained neither budget caps nor block grants for the food stamp program. Nevertheless, it still transferred control over family cash assistance to the states, imposed time limits on welfare benefits, deprived most legal immigrants of aid, and cut spending by more than $54 billion over seven years, $23 billion from food stamps alone. As Chairman Roberts celebrated, "Congress is back in control of spending on food stamps."[44] President Clinton, after much wavering, announced despite reservations that he would sign the measure because of the "historic opportunity to finish the work of ending welfare as we know it."[45] He carefully consulted the public opinion polls before making his decision, which was motivated significantly by electoral politics.[46]

In terms of budget effect, block grants and expenditure caps both freeze program spending while minimizing congressional responsibility for the effects. Block grants shift authority to the states, which then must manage on their own against potential deficiencies in available funding relative to demand. Expenditure caps formally constrain annual appropriations, such that potential funding deficiencies are deemed extraordinary and are remedied by Congress solely as a matter of policy discretion. Both block grants and caps have been justified as tools useful to control runaway federal welfare costs. Despite the apparent political and budgetary attraction of these tools and the ideological insistence from the new Republican majority that one of them be adopted, neither ultimately was applied to the food stamp program as part of the 1996 reform. The most striking conclusion from the preceding discussion is that institutionalization matters. On the one hand, the institutionalization of policy established stakeholders, either as beneficiaries protective of existing program functions or as decision makers protective of their jurisdictional power. The former was exemplified by the odd coalition of nutrition advocates and farm lobbies; the latter by the agriculture committees refusing to cede sovereignty over the policies within their domain. On the other hand, the institutionalization of procedure constructed the policy arena and multiplied the number of actors with effective bargaining capacity. The autonomy of congressional committees enabled Roberts, Emerson, and Lugar to resist pressures from "Contract" loyalists. The threat of filibuster in the Senate allowed Leahy and other Democratic moderates to extract a price for their consent. The president's veto power helped Secretary Glickman to negotiate provisions more acceptable to the Clinton administration. The food stamp policy outcome—a momentous change that never occurred—was hardly the consequence of systematic deliberation and the careful formulation of preferences. Entitlement status was preserved, but not in a manner that suggests permanent resolution.

Bottom-Up or Top-Down Control

In the present era of welfare budget restraint, two alternative strategies have dominated the political agenda. The first emphasizes control from the bottom up, looking at the details of each program in order to enact reforms the sum of which are projected to bring overall costs down to the target level. The second emphasizes control from the top down, imposing a fixed limit on permissible spending backed by a procedure requiring program cuts if total outlays threaten to exceed some specified threshold.

From the standpoint of cost containment, each approach has its own entailed risks. The approach from the bottom is politically more difficult to enact, as it requires legislators to specify all program sacrifices and to construct a viable coalition capable of maintaining the cuts through the congressional labyrinth. After enactment, there will still be temptations toward leakage, as the groups deprived of desired benefits continue to pressure for redress and compensation. Moreover, there is no guarantee that any package of piecemeal reforms from the bottom will actually achieve the desired level of savings. Estimates of future program costs are rarely accurate. This is especially true of welfare entitlements, notoriously sensitive to fluctuations in utilization rates and macroeconomic indicators. The net result, therefore, is often substantial political pain for little budgetary gain.

The approach from the top, by contrast, is especially difficult to enforce. Legislators might be amenable to aggregate restraint as long as the cuts do not have to be identified in the present and the effects are felt only in the future. Mandatory spending ceilings protect against cost misestimation and automatic drift, but only to the extent that elected politicians are truly willing to sustain them when threatened—quite possibly deep into the fiscal year, quite possibly through cuts unpalatable to vulnerable or powerful interests. The net result, therefore, is that aggregate caps are often written to be more symbolic than real, and in emergency conditions they are overridden rather than imposed.

Food stamp reform within the Personal Responsibility Act was increasingly focused upon cutting costs and saving federal dollars. The target figure was set by the budget resolution and the money would be used to help finance the zero-deficit plan advanced by the Republican leadership. At the start of the process, the proposed strategy for cost savings was almost entirely top-down, initially by means of block appropriations to the states and then by ceilings on inflationary adjustments and by annual spending caps. At the end, the cost-cutting strategy was almost entirely bottom-up, based upon a series of particular changes to program provisions. This was a remarkable movement, but it was not unique. A parallel shift, for instance, occurred at the aggregate level, directed at the control of welfare entitlements as a whole.

The "Contract with America" called for a balanced budget constitutional amendment as a form of top-down restraint upon the entire federal government. Defenders refused to specify exactly how zero deficits would be achieved, in part because an amendment should be focused on principles more than details and in part because the specification of details might frighten off potential supporters. Yet the wording of the amendment instructed Congress to enforce and implement the new article through appropriate legislation, which certain proponents assumed meant controls on mandatory spending written to match the Budget Enforcement Act's controls on discretionary spending. The balanced budget amendment easily passed the House, but it narrowly failed to secure a two-thirds majority on the Senate floor in 1995, 1996, and 1997.

In the meantime, Congress and the president were locked in a bitter struggle over deficit reduction. President Clinton proposed only a token reduction in his budget submission of February 1995. In June, he sought to steal some of the Republicans' thunder by proposing to eradicate the federal deficit over ten years, saving enough money from changes in mandatory and discretionary programs to afford a small tax cut for middle- and lower-income class families. In December, at the climax of the battle, he matched the Republican offer with a revised, seven-year balanced budget plan, although it advanced somewhat different fiscal priorities and was grounded on friendly OMB econometric estimates. In February 1996, Clinton accepted the principle of CBO scorekeeping as an element in the temporary truce that was kept until elections. The 1996 election maintained divided partisan control over government institutions, and the consequence was that both sides returned to Washington ready to negotiate. The celebrated budget deal of May 1997 would cut taxes and retard spending, especially health care.[47] Economic growth certainly made it easier to reach accord, as comparatively high revenues and low entailed spending had reduced the projected deficit gap. The agreement in itself indicated the degree to which the Republican agenda had become dominant. Yet the details of the agreement were entirely bottom-up, thus requiring appropriations and reconciliation bills to enact a range of reforms across many separate programs. Predictably, deficit hawks conscious of the original "Contract" were concerned by the disregard for top-down controls.

The anticipated rebellion occurred over the rule bringing to the House floor the reconciliation bill for government spending. Deficit hawks sought to add a title to the bill to ensure strict enforcement of the specified revenue, expenditure, and deficit thresholds, and to obligate an automatic sequester if the actual figures varied from expectation. For mandatory spending, there would be a cap for the total sum and for a series of separate program categories, including food stamps. The annual target would be adjusted for changes in inflation and eligible population. If outlays during the previous fiscal year or anticipated during the current year breached the target, either in the aggregate or for any particular entitlement category, the budget committees had to report new legislation to generate the necessary savings and/or to accommodate the overage. If no explicit action were taken, across-the-board cuts would be imposed. The House Rules Committee, fearing disruption to the tenuous agreement negotiated with the Clinton administration, refused to allow the enforcement provision the privilege of a direct vote on the floor. However, the next day, as the rule on the reconciliation bill appeared in jeopardy, the committee backtracked and agreed to allow the title to be introduced, but only as a separate, free-standing measure.

When the budget enforcement proposal finally reached the House floor one month later, the Republican leadership worked to prevent passage. It prohibited amendments to improve the draft, complained about interruptions to ordinary committee procedures, and warned that the measure would endanger tax reduction, Social Security, and veterans benefits. The defenders of top-down controls complained loudly about hypocrisy, treachery, and duplicity. They argued that a balanced budget required firm discipline to promote responsible behavior. They pointed to the history of previous agreements—including Gramm-Rudman-Hollings and the compact of 1990—which had failed to achieve lower deficits because of the lack of sufficiently strong and encompassing entitlement constraints. The 1997 accord depended far too much on future projections, plausible as they were. Economic shocks were always a risk, but steps could be taken to guarantee that they did not undermine the fiscal promise made to the American people. Although it might sound hard-hearted, they asserted, no federal policy program should be insulated from budget accountability. The arguments were consistent but the supporters were few, even among Republican loyalists. The enforcement bill lost impressively, 81–347. Top-down ceilings on the growth of entitlement spending had been a central element of dissenting budget resolution motions during the 103rd Congress. Now, surprisingly, early in the 105th Congress, with a Republican majority in both chambers and with public opinion favoring a balanced budget, this approach was rejected soundly.

The most recent period of welfare and budget reform thus produced, overall and for many individual policy arenas, a systematic tendency toward disaggregated spending control. From the advance advertising, one might well have predicted the opposite. There was remarkably little debate regarding the merits of alternative strategies for restraint. Political contests were concerned more with partisan position-taking and deal-making than with the presentation and evaluation of fundamental principles of governance. Such is the common nature of American politics. Sometimes, even without careful deliberation, the resolution of thorny problems emerges. In the mid-1990s, AFDC was given to the states as a block grant, ending the direct federal commitment to support poor families with children. However, the vast majority of anti-poverty programs remained in their fundamental structure unaltered. Despite repeated threats, food stamps were left as an uncapped entitlement. Medicaid similarly avoided reconstruction. A balanced budget was promised without procedural fetters on the growth of mandatory spending. The bottom-up strategy imposed a series of deep yet piecemeal spending cuts, but it did not establish new decision-making procedures or redefine entitlement rules. Given the inherent policy tension between responsive welfare provision and encompassing budget regulation, the outcome for the programs remaining within the federal domain appears to have been settled largely in favor of the former.

Nevertheless, there are grounds for skepticism. Entitlement protection and expenditure restraint still represent contradictory principles. Discipline over federal government spending remains popular on the national policy agenda. Welfare costs remain largely stigmatized despite the fact that full entitlement status for most programs has been preserved. The pressure to institute top-down limitations, overall and for food stamps in particular, was escaped but not because of serious consideration of the complications entailed. In an era of pervasive budgetary concern, the bottom-up attempt to control welfare spending might not appear sufficiently strict. It establishes too little guarantee to politicians fixated upon securing a zero-deficit figure. It requires, during economic downturn, that the government either abandon outlay targets or enact explicit new sacrifices upon the needy at a time when welfare demand is increasing. At best, the settlement of the mid-1990s reflects a mere hope that the tension between welfare and budgeting concerns will not soon emerge in a vexatious form. The policy of piecemeal program cuts, conjoined to prosperous macroeconomic conditions, cannot be considered stable.

First, there is a problem with incremental leakages. Sympathetic constituencies and organized interests will pressure for relief from particular provisions intended to reduce program costs. The erosions in food stamps, for example, started almost immediately. In late 1996, $2 billion of projected savings began to disappear as the states used a lenient administrative ruling to exempt nonworking able-bodied individuals with no dependents from the limitation of three months of benefits every three years. The law allowed waivers to communities with high unemployment rates or an insufficient number of available jobs. By December, thirteen states had requested waivers and more applications were expected. The 1997 supplemental appropriations bill gave permission for the states to award food stamp benefits to legal aliens, provided that they reimburse the USDA for the cost. The 1997 reconciliation bill allowed the states to exempt an extra 15% of able-bodied individuals from the work requirement. In 1998, the Agricultural Research, Extension, and Education Act restored full benefits to those aged, disabled, or child noncitizens who were legally in the United States when the 1996 welfare reform was enacted. The provision was not in the original bill but was added in conference partly in response to intense lobbying by Hispanic interests. The Clinton administration strongly supported the measure, and it was backed by a logrolling coalition of farm and nutrition groups that agreed to split the $1.7 billion made available by a reduction in food stamp administrative costs.

Second and more important, welfare restraint through bottom-up adjustments in program benefit and eligibility rules is vulnerable to unexpected economic fluctuations. The effect of program cuts on total spending is merely predicted, and predictions often fall short of actual results. The thriving U.S. economy of the mid-1990s lowered assistance rolls, helping the Personal Responsibility Act to achieve its targets; it lowered the federal deficit, making the balanced budget accord easier to negotiate. The problem is that the prevailing fiscal optimism depends heavily on the assumption that market conditions will remain favorable. The bottom-up strategy alters substantive provisions but does not affect the requirement that the government finance all benefits granted under the terms of prevailing law. The deficit hawks had legitimate grounds for their suspicion of dollar savings claimed on the basis of forecast without procedural enforcement. A policy synthesis proclaiming simultaneously spending constraint and guaranteed payments is inconsistent when intruded upon by renewed budget pressures.

One can imagine a situation where entitlement dominates, in which society agrees to accommodate all entailed obligations on behalf of the poor regardless of their effect on deficits, taxes, or other spending priorities. In the United States, however, recent pressures tilt the other way. The firm promise to balance the budget has diminished fiscal flexibility. Individual discontent has reduced voter willingness to sacrifice tax dollars or program rewards. The perceived imperatives of economic growth, especially in times of uncertain investor confidence, help deter movement toward progressive redistribution.[48] The Clinton administration has been favored by prosperity, which has the capacity to drown away inconsistent imperatives. Yet upturns historically have not enjoyed infinite duration, and in the receding tide tensions often re-emerge among competing policy principles. Unwilling to accept the full implications of welfare entitlement, it is not unlikely that the American federal government will in time rediscover the temptation toward mechanical caps and ceilings imposed upon the assistance it awards to the hungry and impoverished.

Notes—Chapter 9

1. House Republican Conference, "Contract with America," *Legislative Digest,* September 24, 1994, 31.
2. House *Report* 104–77, 17.
3. House *Report* 104–430, 632.
4. William J. Clinton, "Message to the House of Representatives Returning Without Approval Legislation on the Welfare System," January 9, 1996, *Public Papers of the Presidents of the United States, William J. Clinton, 1996,* 23.
5. U.S. House of Representatives, Committee on Ways and Means, Subcommittee on Human Resources, *Contract With America—Welfare Reform,* 104th Cong., 1st sess., 1995, 11.
6. U.S. House of Representatives, Committee on Ways and Means, Subcommittee on Human Resources, *Contract With America—Welfare Reform,* 12.
7. U.S. House of Representatives, Committee on Agriculture, Subcommittee on Department Operations, Nutrition, and Foreign Agriculture, *Reforming the Present Welfare System,* 104th Cong., 1st sess., 1995, 351.
8. *Congressional Record* 141: S 12692.
9. *Congressional Record* 141: S 11601–2.
10. *Congressional Record* 141: H 3615; S 13334.
11. U.S. Department of Agriculture, Food and Consumer Service, "The Nutrition, Health, and Economic Consequences of Block Grants for Federal Food Assistance Programs," in U.S. House of Representatives, Committee on Agriculture, Subcommittee on Department Operations, Nutrition, and Foreign Agriculture, *Reforming the Present Welfare System,* 104th Cong., 1st sess., 1995, 291–301.
12. U.S. House of Representatives, Committee on Agriculture, Subcommittee on Department Operations, Nutrition, and Foreign Agriculture, *Reforming the Present Welfare System,* 694–95.

13. U.S. House of Representatives, Committee on Ways and Means, Subcommittee on Human Resources, *Contract With America—Welfare Reform,* 106–07.

14. William J. Clinton, "Teleconference Remarks and a Question-and-Answer Session With the National Conference of State Legislatures," July 20, 1995, *Public Papers of the Presidents of the United States, William J. Clinton, 1995,* 1126. A former congressional aide put the matter succinctly. "Block grants are one of the best ways to cut the budget. The cuts are so ethereal. You don't have to specify what will really happen to people and programs. You just give the states less money and let them decide." Quoted in Timothy Conlon, *From New Federalism to Devolution* (Washington D.C.: Brookings Institution, 1998): 237.

15. U.S. House of Representatives, Committee on Ways and Means, Subcommittee on Human Resources, *Contract With America—Welfare Reform,* 27–28, 49.

16. House *Report* 104–725, 262.

17. House *Report* 104–651, 1963; David A. Super, Sharon Parrott, Susan Steinmetz, and Cindy Mann, "The New Welfare Law," Center for Budget and Policy Priorities, August 13, 1996.

18. U.S. Department of Agriculture, Food and Consumer Service, "The Nutrition, Health, and Economic Consequences of Block Grants for Federal Food Assistance Programs," 303–15.

19. William J. Clinton, "Remarks to the Iowa Legislature in Des Moines," April 25, 1995, *Public Papers of the Presidents of the United States, William J. Clinton, 1995,* 603; "Teleconference Remarks and a Question-and-Answer Session With the National Conference of State Legislatures," July 20, 1995, *Public Papers of the Presidents of the United States, William J. Clinton, 1995,* 1124.

20. *Congressional Record* 141: S 13336. A comparative study of state AFDC programs operating during the early 1990s under waiver authority concluded that tightened fiscal circumstances plus unfavorable public opinion have meant that autonomous state welfare efforts are "even more likely to fall under the budgetary knife and that the cuts would be both popular and relatively easy to make." Donald F. Norris and Lyke Thompson, *The Politics of Welfare Reform* (Thousand Oaks, CA: Sage Publications, 1995): 220.

21. Judith Havemann and Barbara Vobejda, "Food Stamp Block Grant Eyed as Way of Breaking Welfare Reform Stalemate," *Washington Post,* July 13, 1995, sec. A: 6.

22. *Congressional Record* 142: S 8350–7.

23. House *Report* 104–81, Part I, 13.

24. *Congressional Record* 141: H 3614.

25. U.S. House of Representatives, Committee on Agriculture, *Food Stamp Program,* 104th Cong., 1st sess., 1995, 2.

26. *Congressional Record* 141: S 13336.

27. *Congressional Record* 141: H 3615.

28. Robert Pear, "House Leaders and Republican Governors Agree on an Alternative to Food Stamps," *New York Times,* March 2, 1995, sec. B: 9; Judith Havemann and Barbara Vobejda, "Governors Offered Control of Food Stamps," *Washington Post,* March 2, 1995, sec. A: 4.

29. William P. Browne, *Cultivating Congress: Constituents, Issues, and Interests in Agricultural Policymaking* (Lawrence: University of Kansas Press, 1995): 31–34; John Mark Hansen, *Gaining Access: Congress and the Farm Lobby, 1919–1981* (Chicago: University of Chicago Press, 1991): 201–11.

30. U.S. House of Representatives, Committee on Agriculture, *Food Stamp Program,* 2.

31. U.S. Department of Agriculture. Food and Consumer Service, "The Nutrition, Health, and Economic Consequences of Block Grants for Federal Food Assistance Programs," 300–03.

32. *Congressional Record* 141: S 13339.

33. House *Report* 104–77, 46.

34. *Congressional Record* 141: S 11739; "Panel Trims Nutrition Spending, But Keeps Food Stamp Benefits," *New York Times,* June 15, 1995, sec. A: 20.

35. House *Report* 104–77, 35.

36. *Congressional Record* 141: H 3683.

37. Guy Guliotta and Barbara Vobejda, "Hill Action on Food Programs Reflects Disparity of Influence," *Washington Post,* November 29, 1995, sec. A: 4.

38. *House Report* 104–77, 169–70.

39. U.S. Senate, Committee on Agriculture, Nutrition, and Forestry, *Federal Nutrition Programs,* 104th Cong., 1st sess., 1995, 19.

40. William J. Clinton. 1995, "Message to the House of Representatives Returning Without Approval Budget Reconciliation Legislation," December 6, 1995, *Public Papers of the Presidents of the United States, William J. Clinton, 1995,* 1853.

41. William J. Clinton, "Message to the House of Representatives Returning Without Approval Legislation on the Welfare System," January 9, 1996, *Public Papers of the Presidents of the United States, William J. Clinton, 1996,* 22–23.

42. *Congressional Record* 142: S 901.

43. David Hosansky, "Snare of Competing Interests Entangles Dairy Debate," *Congressional Quarterly Weekly Report,* March 16, 1996, 691.

44. *Congressional Record* 142: H 7753.

45. William J. Clinton, "Remarks on Welfare Reform Legislation and an Exchange With Reporters," July 31, 1996, *Public Papers of the Presidents of the United States, William J. Clinton, 1996,* 1235.

46. Dick Morris, *Behind the Oval Office* (New York: Random House,

1997): 297–304. Senator Moynihan (D-NY) commented, "The Cabinet is against the bill. The pollsters are for it. This is a defining event in his Presidency," quoted in Robert Pear in "Clinton To Sign Welfare Bill That Ends U.S. Aid Guarantees and Gives States Broader Power," *New York Times,* August 1, 1996, sec. A: 22.

47. For a history of the 1997 budget agreement, see Daniel J. Palazzolo, *Done Deal?* (New York: Chatham House, 1999).

48. Ronald F. King, *Money, Time, and Politics: Investment Tax Subsidies and American Democracy* (New Haven, CT: Yale University Press, 1993).

TEN

Re-Caps: Food Stamps and Budget Rules in Retrospect and Prospect

There is an ancient Japanese proverb that observes, "although our mothers and fathers give us life, it is money alone that preserves it." There are millions of individuals in the United States today who do not earn sufficient incomes, judged by the minimal standard we ourselves have established for decent living. Welfare constitutes the set of government transfer payments designed to fill at least a portion of the gap between market earnings and the poverty threshold. The gap exists because, in our capitalist economy, earnings depend upon one's ability to sell a valued factor of production, most often labor power. Yet certain individuals sit outside the labor market because they are elderly or disabled or caring for young children, or there is no market for the productive factor they wish to sell, or the returns from the sale are insufficient to support a minimally decent lifestyle.

One would like to believe that welfare support stems from moral values. An individual, allegedly, is more than a commodity in capitalist markets; there is intrinsic worth to each human being that merits nurture and protection. Moreover, the individual exists as a member of the community. The notion of inclusive, equal membership is contradicted when some participants sink to the level of destitution; the sense of collective whole is destroyed when extreme inequality creates hierarchies in status. The literature on social welfare provision is often more skeptical, unfortunately, regarding motives. The history of welfare is marked by the struggles of the underprivileged to obtain needed benefits. Such struggles in the United States have been compounded by the organizational weakness of the working classes, the fragmentation of societal interests, the established ideology of self-help, and the decentralization of state decision making.

Recent decades have seen the emergence of an additional challenge to welfare provision, the growing fiscalization of public policy. Increasingly, Americans believe that budget funds cannot be supplied sufficient to meet the transfer obligations incurred. Tax resistance has deepened, in part the consequence of stable real household incomes and unstable future expectations. Welfare as a share of federal outlays has risen, in part the consequence of an aging U.S. population. Deficit concerns, especially pronounced from the period 1981 to 1996, have made Americans sensitive to fiscal constraints and suspicious that their elected leaders will disregard responsible choice in the pursuit of short-run popularity. Hopes for budget relief depend largely on continued robust economic performance, which before has proved fleeting given competitive international conditions.

Fiscalization has helped to put welfare advocates on the defensive, shifting attention to the amount society will afford rather than the amount the disadvantaged might require. It gives prima facie justification to those who do not wish to spend more money on the impoverished, and makes those who may otherwise be sympathetic become hesitant regarding social welfare commitments. In its political logic, fiscalization implies that there exists an encompassing national financial problem to be solved, with sufficient importance to the whole that it can restrict the benefits granted to dependent subpopulations within the whole. It begins with a truism, that the capacity of the state is always limited, and concludes with a policy platform, that those limits are in danger of breach as a consequence of public generosity.

This book has explored certain dimensions of the growing fiscalization of U.S. welfare, focusing especially on the concept of entitlement. Entitlement, according to the interpretation adopted here, is not an inviolable moral or constitutional right. It is conferred by the provisions of statutory law and can be altered by legislative enactment. Seen as a form of budgetary rule, entitlement comprises one of the ways in which the federal government appropriates funds. It establishes direct spending, obligating Treasury outlays to all individuals specified as eligible under the terms of the authorization. Unlike ordinary discretion, the annual budget merely estimates projected spending rather than allocates a fixed program amount. Unlike discretion, the consequence of no new legislation from Congress is still full payment to all qualified beneficiaries. Entitlement within the budget system entails different institutional processes and actor strategies, but it is a plausible arrangement for policies awarding government cash subsidies, particularly for the purpose of behavioral incentive or income supplementation. Nevertheless, the relatively uncontrollable aspect of entitlement budgeting helps to simultaneously prompt fiscalization worries while ensuring escape from the conventional means of annual cost management. Reconciliation instructions sometimes are incorporated into congressional budget resolutions, but restraint depends on the acceptance of detailed changes written into program regulations and their effect on the benefits granted. The PAYGO provision of the Budget Enforcement Act integrates entitlement programs within the overall framework for expenditure control but imposes no limits upon spending growth entailed under the operation of prevailing law. As a result, we have seen proposals arise periodically, especially from fiscal conservatives, for new budget procedures imposing far stricter constraints.

The food stamp program has functioned under discretionary, entitlement, and expenditure cap rules, providing a natural experiment for social science analysis. The chronological account presented through the chapters of this book examines food stamp politics and policy over the various periods of its existence, defined by the character of the budget system in operation. Certainly, all entitlements are not alike. Yet there are general lessons to be learned from this extended case study: methodologically regarding the use of rational choice models in policy research and of the specific framework applied here to the analysis of welfare budgeting; theoretically regarding the inherent and apparently irresolvable tension between entitlement protection and fiscal control, which remains a problem despite the flurry of recent procedural reforms; and substantively regarding the practical effect of expenditure caps upon strategic play and collective outcomes, which in this assessment is not especially favorable. The argument in each of these areas is controversial, as is the general perspective asserting the relevance of budgeting for contemporary social welfare policy. Although the topic for discussion has been food stamps, the underlying concern is the American welfare state, which is under pressure to exercise greater central regulation and restraint. Meanwhile, according to U.S. government estimates, more than thirty million Americans each year subsist under the official poverty threshold.

Method, Theory, and Subject

Social science is inherently three-dimensional, advancing claims simultaneously at the level of method, theory, and subject. Regarding subject, it is necessary to tell a detailed, interesting, and salient story. Regarding theory, it is necessary to explore the inner meaning of the story and its relationship to other stories, thereby confirming, supplementing, or challenging certain broadly held beliefs. Regarding method, it is necessary that the story be told in a structured manner and that the findings be rigorous and sound. All three dimensions were intrinsic to the preceding narrative. The object now is to make them explicit.

Method

This book has sought to illustrate and give plausibility to a pair of models, simple in their construction but valuable for highlighting differences across the main forms of budget rule—discretion, entitlement, and expenditure caps. At the core of the models is the notion of a reversion point, the outcome that will prevail by default if no negotiated agreement is reached. By backwards induction, differences in the reversion point will affect the strategies of players in the game of budget politics and the probable results from play.

One model is institutional in focus, emphasizing the sequence of U.S. fiscal decision making and the incentives generated by the various budget rules for honesty or dishonesty when estimating program costs. Under discretion, assuming no dramatic ideological conflict, agencies will tend to overestimate costs in order to better promote program expansion, but the president and Congress should play relatively honestly as a means of reinforcing the confidence needed for incremental bargaining. This, for example, was the pattern beginning to emerge for food stamps during the early Nixon administration, after the program won substantial legitimacy but before entitlement rules were introduced. Under entitlement, the president should play dishonestly, underestimating costs for the appearance of fiscal restraint. For food stamps, this was evident during the Ford administration and again under Bush after the expenditure caps were eliminated. Under caps, Congress should play dishonestly, underestimating costs in order to expand its oversight role when expenditures grow rapidly yet be able to take credit for any subsequent remedial action. This was the situation for food stamps during the Carter administration. The institutional hypotheses developed in chapter 2 are thus well supported by the data. The only emendation, based on the evidence presented, occurs in the case of budget caps when spending is predicted to fall well short of the cap threshold. With the reversion point unlikely to ever threaten program obligations, welfare finance assumes an entitlement-like pattern and therefore the president, as seen in the case of food stamps during the middle and later Reagan years, safely can return to systematic cost underestimation.

The other model is ideological in focus, emphasizing the location of the actors' preferred positions along a linear policy map and the effect of the various budget rules on the bargains they will construct in pursuit of the best feasible outcome. Under discretion, spending will reflect the balance of competing forces. Thus the food stamp program in its formative period during the Johnson administration had to fight for funds against entrenched agriculture interests, and it expanded only gradually, benefiting from logrolling deals and a popular campaign publicizing the extent of hunger in America. Entitlement provided a useful escape from annual appropriations battles and facilitated dramatic expenditure growth despite political contention. Under entitlement, the opposing sides will freely practice rhetorical excess and policy intransigence since they understand that stalemate at the reversion point is preferable to any compromise. This is the pattern that occurred during the Ford administration and then, with somewhat lesser intensity, during the latter Bush period. Under budget caps, advantage goes to any conservative actor willing to invoke the cap reversion point unless given compensating program reforms. This was the threat made by the Reagan administration during its first years in office, which effectively altered the strategy of food stamp advocates. Again, the hypotheses developed in chapter 2 are well supported by the data. The only addition, from the evidence presented, stems from the interaction of the two models because sometimes they hypothesize behavior in contradictory directions. Thus, for example, a moderate Congress under a cap arrangement might see value institutionally from underestimating costs for purposes of oversight, but might hesitate ideologically for fear that an approaching reversion point would give advantage to the conservative president. This was the situation that prevailed during the second Reagan administration.

Congress deliberately imposed loose food stamp expenditure caps, sacrificing much of its procedural opportunity in order to minimize the risk of renewed substantive program cuts.

The rational choice approach to social science builds analysis from the logical microfoundations of individual behavior.[1] It is assumed that individuals act intentionally, formulating preferences across various possible outcomes and adopting the means believed most effective for realizing those preferences. As strategic calculators, they are expected to respond to the incentives and disincentives found in the environment. Outcomes result from the combination of separate individual actions. The universe is populated by many individuals, each capable of choice yet aware that others are similarly capable. Thus no outcome is completely under one's control, although players tend to perform best as utility maximizers when they anticipate the probable reactions of others. The social scientist seeks to model common decision situations, highlighting the objective structure confronting the various players, the choices existing within it, and the probable results from joint intentional play. The model is an abstraction, a broad construction based on constraints and opportunities. It is not designed for complete description of each event and each personality. Rather, the object is to enhance conceptual clarity—to capture the essence of a relationship, controlling for both random variation and exogenous systematic influences, and thus to permit rigorous deductions. A model suggests explanation for social behaviors and outcomes, and it can be thought plausible to the extent that the premises are logical and the entailed hypotheses are confirmed by empirical testing.

Certain of the models offered within the rational choice tradition have been criticized for their questionable practical relevance. Designed with mathematical elegance, they are sometimes abstruse and sometimes offer too many logical solutions to permit efficient testing. The orientation adopted here is just the opposite. The models are elementary intentionally, designed for application to a pressing problem in U.S. public policy. They are not comprehensive for all possible forms of budget rule, nor for all possible versions of expenditure cap, nor even for all possible political configurations affecting the cap versions considered. The models were chosen explicitly for their pertinence to the food stamp program as it has evolved historically. Their aim is to direct attention to the connection between rules and results, operating through the intermediary of individual actors who adapt tactically to the structured opportunities for gain and the bias in political advantage for achieving it. As such, the models present a general framework, given the evidence supporting their credibility, useful for investigating the inherent policy dynamics of welfare budgeting. Other variants can be developed by extension. Research in the field of public policy, far too often, is either narrowly descriptive regarding actual outcomes or narrowly prescriptive regarding the outcomes the author may wish to occur. This book offers a more analytic alternative. By illustration, it hopes to contribute to a growing number of policy studies based on rigorous social science, thereby forging stronger links between abstract conceptualization and concrete application.

Theory

Political actors searching for the public good have long been caught by the tension between procedural and substantive justice. Procedurally, justice entails responsive decisions. They should be inclusive, based on the broadest feasible amount of participation over the broadest feasible set of issues. They should also be deliberative, utilizing institutions that encourage reason, debate, and accommodation. By implication, there are no privileged beneficiaries; all interests must compete for the rewards they wish to receive. There are no privileged benefits; all spending is equally subject to political choice. Value is defined internally to the political system. The public good is simply the policy that results from unconstrained and unbiased procedures. By contrast, substantive justice defines good by means of external standards. Most often these are fundamental rights that must be protected and fundamental goals that a political system worthy of respect ought to pursue. Institutionalized agreement is not sufficient by itself to legitimate the use of coercive government power. According to the substantive point of view, justice requires that the product of political decision making has essential merit, that it promotes social ethics or contributes to human fulfillment.

Normative theory accepts both ideals, seeking participation from a citizenry that is simultaneously encompassing yet capable, empowered yet wise. Each of the ideals, of course, is ambiguous. Moreover, there is no guarantee that they will progress together. Skeptics since ancient times have proclaimed the incompatibility between mass government and good government. The conflict in the modern era is quite visible with regard to social welfare. The question is whether the majority will acknowledge its obligation to assist those members of the community deserving of aid, and whether the deserving poor can establish sufficient political capacity to extract needed benefits despite potential opposition. The answer depends on the perceived relationship between power and poverty. According to the most optimistic commentators, American politics is commendable for its multiplicity of interests and the permeability of the government apparatus to those interests. Under normal conditions, all legitimate groups can make themselves heard "at some crucial stage in the process of decision."[2] Representatives for the poor are therefore not debarred from power. They should and ordinarily do organize their constituency, muster resources, obtain access, and exert pressure over the collective outcome, engaging actively in the process by which the American polity defines its collective will. Critics instead reply that the pluralist chorus sings with an "upper-class accent."[3] The contested game allegedly reflects more bias than balance, as the poor cannot necessarily understand, articulate, mobilize, and struggle effectively on behalf of material objectives. Inequality of income leads to inequality of power, which in turn reinforces inequality of income. From this latter perspective, moral obligation requires more from society than mere competitive political participation. From the former perspective, competitive political participation removes from society the obligation to give special consideration to morality. The debate between these two positions is fundamental, for at stake is the essential compatibility or incompatibility of welfare provision with democratic practice.

Within the social welfare arena, the tension between procedural and substantive justice is especially salient with regard to finance. In a sense, discretionary budgeting is based on procedural principles, subjecting each program each year to potential legislative review and restriction. Entitlement budgeting is more based on substantive principles, ensuring adequate outlays for all individuals declared eligible and enrolled under prevailing law. Discretion overtly enhances the domain of democratic decision making over government appropriations. The maximum figure for each fiscal year and thus the scope of program operations is determined by political choice; no spending is permitted without extensive agreement regarding such choice. Entitlement, by contrast, signifies a degree of self-restriction over government appropriations. The political system must specify in advance who has legitimate claims to benefits, of what sort, and at what level of generosity; it then is obliged to honor those claims, regardless of short-run democratic preference, until the authorizing law is altered or abolished.

Yet this picture of two separate budgetary realms, organized by two distinct policy principles, is somewhat too simplistic. The tension between procedural and substantive justice is pervasive and thus penetrates both of the realms. Within discretion, the fear that annual decision-making will upset the stable agency foundations necessary for substantive policy implementation has led to the establishment of incremental budgeting. Despite the range of potential choice, contention is usually confined to the margins and spending proceeds by accretion. Equally, within entitlement, the fear that public resources are entirely vulnerable to unanticipated cost expansion, with potential consequences for financial balance and macroeconomic policy, has led to new forms of procedural restriction.

In recent decades, most U.S. welfare programs have won permission to operate under entitlement status. Yet society has often balked at the fiscal implications of this commitment. Unwilling to renege on specific poverty protections but equally unwilling to abandon overall budget management, politicians caught in the middle have sought to exert somewhat greater democratic control over the relatively uncontrollable. Expenditure caps then become an attractive option, functioning as if entitlement rules apply until the specified threshold is breached, at which point they force discretionary choice. Congress can override the cap, all or in part, and it can alter program operations to save money, but without explicit action benefits will be slashed to keep total spending within the cap reversion point. Expenditure caps thus integrate welfare into aggregate budgeting through a mechanism that compels programs to compete for funds, but only under conditions of extraordinary growth. Advocates defend the scheme for maintaining substantive protections up to a reasonable level of outlays, and then for introducing more inclusive procedural choice under which priorities can be weighed and compromises introduced in accord with the popular will. Critics reply that any spending threshold is arbitrary; that it endangers essential benefits during times of unintended cost misestimation; that the risks from popular prejudice are high; and that even when not invoked the cap procedures can lead to perverse political play and to the stigmatization of a social constituency that, given the rising level of need, should otherwise deserve our sympathy.

Regardless of one's evaluation of expenditure caps, it is necessary to understand that their implementation represents an opposition inherent to democratic policymaking. We want to believe both that the public good entails the satisfaction of individual demands and that it should transcend majoritarian disposition, that it should be based on the participation of citizens and that it should be commanding of their allegiance, that it should be constructed synthetically from different points of view and that it is a unified vision that admits no inconsistency or contradiction. The public good needs to be defined both internally and externally to the political system, a tension in this country that has been inescapable since the American founders first declared their attachment to both popular sovereignty and self-evident rights. The conflict between "what-we-want" and "what-we-should-want" becomes manifest most often under conditions of scarcity. Not surprisingly, it is found in budgeting, especially budgeting with regard to social welfare. Recent reforms can be interpreted as part of an ongoing effort to adjust the balance. Respite in the late 1990s has come not from innovative policy solution, but instead from macroeconmic relief of intense fiscal scarcity. We should not assume that the matter has been resolved. Just the opposite—active confrontation with the issue, attending to the theoretical complications on each side, should be understood as a fundamental and continuing obligation of an engaged citizenry.

Subject

Supported by method and theory, this book has provided a detailed account of budget rules and spending constraints as they affected the U.S. federal food stamp program. Toward the beginning of the story, the emphasis was on the limitations imposed by procedural discretion upon program expansion. Agricultural interests and welfare opponents used institutional leverage to obstruct government assistance to the hungry, keeping spending below the level desired by the congressional median. A decade later, the emphasis was on the benefit guarantees created by entitlement. Protected recipient payments during times of macroeconomic fluctuation led to spending higher than anticipated and above the level sought by the political median. Concerns over program efficiency and runaway outlays eventually led to procedural innovation. Mainstream legislators, regardless of political party, wanted greater budgetary control without abandoning their commitment to the needy. Although triggered by the threat of across-the-board benefit cuts, the food stamp expenditure caps were advertised as a means to promote more responsible government. According to proponents, the caps would encourage administrators under normal circumstances to improve program management and limit costs; and it would force politicians on those occasions of extraordinary growth to confront the tradeoff between spending restraint and welfare provision, to declare a clear preference, and to justify it.

Somewhat predictably, the food stamp caps did not perform as promised. Institutionally, given multiple decision-making stages—including amendments to budget, authorization, appropriations bills, numerous committees, last-minute cost estimations, and conflicting interests—the consequence was a series of crisis enactments approved under deadline to prevent benefit reductions. Administratively, they created the incentive for excessive tinkering with program rules and requirements, since it would appear irresponsible for Congress merely to approve any overage without also claiming that efficiencies had been added and waste trimmed. Politically, the caps expanded the opportunity for partisan maneuvers and strategic gimmicks, favoring those players willing to use brinkmanship tactics threatening legitimate benefits in order to compel extraneous concessions. Under the best circumstances, when override faced little inherent policy disagreement, the cap system was unwieldy and complicated. Under the worst circumstances, institutional deadlock and conflicting political purposes augured considerable hardship to poor families.

Moreover, the caps proved to have dubious enforceability. They were most plausible when their potential effect was relatively minor. During the late 1970s, the announced aim was to reduce program waste and fraud. When costs accelerated due to economic crisis, legitimate benefits were protected and emergency overrides were enacted without much pleasure; the piecemeal reforms were reasonable but certainly not dramatic. Thus it could appear to the casual observer that the food stamp expenditure caps were failing, as their net effect was to legitimate, rather than constrain, the sum of unanticipated program outlays. In the early 1980s, the announced aim for cap proponents shifted from control over program operations to control over the growth in welfare spending. By the mid-1980s it widened even further, to control over the aggregate federal deficit. As concern moved from internal budget administration to external budget costs, demands upon the cap arrangement increased but the ability to comply, both technically and politically, diminished.

Technically, it was difficult under changing market conditions to keep annual food stamp costs within the cap threshold. Successful containment within the threshold, however, would contribute only a minuscule amount to restrained welfare growth and even less to deficit reduction. Politically, it was difficult to impose specific and harmful benefit restrictions upon qualified recipients as part of the attempt to help advance diffuse national fiscal policy goals. Just a few years earlier, it was assumed that sufficient cost restraint simply involved defining legitimate qualifications better and then removing the unqualified from the rolls. Now, instead, legislators had to confront the possibility that nutritional aid might have to be reduced for deserving households. From the evidence, most were uncomfortable with the prospect. Simultaneously wishing to enact visible spending limits but not wanting to impose them on the truly needy, Congress during the mid-1980s sought ways to both establish cap provisions yet escape their restrictions. Caps become largely unenforceable when the apparent gain is a slight contribution to some broad and difficult-to-obtain national aspiration but the pain is narrowly targeted to an identifiable constituency that would suffer due to no special fault of its own. Politicians, naturally hesitant when forced to decide between the general good and particular sacrifices, also do not want to be thought incapable of making such decisions—especially late into the fiscal year whenever entailed welfare costs unexpectedly exceed well-publicized boundaries. In 1990, the food stamp expenditure caps were permitted to expire as an unnecessary complication that brought neither budgetary nor political relief.

Nevertheless, the underlying conditions that made expenditure caps initially attractive continued unchanged. On the one hand, entitlement spending was still susceptible to great cost accelerations, free from the harness of explicit appropriations. On the other hand, mounting fiscal pressures and deficit fears prompted concern whether the federal government could successfully manage its own affairs. Renewed cap proposals, both in the aggregate and narrowly targeted to food stamps, soon made their way back to the active political agenda. They remain on the agenda today, in reserve awaiting the next budgetary crisis to arise. Ideologues can foresee new opportunities for entitlement restraint, which is viewed either with relish or alarm. Cynics anticipate symbolic gain, making a visible show of entitlement control that is never intended to be effective. Proceduralists hope for more encompassing budget review, in which priorities are weighed and reasoned deliberation guides the collective conscience. The results from this historic review suggest that none of these expectations are likely to be fulfilled. Caps are virtually impossible to enforce when they entail benefit reductions to otherwise deserving households; yet their very existence, given economic uncertainty, means that some threat against legitimate benefits will eventually arise; and under those conditions mainstream politicians will hesitate to make a decisive choice because of the evident electoral risks on either side.

Ultimately, the food stamp expenditure caps failed because they hoped to resolve, simply through the insertion of a new institutional rule, an issue that could not be decided by existing budget politics. Contrary to the somewhat naive assertions of Congressman Mathis, food stamp cost acceleration was caused minimally by program inefficiencies and abuses; political hesitance to address the tradeoff between spending control and welfare protection was not primarily caused by mere weakness of will. Rather, the problem was far more fundamental, for legislators representing the views of the American public wanted to both guarantee nutritional assistance to the hungry and promote flexible apportionment within the guidelines of fiscal restraint. The inability to select between these two accepted principles helped prompt recourse to the cap mechanism in the first place. It requires a leap of faith to believe, in situations when the cap thresholds were breached (especially if unanticipated and late into the budget year), that political consensus would suddenly emerge whereas previously it had proved intractable. The greater the demand for cap effectiveness, the less the caps were able to provide; and in the meantime legislative complexity and politically gimmickry found opportunities to flourish. The food stamp budget caps are the product of a nation that made a clear commitment to feed impoverished households but was uncertain whether to shoulder the entire cost of that commitment under all financial circumstances and political configurations. They are simultaneously the reflection of a deep policy ambiguity and an attempt, through a mechanical procedure invoking substantive threat, to force a solution to that ambiguity. Paradoxically, the caps could not be effective during times of unanticipated cost pressures until the dilemma that made them attractive was somehow resolved; if the underlying dilemma were ever resolved, the caps would no longer appear valuable as a means of compelling political choice. The ultimate assessment is that the food stamp expenditure caps were both politically perverse and conceptually misconceived. There is no reason to believe that the outcome would be substantially different if the design were altered or the application shifted to some other welfare policy arena.

On Budgeting Entitlements

Alexander Hamilton, in *Federalist* 78, wrote that democracy requires safeguards "against the effects of occasional ill humors in the society."[4] Entitlement status for social welfare programs is, in a sense, a form of essential safeguard protecting legitimate beneficiaries against the fluctuations of market and political fortune. Entitlement for welfare makes eminent sense. The American people have accepted the obligation to give material support to deserving members of the community determined to be in need.[5] They especially believe that there is no justification, in this land of abundance, that individuals should go hungry or suffer the health hazards of malnutrition. There is always debate at the margins, deciding exactly who should be declared needy and what is the extent of their need. Yet at the core of the obligation is a feeling that legitimate recipients should not be allowed to fall below some specified standard, which in the case of nutrition is the ability to purchase with no more than 30% of one's net income the equivalent of the USDA's Thrifty Food Plan. Given this standard, annual budgeting with fixed maximum amounts per fiscal year is an unnecessary fetter. The extent of authorized individual assistance, and thus the public price to provide that assistance, is highly sensitive to changing inflation and unemployment rates, to recipient enrollments and social characteristics. One can always try to make adjustment by means of supplemental appropriations, but that is complicated, and even the best technical estimates sometimes err. In addition, there is always the possibility, with initial appropriations and possible supplementals, that the political system will not respond up to the level of its declared obligation—that the ill humors of the moment will dominate over good conscience. Entitlement is a budgetary means by which citizens can bind themselves to help ensure that they act responsibly, in this case to provide the funds up to the standard that was promised.[6] Such self-commitment is familiar to the American constitutional tradition, and to many strictures existing below the constitutional level.

Are there conditions under which one should break the commitment and not fully fund promised benefits? One can always imagine a dire national emergency, in which the needs of the whole far transcend the obligations to the segment. Equally, are there conditions under which one should fear that society would break its commitment to the poor for less than worthy purposes? In times when the comfortable feel constraint, when their incomes are not rising yet the burdens of assistance remain relentless, there is a temptation toward self-interested neglect. Often when there is the greater need for poverty support, when market circumstances push welfare costs entailed under existing law unexpectedly above the predicted level, there is also the greatest tendency to blame the poor, distort equity, forget former obligations, and focus on the amount of budget savings rather than their human consequences. Such action is always justified in terms of the broad allocation of sacrifices. Yet practical experience shows that during somewhat tight economic times, voters are most averse to tax increases and organized interests struggle hardest to defend established subsidies. Thus the burdens of restraint fall disproportionately on those politically weakest and least able to bear them.

Not surprisingly, therefore, when the budgetary pre-commitment established through entitlement is most critical, entitlement programs regularly come under assault. One strategy is to redefine the promises made to needy households, by declaring certain of them suddenly undeserving or by reducing the standard from which need is calculated. Such tinkering with program regulations is morally suspect. A community should determine its obligation to the hungry and destitute apart from short-run pressures; it is least trusted to evaluate wisely when the taxpayer cost from this obligation is temporarily vexatious. Moreover, the effect of program tinkering, given the persistence of entitlement status, is uncertain since government still must make full payment to all legally qualified beneficiaries, and thus cuts from baseline can coexist with rapidly rising actual outlays.

Under strategic redefinition, benefit promises are reduced but spending remains unconstrained. By contrast, budget caps are an alternative strategy that maintains all promised benefits but places limits on available funding support. The contradiction inherent to the cap format is apparent. Morally, either one adjusts the promises made or one keeps them. The standard for minimum individual well-being has not been altered; caps merely place the satisfaction of that standard in jeopardy when a large number of people unexpectedly have private incomes below the minimum. Welfare advocates might accede to budget caps in exchange for valued program reforms (i.e., the repeal of the food stamp purchase requirement) or as a concession preferable to an even worse option (i.e., instead of block grants). Welfare opponents might seek budget caps as an oblique weapon of attack, useful for cutting individual allotments without saying so explicitly. Yet mainstream politicians should be wary, particularly regarding the temptation to consider caps as an instrument of inclusive choice, a means advertised to help legislators deliberate and apportion priorities when costs seem excessive. The cap reversion point puts the onus on the needy to muster the support necessary to override legal spending limits; reciprocally, it makes it easier procedurally to compromise with obligations that politicians and their public would prefer not to afford. The bias of policy should be structured in the reverse direction. Voluntarily accepted rules to safeguard against the self-interested whims and inclinations of the majority, according to the Hamiltonian dictum, can constitute the most responsible form of political behavior.

From this perspective, the negative consequences observed from the food stamp case study might fortunately be considered moderate. During the late 1970s, the caps were overridden, albeit cheerlessly, to ensure adequate nutritional benefits to poor households. During the early 1980s, they helped instigate benefit reductions that were painful but less severe than advocates had feared. During the middle 1980s, they were loosened to produce an impact more symbolic than real. Nevertheless, as recent welfare and fiscal policy debates have shown, budget caps to constrain allegedly extraordinary growth in entitlement spending remain an attractive idea. While not imposed during the mid-1990s, caps in a number of different variants—in the aggregate for most welfare programs or for a single program in particular; with fixed annual dollar amounts or variable thresholds to accommodate certain types of social and market changes—persist in the repertory of procedural reforms advanced by many active partisan and policy interests. It is implausible to believe that future budget cap experiments would fare better than the one previously undertaken with food stamps. Budgeting and welfare pose incongruous objectives. The former is focused on fiscal planning and control; the latter on guaranteed minimum consumption for designated needy households. The two diverse objectives increasingly have come into conflict in the modern era, exacerbated by recurrent deficit pressures and persistent poverty. The consequence is a policy dilemma that goes to the core of our vision as a democratic society.

Notes—Chapter 10

1. Jon Elster, *Nuts and Bolts for the Social Sciences* (Cambridge, UK: Cambridge University Press, 1989).

2. Robert A. Dahl, *Preface to Democratic Theory* (Chicago: University of Chicago Press, 1956): 145.

3. E. E. Schattschneider, *The Semi-Sovereign People* (New York: Holt, Rinehart and Winston, 1960): 35. Also, for example, Peter Bachrach and Morton S. Baratz, *Power and Poverty* (New York: Oxford University Press, 1970); John Gaventa, *Power and Powerlessness* (Urbana: University of Illinois Press, 1980).

4. Alexander Hamilton, "Number 78," *The Federalist Papers* (New York: New English Library, 1961): 470.

5. For an elaborate defense of this position, see Michael Walzer, *Spheres of Justice* (New York: Basic Books, 1983): 64–94.

6. Jon Elster, *Ulysses and the Sirens* (Cambridge, UK: Cambridge University Press, 1979).

APPENDIX

Food Stamp Program, Fiscal Years 1961–1998

Authorization Ceilings, Appropriations, and Outlays (in thousands of dollars)

FY	*Authorization*	*Appropriation*	*Outlays*	*Legislation*
1961	none	3,725	857	Pilot program, discretionary budgeting
1962	none	48,900	13,700	
1963	none	50,000	20,000	
1964	none	45,000	30,015	
1965	75,000	60,000*	34,395	Authorized, 3-yrs, annual budgeting
1966	100,000	100,000	69,491	
1967	200,000	139,525	114,095	
1968	200,000	185,000	184,727	Reauthorized, 2-yrs, annual budgeting
1969	315,000*	280,000*	247,766	
1970	610,000*	610,000	576,810	Reauthorized, 1½-yrs, annual budgeting
1971	1,750,000	1,679,000*	1,567,767	Reauthorized as national program
1972	none	2,289,214	1,909,166	Open-ended budget authority begins
1973	none	2,500,000	2,207,532	
1974	none	3,000,000*	2,844,815	Reauthorized, 4-yrs, open-ended authority
1975	none	4,874,600*	4,598,956	
1976	none	5,203,000*	5,681,954	
TQ	none	1,239,117*	1,325,159	
1977	none	5,514,000*	5,398,795	
1978	5,847,600	5,627,000	5,548,752	Reauthorized, 4-yrs, with caps
1979	6,778,900*	6,679,200*	6,866,287	
1980	9,191,000*	9,191,000*	9,163,946	
1981	11,480,000*	11,480,000*	11,303,025	
1982	11,300,000	11,300,000*	11,064,157	Reauthorized, 1-yr, with cap
1983	12,874,000	12,830,141*	12,700,882	Reauthorized, 3-yrs, with caps
1984	13,145,000	12,441,705*	12,375,249	
1985	13,933,000	12,593,856*	12,525,738	
1986	13,037,000	12,637,703	12,443,135	Reauthorized, 5-yrs, with caps

FY	*Authorization*	*Appropriation*	*Outlays*	*Legislation*
1987	13,396,000	12,684,665	12,407,465	
1988	14,741,000	13,557,757	13,145,225	
1989	15,435,000	13,823,579*	13,725,093	
1990	15,970,000	16,907,096*	15,923,350	
1991	none	20,550,901*	19,649,558	Reauthorized, 5-yrs, without caps
1992	none	23,362,975	22,799,659	
1993	none	28,115,357	24,602,431	
1994	none	28,136,655	25,440,750	
1995	none	28,830,710	25,554,000	
1996	none	27,597,828	25,422,000	Reauthorized, 7-yrs, without caps
1997	none	27,618,029	22,857,000	
1998	none	25,140,479	20,141,000	

*adjusted midyear

Index

www.ingramcontent.com/pod-product-compliance
Lightning Source LLC
LaVergne TN
LVHW090145080826
844660LV00013B/671/J

* 9 7 8 0 8 7 8 4 0 7 9 7 2 *